UK Politics Today

Peter Fotheringham
(Lecturer, Department of Politics, University of Glasgow)

Pulse Publications

CONTENTS

Published and typset by
Pulse Publications
45 Raith Road, Fenwick,
Ayrshire, KA3 6DB

Printed and bound by
Ritchie of Edinburgh

British Library Cataloguing-in-Publication Data
A Catalogue record for this book is available from the British Library

ISBN 0 948 766 48 4

ACKNOWLEDGEMENTS

The author and publishers would like to thank the following for permission to reproduce copyright material.
Mirror Syndication for photographs on pages 42,44, 60, 71, 73, 78, 83, 99 and 117.
PA News for photographs on pages 20 and 70.
FPN for photographs on pages 40 and 80.
National Pictures for the photograph on page 6.
Cover photograph by Chris Walsh, Britstock-IFA.

CHAPTER 1 The Changing Shape of UK POLITICS

IN THE APPROACH to the 21st century, UK politics exhibits several significant changes compared to the middle of the twentieth century. Economic, ideological and social developments within the UK itself and the changing impact of the world beyond have transformed the British political system. There is no end in sight to the processes of change. UK politics in 2010 may be radically different compared to politics in 2000.

Change in UK Politics

There are two sources of change in UK politics—the external and the internal. A highly publicised example of an external development affecting an important area of British life is the famous 'Bosman Ruling' which has totally transformed the football transfer market and stimulated other changes in the world of football. An important example of an internal development which has significantly altered British politics has been changing class structure. The middle class has been expanding at the expense of the working class in response to changes in manufacturing methods and occupational structure. 'New Labour', the dominant political force in British politics in the wake of the 1997 General Election, is to some extent the product of the changing class and occupational structure.

The impact of external forces on UK politics since 1945 may be conveniently summed up in three phrases:

- ☞ Globalisation
- ☞ European Integration
- ☞ Cold War

1 **Globalisation:** This means that, increasingly, economic (the international marketplace), social (for example, religion), technological (eg. satellite broadcasting) and cultural (for instance FIFA as football's ruling body) activities cross state borders and influence decision making processes within the nation states which have been the major political units of international society for over three hundred years. The British debate about Labour's proposal to introduce minimum wage legislation appears at first sight to be a traditional conflict between Labour and Conservative. Labour and the trade unions support a minimum wage in order to improve the earnings of the poorest members of society who tend to be Labour supporters. The Conservatives and employers oppose the move which they claim would lead to higher costs and lower profits. However, the issue has acquired a global dimension. Opponents of a minimum wage argue that its introduction will make British firms less competitive in the international marketplace because of higher wage costs. They argue that these will also deter American, Japanese and other foreign firms from undertaking further inward investment which has been a feature of British economic recovery in the 1990s. Thus a 'global' dimension enters the national decision making process. Many political commentators in the last decade have predicted or even proclaimed the end of the 'nation state' in response to the many examples of 'globalisation'.

2 **European Integration:** This refers to the process whereby the institutions of the European Union, particularly the Council of Ministers, increasingly take significant economic and political decisions which automatically are binding on the member states. Policies regulating agriculture and fishing in Britain are now formulated in Brussels rather than in London or Edinburgh.

3 *Cold War:* The Cold War, which developed between the former Soviet Union and its capitalist rivals in North America and Western Europe almost before the Second World War was ended, and its demise in the late 1980s have profoundly affected the defence and foreign policies of British governments for over 50 years.

The principal changes in United Kingdom politics, most of which will continue to develop in the next decade, may be summarised under 5 headings.

1 *Electoral Politics:* A weakening two-party system and electoral volatility can be seen.

2 *The Party System:* It is important to look at the ideology of the Conservative Party under Margaret Thatcher and the Labour Party under Tony Blair, and the internal organisation of the Labour Party since the mid-1980s.

3 *Constitutional Reform:* The main reforms are the introduction of a Parliament for Scotland and an Assembly for Wales and the introduction of proportional representation for some elections.

4 *Britain's Relationship with Europe (through membership of the European Union):* This has had a constitutional effect, given the shift of significant decisions affecting our everyday lives from British to European Union government institutions. It has also affected the UK politically. For example, the intense divisions within the ruling Conservative Party after 1992 over proposals for monetary union and a common currency.

5 *The Role of the State:* Politics in many Western democracies centre on a debate about what and how much the state should provide for its citizens by way of welfare, health care and pensions and how such services should be financed.

The external and the internal are inextricably intertwined. At the international political level, Britain experienced a transition from being a front rank Great Power in a Eurocentric international system to being a second ranking Power in a bipolar world dominated by the USA and the USSR and by the Cold War between them. In the 1950s Britain stood aloof from efforts on the Continent to create a supranational political community which would retain for Europe and Europeans a

significant measure of economic and political independence in a changing world. Within Britain, the first 20 years after 1945 were notable for a 'postwar consensus' as both parties supported a welfare state, a national health service and a mixed economy. Keynesian economic theory, which claimed that the provision of such services by the state for its citizens was beneficial for the economy as a whole, was accepted by both Labour and Conservative governments from Clement Attlee to Harold Macmillan (1945–1963).

The Postwar Period in UK Politics

The first 20 years of the postwar era were dominated by economic recovery from the hardships of the Second World War. Britain moved so far from the economic austerity of the immediate postwar years that a Conservative Prime Minister could assure the electorate during the 1959 General Election campaign that "You've never had it so good". Even as he said this, international comparisons suggested that Britain's economic performance in the international marketplace was poor compared to that of such major rivals as Japan and West Germany. Britain's problems were not unique. In the 1960s and 1970s most Western gov-

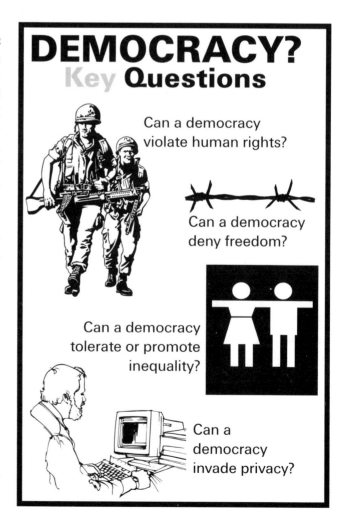

4

ernments had to confront the twin problems of inflation and employment. Hitherto most politicians had subscribed to full employment and low inflation. Suddenly, full employment was associated with unacceptable levels of inflation, partly stimulated by rising public expenditure as more and more demands were placed on the state. Public expenditure (what the state should provide for its citizens) and taxation (how to pay for the functions of the state) became central political issues.

Economic Decline

Britain's economic and political problems coincided with significant worldwide developments in production methods which changed industrial and occupational structures. An industrial society, characterised by mass production assembly lines and by heavy industries such as coal mining, shipbuilding and steel production, was giving way to a 'post industrial' society, in which economic activity was concentrated in more highly skilled technological 'silicon glens' and in service industries. The work force was becoming more skilled and society was becoming more middle class.

The most dramatic short-term consequence of an awareness by British politicians of relative economic decline and an ever-changing world was that Britain joined the European Economic Community, as the European Union was then called, in 1973. Both major parties had applied for membership in the 1960s in an effort to cope with Britain's economic and political difficulties. Those applications were rejected by the French President de Gaulle who regarded Britain as too closely tied to the United States with whom Britain claimed a 'special relationship'. When de Gaulle left office, Britain was allowed to join along with Denmark and Ireland in the first of several 'enlargements' of the world's most advanced experiment in the economic and political integration of nation states.

Britain's entry into the EEC coincided with other decisive economic and political upheavals in the 1970s. The 1973 Arab–Israeli War provoked an energy crisis and inflation accelerated in the capitalist world. New methods of manufacturing production ('lean production' and 'just in time'), pioneered by Japan, and the industrialisation of some Third World countries such as South Korea and Taiwan led to intense competition within the global marketplace. Sections of the more mature industrial economies of the USA and Western Europe suffered badly. Heavy manufacturing industries such as shipbuilding on the Clyde, steel production in Lanarkshire and coal mining throughout Britain all but disappeared. The increasingly global nature of the marketplace led to uncompetitive British motor car manufacturers giving way to American, German and Japanese firms all of whom set up plants in different parts of the United Kingdom.

Restructuring of UK Politics

The British electorate moved from granting the Conservatives 13 years in office from 1951 to 1964 to rejecting (1970, 1974 and 1979) the governments of both parties after six or fewer years in office. The second half of the 1970s and the early 1980s proved a difficult time for government in many countries. Significant elections rejected Labour in Britain, Democratic President Carter in the USA and a right of centre administration in France. The Social Democrats lost power in West Germany. Electorates reacted against high levels of taxation, but expected the state to provide welfare, pensions and health care nonetheless.

The longer term consequence of the international and domestic difficulties of the 1970s was a restructuring of UK politics which began with the election of a Conservative Government in June 1979 under the leadership of Mrs Thatcher who was to give her name to a radically new vision of politics and the state. 'Thatcherism' challenged the essential characteristics of the 'postwar consensus' without undermining it completely. The Conservative Government became embroiled in major conflicts with the trade unions, especially the miners, and with local authorities, especially those under Labour control, over issues such as the sale of council houses and local authority spending. Conflicts also arose with the population generally over the provocative poll tax and with Britain's European partners as they sought more and more economic and political integration which Britain under the Conservatives resisted.

Conservative electoral success under Margaret Thatcher and then John Major forced Labour, which had swung left after the 1979 Election defeat, to reconsider its policies, its organisation and its electoral strategies. Labour lost the April 1992 Election in spite of economic circumstances which were widely considered to make a change of government likely. Similar economic circumstances contributed to the defeat of President George Bush in November 1992. Repackaged un-

Women in the House

der Tony Blair as 'New Labour' and benefiting from the Conservatives' disastrous flirtation with the European Exchange Rate Mechanism (ERM) which ended in withdrawal and devaluation of the pound in September 1992, Labour won the 1997 Election by a massive margin.

There is a fundamental difference in the political strategies of the Conservative Government led by Thatcher in the 1980s and the New Labour Government elected in 1997. The Conservatives attempted to apply ideological principles to politics by increasing the role of the market in economic decision making and on 'rolling back' the state. New themes in UK politics under Mrs Thatcher included internal markets in health and education, privatisation of public utilities, sale of council houses, and the development of a property-owning, share-owning democracy.

Constitutional reform did not interest the Conservatives. Both Mrs Thatcher and Mr Major opposed widespread Scottish demands for devolution. Labour, having had to accept some of Mrs Thatcher's achievements such as the lowering of income tax, which imposes severe constraints on government revenues and on public expenditure, is concentrating on Constitutional Reform. Devolution, the introduction of proportional representation systems for some elections (the Scottish Parliament, the European Parliament, and possibly the Westminster Parliament), and the abolition of the right of hereditary peers to sit and vote in the House of Lords are all in Labour's redesign of the constitutional foundations of UK politics as the millennium approaches.

The chapters to follow enlarge on the themes introduced above which are likely to dominate UK politics for the foreseeable future.

CHAPTER 2 The Electoral SYSTEM

ELECTIONS ARE CENTRAL to democracy. Elections permit the people collectively to decide who should govern them. British democracy is representative and indirect. The people do not rule or govern directly. Rather the people are governed by the individuals they have elected to represent them in the legislature, the House of Commons, some of whom also become members of the executive.

Democratisation, the process whereby countries become democratic, is characterised above all by two achievements—*universal suffrage* and *free elections* devoid of corruption. The process of democratisation in Britain took a long time. In the 19th century the right to vote was extended to most males. Women did not get the right to vote until the 1920s.

The electorate used to decide only who should represent them in the Commons and on local government councils. Today, voters take part in elections to the European Parliament, and, if they live in Scotland and Wales to the Scottish Parliament or the Welsh Assembly.

The principal election in Britain remains the General Election which must be held once every five years. The Prime Minister may call a general election before the five year period is up if that is likely to increase the Government's chances of reelection. Formally the Prime Minister must ask the Monarch to dissolve Parliament before the election can be held. However, circumstances may leave the Prime Minister with little choice on the election date. Such was the case in May 1979 when James Callaghan went to the country after losing control of the House of Commons as a result of being defeated in a Motion of Confidence. The Prime Minister may also be forced to wait until almost the last possible moment of the five years allowed if opinion polls suggest that his or her

party will not be re-elected (for instance, Mr Major in 1997).

When a general election is held, all 659 Members of Parliament are elected. Every one of the 659 constituencies in Britain is represented by a single MP. Constituencies do not all have the same number of voters. The Western Isles has the smallest number (22,983 in 1997) while the Isle of Wight has the most voters (101,680 in 1997). In 1997 the average constituency had 68,927 voters in England and Wales and 54,800 voters in Scotland. The voters in each constituency choose one individual from a number of candidates for the job of MP in that constituency. Although voters are officially voting for an MP, they tend to think more about which party they support and who will form the government. A candidate's party affiliation is now noted beside his/her name on the ballot paper. In addition to selecting their own candidates, the major political parties effectively organise the election campaign.

Under the procedures established over many decades, candidates are required to submit their nomination papers together with a deposit of £500 to the Returning Officer, who has responsibility for managing the smooth running of the election. The regulations require that any candidate who fails to gain at least 5% of the votes cast in the election will lose his or her deposit. This is a considerable sum of money for any individual to lose, be it large or small. In 1992, a total of 2,946 candidates contested the Election, of whom 903 (30.6%) lost their deposits. This total included one Labour candidate, 3 Conservatives and 11 Liberal Democrats, so the great majority of deposits lost were by the candidates of minor parties with no hope of winning seats.

On general election day, polling stations up and down the country will be open from 7.00 am until

10.00 pm. Voting is fairly straightforward with the electors marking an X beside the name of their preferred candidate. At the close of the polls the ballot boxes are carefully sealed and sent on to the numerous counting centres which have been set up. It is here that the votes are counted and the results announced. Any voting slips which have been agreed as being 'spoiled' are set aside and not counted. Results are announced from midnight onwards, with the outcome of the election usually being fairly clear by about 3.00 am.

The Purpose of Elections

What is it, then, that voters hope to gain out of a general election? A change of Prime Minister and Cabinet? A new MP to represent their views at Westminster? Manifesto promises carried out? In many ways the voting public will get all of these things. They certainly get a constituency MP who will represent them whether they voted for him/ her or not. These constituency representatives select the government. That government will, during its lifetime, find time to carry out some of its manifesto promises.

Governments are decided by the electoral process, even though in the British parliamentary system only members of the legislature (ie. the MPs) are elected directly by the people. Which political party makes up the government is effectively decided by the collective voice of individual voters who usually return to the Commons a majority party from whose ranks the Prime Minister, Cabinet and junior ministers are drawn. The government receives legitimacy from being elected. The rule of law is much easier to achieve when those who make the law have been elected by the people who must obey the law.

The voice of the people is turned into political reality by the electoral system, ie. by the rules governing general elections. The way that a country is divided into constituencies, the number of representatives per constituency, the way votes are counted, and the number of votes required for election all influence the representation of parties in the legislature and the party composition of the government to emerge from the legislature after an election. Electoral systems are not neutral. Different rules lead to different results in terms of the number of parties with significant representation in the legislature and the way in which these parties make up the government which emerges from the legislature. There is a conflict between two of the principal purposes of an election—represen-

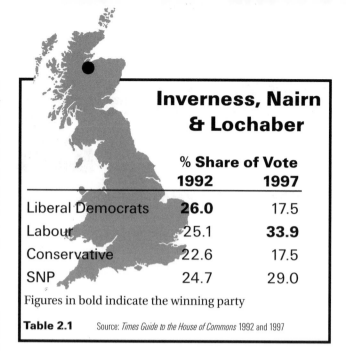

Inverness, Nairn & Lochaber

	% Share of Vote 1992	1997
Liberal Democrats	**26.0**	17.5
Labour	25.1	**33.9**
Conservative	22.6	17.5
SNP	24.7	29.0

Figures in bold indicate the winning party

Table 2.1   Source: *Times Guide to the House of Commons* 1992 and 1997

tation of the people and the establishment of a government. How representative is the House of Commons *and* the government following a general election? What is the best type of government—one based on a single majority party or one based on a coalition of two or more parties none of which individually enjoys a majority in the legislature?

The British Electoral System

Britain has a long history of two major parties along with single majority party government. The rules of the electoral system contribute in no small measure to these central features of British politics. The British electoral system has developed into a controversial political issue in recent decades for a number of reasons.

1 The apparent electoral invincibility of the Conservative Party from 1979 until 1992 led some to believe that the only way to overcome Conservative strength was to change the electoral system.

2 The devolution question focused attention on the issue of how to elect the parliaments proposed for Scotland and Wales.

3 Every EU member state except Britain uses proportional representation in elections to the European Parliament.

4 The two-dimensional nature of the British party system at the electoral level is weakening. (See Table 2.1.)

The British electoral system depends on majorities rather than proportion. It is popularly known as a first-past-the-post system or plurality system because the winning candidate is the one with the most votes in each single member constituency.

The British Two-Party System and the Electoral System: 1945–1997

| | % Share of the Vote | | | % Share of Seats | | | Libs. | Libs. | Overall |
| | Con. | Lab. | C+L | Con. | Lab. | C+L | %Votes | %Seats | Majority |
	1	2	3	4	5	6	7	8	9
1945	39.8	**47.8**	87.6	33.3	61.4	94.7	9.2	1.9	146
1950	43.5	**46.1**	89.6	47.7	50.4	98.1	9.1	1.4	5
1951	**48.0**	48.8	96.8	51.4	47.2	98.6	2.5	1.0	17
1955	**49.7**	46.4	96.1	54.7	43.9	98.6	2.7	1.0	58
1959	**49.4**	43.8	93.2	57.9	40.9	98.8	6.0	1.0	100
1964	43.4	**44.1**	87.5	48.1	50.3	98.4	11.2	1.4	4
1966	41.9	**47.9**	89.8	40.2	57.6	97.8	8.5	1.9	96
1970	**46.4**	43.0	89.4	52.4	45.6	98.0	7.5	1.0	30
1974	37.9	37.1	75.0	46.6	47.4	94.0	19.3	2.2	—
1974	35.8	**39.2**	75.0	43.5	50.2	93.7	18.3	2.0	3
1979	**43.9**	36.9	80.8	53.4	42.2	95.6	13.8	1.7	43
1983	**42.4**	27.6	70.0	61.0	32.2	93.2	25.4	3.6	144
1987	**43.4**	31.7	75.1	57.7	35.2	92.9	23.2	3.4	101
1992	**41.9**	34.4	76.3	51.6	41.6	93.2	17.9	3.1	21
1997	30.7	**43.2**	73.9	25.0	63.6	88.6	16.8	7.0	169

• The figures in bold denote the share of the vote of the party which won a majority of seats in the House of Commons. In 1974(Feb), no party won a parliamentary majority.

• Shares of votes and seats are based on results in the United Kingdom as a whole. Until 1970 Northern Ireland votes are included under the appropriate British parties. From 1974 this is not done because the Northern Ireland parties broke away from their British counterparts which did not, by and large, campaign in the province.

Table 2.2 Source: Butler and Butler, *British Political Facts 1900–1994* and *Times Guide to the House of Commons 1997*

In other words the one winner in each constituency is the candidate with more votes than any other rival candidate. The required number need not be an absolute majority. Indeed, if there are candidates from the three leading parties in England or the four in Scotland and Wales, then the winner may not gain an absolute majority. In the 1992 General Election 392 MPs, 60% of the membership of the House of Commons, received more than 50% of the votes cast in their constituencies. In Scotland, where the SNP means that there are four significant parties competing in many constituencies compared to only three in England, only 21 MPs, 29% of Scotland's 72 representatives at Westminster, won over 50% of the votes cast. The Scottish MPs winning an absolute majority of the votes cast were all Labour candidates representing urban constituencies. In total, 7 of Glasgow's 11 seats fell into this category.

A major criticism which can be made of the first-past-the-post system of voting is that it creates a situation whereby many individual MPs and the victorious party overall, which goes on to form Her Majesty's government, do not receive the support of a majority of the electorate. The people who vote for those parties which form the opposition may still have their views represented by the opposition MPs. They will not, however, see these representatives create policy which will be passed as law. Since there are no prizes for coming second they get nothing in terms of power or influence. As we will see, those who get nothing comprise a substantial proportion of the electorate.

Election results based on the first-past-the-post principle, such as those reported in Tables 2.1–2.3, give rise to claims that the electoral system used to elect members of the House of Commons is essentially unfair and that it leads to many individual votes being 'wasted'. Election results, whatever the electoral system in use, are not determined absolutely by that system alone. Rather, election results emerge from the interaction between the collective voice of individual voters and the rules of the electoral system. Tables 2.1–2.3 clearly illustrate how the electorate and the electoral system combine to influence how representative British democracy is. This is shown at three distinct territorial levels, namely individual constituencies, the national level (Scotland and Wales), and the overall (UK-wide) level.

The three most striking features of the general election results reported in Tables 2.1–2. 3 are:

1 The clear discrepancy between the proportion of votes gained by a particular political party and the proportion of seats it has in the House of Commons. The difference varies from one election to another.

2 The clear parliamentary majority achieved by one single party in 11 of the 15 elections since 1945. The exceptions are 1950,1964, February 1974 and October 1974. (See column 9, Table 2.2)

3 The persistence of a two-party system at the parliamentary level in spite of the decline in the combined Conservative and Labour share of the popular vote. (Compare columns 3 and 6, Table 2.2.)

ALLEGED DEFICIENCES
OF THE PLURALITY SYSTEM
General election results, including national and regional variations, are combinations of results in individual single member constituencies. Table 2.1 illustrates what can happen to the winner's share of the vote in a constituency such as Inverness and Lochaber when three or even four candidates are fairly evenly matched. In 1992 Sir Russell Johnstone won the seat with only 26% of the votes cast. Four candidates were each within 2% of a quarter of the vote. Johnstone was the only MP to win with less than 30% of the votes cast. The Liberal Democrats lost Inverness to Labour in 1997 following Sir Russell Johnstone's retirement. The Labour candidate won with one-third of the popular vote. In 1992, seventeen MPs were elected with less than 40% of the vote—8 were elected from Scotland and 5 from Wales where nationalist strength created four effective parties at the local level. The MP with the highest share of the vote in 1992 was L Smith of Blaenau, Gwent, who won 79%. Four MPs, all Labour, won over 75% support in their constituencies.

Table 2.2 illustrates trends in the percentage shares of votes and seats won by British political parties in general elections since 1945. The discrepancies between party shares of individual votes and number of seats in the legislature, based on the combination of results in 651 single member constituencies, define the 'representative' character of the electoral process in Britain. There are three main conclusions to be drawn from the data presented in Table 2.2.

All rewards to the victor
Firstly,the winning party always wins a bigger share of seats than of votes. In 1992, the Conservatives won 41.9% of the popular vote and 51.6% of the seats in the House of Commons. Labour also won a bigger share of seats than of votes. The party coming second overall in the share of the popular vote usually benefits from the first-past-the-post system by winning proportionately more seats than votes. The impact of the electoral system is evident when the two-party or major-party share of the vote (ie. the combined Conservative and Labour share) is compared with the major-party share of seats in the Commons. The decline in popularity of the two major parties is shown in column 3. Conservative and Labour together won close to 90% or more of the popular vote from 1945 until 1970. However, in the 1974 Elections their share fell well below 80%. Their lowest share was recorded in 1983 when they won less than three-quarters of the popular vote. Column 6, which gives the major-party share of seats in the Commons, shows that, despite this decline in their share of the vote, the number of seats won by the two major parties has remained stable.

It is true that, since 1974, the two major parties have won fewer seats than before, but they still won over 90%. In 1997 the much stronger Liberal Democrat performance in winning 46 seats reduced the Conservative–Labour share of seats (88.6%) to less than 90% for the first time in the postwar era. Such trends suggest that the electoral system protects the parliamentary representation of the two major parties from limited and temporary declines in their popular support.

The 'winning' party, ie. the party with the most seats, nearly always wins more votes than any other party. However, in 1951 the Conservatives won more seats than Labour in spite of winning a slightly smaller share of the popular vote. This can happen because of single member constituencies. A party winning some of its seats by large margins may win fewer seats but more votes than a party which wins its seats by narrower margins. In February 1974 these positions were reversed. The Conservatives, who had called the election after three years and eight months in office, won almost 230,000 more votes than Labour. This difference in number of votes represented less than 1% of the total vote in the United Kingdom. Nevertheless, the Conservatives won four seats fewer than Labour. However, no party won an overall parliamentary majority, the only time this has happened in the 14 general elections since 1945. Overall majorities were less than 10 in 1950, 1964 and October 1974.

Third parties smothered

Secondly, the first-past-the-post system makes it difficult, though not impossible, for 'third' parties to gain significant representation in the House of Commons. In Table 2.2, Columns 7 and 8 illustrate the mixed electoral fortunes of the most significant 'third force' in postwar British politics, the Liberals from 1945 to 1979, the Liberal/SDP Alliance in 1983 and 1987 and the Liberal Democrats in 1992 and 1997. The two major parties won a larger share of seats than votes. In sharp contrast, the third party has been winning a lot more votes than seats for many years. In 1951 the Liberals won 6 seats with 2.5% of the vote. In 1992 the Liberal Democrats won 23 seats with 17.9% of the vote; ie. the third party vote share went up 10 times but its share of seats went up only 4 times. The 'third party' fared particularly badly in 1983 when it took the form of the Liberal/SDP Alliance (an alliance of the old Liberal Party and the newly formed Social Democratic Party which had broken away from Labour in 1981). The Alliance won 25.4% of the vote in Britain compared to Labour's 27.6%. Yet the Alliance won only 23 seats (3.6%) compared to Labour's 209 (32.2%). After the 1997 Election, which produced the largest overall majority of the postwar era, 'New' Labour and the Liberal Democrats appeared to be discussing a common approach to issues of constitutional reform, including reform of the electoral system.

The electoral system encourages long-term two-party domination at the parliamentary level, but a particular two-party system may not be indestructible. It took the Labour Party, established by the trade union movement in 1900, 45 years to win a general election. During that period Labour replaced the old Liberal Party as the second major party as it gained the support of an increasing proportion of the working class. To overcome the biases of the first-past-the-post electoral system, third parties have to attract the support of significant sections of the electorate. Labour accomplished this task very gradually during the first

THE ELECTORAL SYSTEM: A Scottish Dimension

Election Results in Scotland: 1992 & 1997

	1992			1997		
	% votes	% seats	Nº of seats	% votes	% seats	Nº of seats
Labour	39.0	68.0	49	45.6	77.8	56
Conservative	25.7	15.2	11	17.5	0	0
Liberal	13.1	12.5	9	13.0	13.9	10
SNP	21.5	4.2	3	22.1	8.3	6

Table 2.3

thirty years of the 20th century.

The influence of third parties depends as much on the gap between the two major parties as on their own strength in the Commons. The narrower the margin between the major parties in the legislature and the smaller the winning party's overall majority, the greater is the influence of the small parties which have some representation in the Commons. The contemporary Conservative–Labour two-party system has tottered sometimes, particularly in the 1970s when on two occasions no party enjoyed a Commons majority. In the February 1974 Election, no party won a parliamentary majority. Labour formed the government because the Liberals made it clear that they would not support the continuation of Edward Heath's Conservative Government. In October 1974 Labour 'won' with a majority of only three. Labour lost its majority in by-elections and had to rely on a 'Lib-Lab Pact' to survive in Parliament until the summer of 1979.

Comfortable government

Thirdly, the electoral system and the electorate usually combine to produce a government with a comfortable working overall majority in the House of Commons. (Column 9 in Table 2.2.) 'Comfortable' is a variable which depends upon such factors as how the governing party fares in by-elections and whether a suitable opportunity arises for the government to call a general election which will increase its parliamentary majority. Labour's majority of five in 1950 was not sufficient to withstand a determined Conservative Opposition which forced all-night sittings and brought the government to its knees. The Labour Government which won narrowly in 1964 after 13 years of Conservative rule was able to call an election after 18 months and win a large Commons majority. In contrast, the Labour Government elected in October 1974 with an overall majority of three never found an opportunity to go to the country to strengthen its mandate (though there is a belief in some Labour Party quarters that Prime Minister Callaghan should have called an election in the autumn of 1978 when the Party would have had a better chance of winning than it did in May 1979).

The three Conservative victories in 1979, 1983 and 1987 were all 'comfortable'. The somewhat unexpected victory for the Conservatives under John Major in April 1992 provided a majority of 21 which was whittled away by by-election defeats and the defection of three Conservative MPs until, at the beginning of 1997, the Government lost its overall majority. However, the Government survived some votes of confidence because the Ulster Unionists did not vote against it. A Government without an overall majority can survive if some third party MPs vote for it or do not vote against it. Prime Minister Major was unable to call an election until the last possible moment because the polls had suggested for several years that Labour would win.

The present system suits parties with significant socioeconomic support nationally (Labour and Conservative) or strong, if limited, regional support (the nationalist parties in parts of Scotland and Wales in 1974). Such support leads to the parties coming first in certain types of constituency. For example, Labour dominates in the central cities such as Glasgow where all the seats were won by Labour in 1992 and 1997. It does not suit parties whose vote is spread evenly, but thinly, throughout most of the country (the Liberal Democrats in England and the SNP since 1979).

Table 2.3 illustrates further variations in the results possible in the first-past-the-post electoral system. Labour has been the dominant party in Scotland since 1959. Its dominance in terms of seats has grown in spite of the increase in support for the two smaller parties which now contest all Scottish constituencies. In 1966 Labour won almost 50% of the Scottish vote and 46 seats. In 1992 Labour won less than 40% of the vote but won 49 seats. Labour's social base has remained sufficiently loyal to ensure that Scotland's parliamentary delegation consistently contributes a sizeable majority to Labour's overall strength in the House of Commons. In contrast, the Conservative Party, which won 50.1% of the Scottish vote in 1955, has experienced a massive loss of votes which reduced its share of seats to 15% in 1992 and no seats in 1997.

The Conservative decline is due, in part, to the increase in support for the SNP and the Liberal Democrats whose strength has been most evident in the rural periphery of Scotland outside the industrial and urbanised belt in Central Scotland. The Conservatives have, since 1959, progressively lost out to Labour in urban and industrial Scotland.

The advantages of having your votes concentrated in certain areas can be seen in the changing electoral fortunes of the third and fourth party challenges to Labour and Conservative. The Liberal Democrats have been winning more seats than the SNP in spite of a much smaller share of the Scottish vote because their support is greatest in rural areas. The SNP has much more support than the Liberal Democrats in most parts of Scotland outside the seats won by the Liberal Democrats. In 1997 the SNP came second in every one of Glasgow's 10 constituencies and won 19% of the vote compared to the 7% won by the Liberal Democrats. However, such strength goes only to increase the SNP's share of the popular vote without winning the Party any seats in urban Scotland. In contrast, the Liberal Democrats' parliamentary representation (13.9% of Scottish seats) was directly proportional to its share (13%) of the popular vote.

PROPORTIONAL REPRESENTATION
Majoritarian (that is one candidate wins because he/she has a majority of the votes cast) or plurality electoral systems like the British one often lead to wide differences between shares of votes and shares of seats won by the competing parties. Plurality systems, which are also used in the United States, are in sharp contrast to Proportional Representation Systems (PR) which are outlined below. PR is based on the principle that every party winning an agreed minimum number of votes should be awarded a number of seats in the legislature. This number should be approximately proportional to the number of votes the party receives in the country as a whole. Some small parties, who have gained very few votes, will not be awarded any seats at all.

In Scotland the electoral system works massively in favour of Labour compared to the shares of seats which would emerge from any type of proportional representation. Exactly how important the principle of proportionality is in determining the number of seats won by each party can be clearly seen by comparing the results in Scotland in Table 2.3 with the results of the 1992 and 1997 Elections in Ireland (Table 2.5) where a form of PR is used. If the shares of the vote won by the parties in Scotland in 1992 (Table 2.3) were to be translated into shares of seats on the basis of pro-portionality, there would have been no majority of seats for the Labour Party, the SNP would have won more seats than the Liberal Democrats and the Conservatives would have won 18 seats rather than 11.

However, a change in the electoral system might lead to significant changes in voting behaviour. It cannot be assumed that if Scotland had voted in 1992 with a system of proportional representation in place the results would have been the same. Some voters, aware of a reformed electoral system, might have made different decisions, especially if they were 'protest' or 'tactical' voters. Individuals believing that in the first-past-the-post system a vote for a smaller party is a 'wasted' vote might also behave differently in a proportional electoral system.

The Alternative Vote (AV)
The alternative vote, is in effect, only a modified form of the first-past-the-post system. It would not require any boundary changes and the con-stituencies would still return one MP. Where the alternative vote system differs is that voters would have *two* votes instead of one. The voter would indicate his or her preference among the candi-dates. In this situation the winner would be that candidate who secured an absolute majority of the votes cast. Should this not happen after the first count, then the candidate with the fewest votes would be eliminated with his/ her second prefer-ences being distributed among the other candi-dates. If this did not produce a candidate with more than 50% of the votes, the procedure would be repeated until it did. The alternative vote sys-tem has been criticised on the grounds that it would fail to give a fairer share of the votes to the smaller political parties.

The Additional Member System (AMS)
The Additional Member System is of great inter-est in Britain because it has been chosen as the system to be used for elections to the Scottish Par-liament to be established by elections in May 1999. This system is currently used in Germany. The voter in the additional member system casts two votes. First the voter selects the candidate whom he/ she wishes to represent him/ her in the local constituency. In Germany, half of the MPs in the legislature, the Bundestag, are elected on the ba-sis of first-past-the-post in single member con-stituencies. The rationale here is to maintain a link between constituencies and their elected repre-sentatives. Therefore, the first 73 members of the Scottish Parliament will be elected from 73 single

THE GERMAN ADDITIONAL MEMBER SYSTEM: 1994

PARTY	FIRST VOTE		SECOND VOTE			
	% Share of Vote	N°. of Seats Won	% Share of Vote	N°. of seats allocated (PR)	% of Seats Won	N°. of seats added from party list
Christian Democrats	44.8	221	41.5	294	43.7	73
Social Democrats	38.3	103	36.4	252	37.5	149
Free Democrats	3.3	0	6.9	47	7.0	47
Greens	6.5	0	7.3	49	7.3	49
Party of Democratic Socialism	4.1	4	4	30	4.5	26
Others	3.0	0	3.7	0	0	0
TOTAL		328		672		

1 The first votes produced a typical first past the post result: the CDU/CSU alliance won a comfortable majority of the 328 members elected to represent constituencies. But these members make up only about 50% of the legislature.

2 The second votes are counted in such a way as to provide a high degree of proportionality between shares of votes and seats. Parties are allocated 'additional members' from their lists of candidates to bring their overall representation into line with their relative showing in the second vote. All the parties except the strongest party (the Christian Democrats) receive most of their seats from the party list system. A party has to win 5% of the second vote or 3 constituencies in the first vote to qualify for the proportional share of seats. The Party of Democratic Socialism won only 4.1% of the second vote but did nevertheless win its proportional share because it won 4 seats in the former East Berlin.

3 No party won a majority in the legislature. The Christian Democrats and the Free Democrats formed a coalition.

4 The smaller parties were treated 'fairly' in that their share of seats were more or less perfectly proportional to their per-centage share of the second vote. The Free Democrats and the Greens did not win any seats in the first vote.

Table 2.4

Proportional Representation in Action
Case Study: Ireland

1992 & 1997 General Elections in Ireland

	1992			1997		
	% Share of Votes	N°· of Seats	% Share of Seats	% Share of Votes	N°· of Seats	% Share of Seats
Fianna Fail	39.2	68	40.9	39.3	77	46.4
Fine Gael	24.5	45	27.1	27.9	54	32.5
Labour	19.3	33	19.9	10.4	17	10.2
Progressive Democrats	4.7	10	6.0	4.7	4	2.4
Democratic Left	2.8	4	2.4	2.5	4	2.4
Others	9.6	6	3.6	9.9	7	4.2
Green Alliance	—	—	—	2.8	2	1.2
Sinn Fein	—	—	—	2.5	1	0.6

Note: The Irish Parliament has 166 seats, so 84 seats are needed for an overall majority.

Table 2.5

LOOKING at Table 2.5, you can see that shares of seats are clearly much closer to shares of votes. The result is that no party wins a majority of seats which means that coalition government is necessary. Smaller parties receive much greater representation in the legislature. The government which was formed after the 1992 Election included members of Fine Gael, Labour and the Democratic Left. The largest party in terms of both votes and seats, Fianna Fail, was not represented in government. The Irish coalition government, based on three parties, enjoyed majority support in the legislature from 1992 to 1997. The 1997 Irish Election produced a different type of coalition government, *a minority coalition.* The two major parties both won more votes and more seats. However, Fine Gael's main coalition partner, Labour, lost both votes and seats. Consequently,

the Fine Gael Prime Minister resigned. The new Prime Minister, Bertie Aherne, formed a coalition with the Progressive Democrats (who were given one single seat in the Cabinet).

In proportional representation systems, shares of seats allocated to parties are clearly much closer to shares of votes won. Seldom does one party win a majority of seats. Smaller parties receive greater, and therefore 'fairer' representation in the legislature than is usually achieved in first-past-the-post systems. One result of proportional representation is that elections frequently lead to coalition or minority government. The Irish Government formed after the 1992 Election included members from three political parties—Fine Gael, Labour and the Democratic Left—whose 88 seats gave an overall majority of 10. The largest party in terms of both votes and seats, Fianna Fail, was not represented in government.

The 1997 Irish Elections led to a change of government and to a minority coalition government. The major change in voting behaviour was a severe decline (almost 50%) in support for Dick Spring's Labour Party. Although Irish Prime Minister Bruton's Fine Gael Party increased its share of both votes and seats, the coalition formed after the 1992 Election could not hold on to its legislative majority in the face of Labour's loss of 16 seats. Fianna Fail once again emerged as the biggest single party and its leader, Bertie Aherne formed a minority government along with the Progressive Democrats who won only four seats. One Cabinet seat went to Mary Harney of the Progressive Democrats. The new Government, which had three seats short of an overall majority, depended on the votes of the five Independents.

member constituencies with Orkney and Shetland both electing one MP.

In addition to voting for a local constituency MP, the voter also votes for a party list which contains the names of individuals in an order of preference decided by the parties. These second votes determine the overall composition of the legislature. The additional members are chosen in such a way as to ensure a high degree of proportionality in the final allocation of seats to parties. (An example of how this system will work in Scotland is given on page 106.) In elections to the Scottish Parliament, the existing 8 Euro-constituencies, which each are made up of 9 British parliamentary constituencies, will be used to elect 56 additional members.

National List / Regional List
This form of PR is used in many European countries most of which consider it to be fairer than the first-past-the-post system. Denmark and Sweden, however, feel that it is not proportional enough and use it along with the Additional Member System. Under this system, voters do not vote for individual MPs—they simply vote for a party. When the votes have been totalled throughout the country, each party standing in the election is told the percentage of seats to which it is entitled in Parliament. (If a party receives 20% of the vote, it will receive 20% of the seats in the legislature). Before the election, each party will have published a list of people who will be eligible to become MPs. The party leadership and major party figures will hold the top places, thus ensuring their election. The least experienced people will come bottom of the list and will probably not be elected. A more popular form of the party list system is to produce regional lists which operate in a similar way to national lists. As with the STV system described below, constituencies tend to be bigger that those which operate under the single member system.

The Single Transferable Vote (STV)
This system is often described as the most complex form of proportional representation. Using a quota system and multi-member constituencies (possibly 5 MPs per constituency) STV introduces a much higher degree of proportionality to the electoral process. In a five member constituency, voters would indicate their preferences 1–5 among the possible 12 or 13 candidates standing. Finding the winning candidates using STV is certainly more complicated. It is done using a mathematical formula to calculate the minimum number of votes each candidate would need in order to be successful in gaining a seat.

STV Formula

$$\text{Quota of Votes} = \frac{\text{Number of Votes Cast}}{\text{Number of Seats} + 1} + 1$$

In a five member constituency where 180,000 votes were cast a candidate would require 30,001 votes to be elected. If, for example, the candidate attracted 33,000 votes the 'surplus' 2,999 votes would be taken and redistributed to the other candidates according to the second preferences of *all* the votes cast for the winning candidate. Therefore, if 10% of the second preferences went to a particular candidate, that candidate would receive another 299 votes which would be added to the votes he or she had already received in the first count. If, after this, no other candidate had managed to reach the quota, the candidate with the fewest first preference votes would be eliminated and his/her second preference votes distributed among the remaining other candidates. Eventually, through this process of redistribution, five candidates would be elected for this constituency.

ELECTORAL REFORM IN THE OFFING?

"WE ARE COMMITTED TO A REFERENDUM ON THE VOTING SYSTEM FOR THE HOUSE OF COMMONS. AN INDEPENDENT COMMISSION ON VOTING SYSTEMS WILL BE APPOINTED EARLY TO RECOMMEND A PROPORTIONAL ALTERNATIVE TO THE FIRST-PAST-THE-POST SYSTEM." (Labour Party Manifesto, 1997)

The Labour Government elected in May 1997 followed up on its Manifesto commitment by establishing an independent commission on voting systems to be chaired by Lord Jenkins of Hillhead. Lord Jenkins, a one-time Labour MP and Cabinet Minister, left the Labour Party in 1981 to set up the Social Democratic Party to represent right-wing Labour supporters dismayed at the Party's move to the left after the 1979 Election defeat. Lord Jenkins subsequently joined the Liberal Democrat Party which in its previous identity as the Liberal Party had long campaigned for electoral reform. Other members of the commission are thought to be favourable to proportional representation.

Labour has already committed itself to introduce legislation which will lead to proportional representation replacing the first-past-the-post electoral system in time for the 1999 elections to both the Scottish and the European parliaments.

If the Labour Government and the voters in a referendum on the issue were to support proportional representation, this would be the most significant constitutional reform since the 1911 Parliament Act with far-reaching implications for representation and government in Britain.

proportional
REPRESENTATION

The sustained increase in the Liberal share of the vote from 1974 onwards (see Table 2.2) stimulated a debate about which type of electoral system Britain should have. Successive Conservative election victories, beginning in 1979, convinced some Labour supporters that reform of the electoral system was one way of preventing a recurrence of long-running Conservative government (as happened from 1951–1964 and 1979–1997). The 1997 Labour Party Manifesto included the electoral system in its list of British institutions in need of reform. It moved quickly to propose one of several variants of proportional representation, the additional member system, for elections to the Scottish Parliament, the first of which will be held in 1999. Labour also decided to fall into line with the rest of the European Union by committing itself to some form of proportional representation for elections to the European Parliament in 1999.

The 'independent commission' (see page 15) will have several alternative voting systems to consider. Different electoral rules tend to produce different outcomes. In particular, the number of major parties, the influence of minor parties and whether there is a single majority party in the legislature are largely determined by the electoral system. The first-past-the-post system used in Britain has tended to produce two-party politics and an executive branch (Prime Minister and Cabinet) drawn from one party only. In sharp contrast, electoral systems based on proportional representation, such as the German additional member system or the Irish single transferable

vote system, tend to produce multi-party systems, which give minor parties more representation in the legislature and more participation in government. They tend to produce more coalition or minority government. (See Table 2.5)

Following Labour's 1997 electoral triumph, the United Kingdom could possibly be operating *four* different electoral systems by the turn of the century.

1 *General Elections*–Traditional first-past-the-post system to be the subject of an independent inquiry.
2 *Scottish Parliament*–Additional member system.
3 *European Elections*–Labour committed itself to PR in 1999.
4 *Northern Ireland*–Single transferable vote in a three member constituency in elections to the European Parliament.

The 1997 Labour Manifesto promised that the British people would be asked to state their views on the 'voting system'. It is likely that the following arguments will be presented to them by the supporters of the rival systems available. Voters in the proposed referendum on the voting system will have to decide whether proportionality, which certainly seems fairer in terms of representation, is also capable of producing governments as 'good' or as 'strong' as the government Britain has enjoyed or endured under first-past-the-post.

First-Past-The-Post (Strong Government)

1 Usually produces a strong government drawn from one party enjoying a majority in the House of Commons.
2 Single party government allows the Prime Minister and Cabinet to pursue policies clearly stated

in the Manifesto without having to compromise with smaller parties in the coalitions associated with PR.
3 There is no tradition of coalition government in Britain. PR encourages coalitions or minority government which may allow minor parties to hold larger parties to ransom.
4 PR may lead to coalition between a minor party or parties and the second largest party outside the government. This leaves the largest section of public opinion unrepresented. (See Table 2.5)
5 Coalitions encourage compromise so that fewer voters, namely Conservative or Labour voters, get what they really want.

Proportionality (Fair Representation)

1 PR is 'fair' because it produces a close correlation between shares of votes and shares of seats and avoids such results as Labour winning 74% of European Parliament seats with 44% of the popular vote as it did in 1992.
2 PR gives minor parties more parliamentary representation and encourages voters to vote for them without feeling that their votes will be wasted.
3 Coalition government increases the percentage of the electorate supporting the government parties.
4 Coalition government gave Germany better government than Britain for many years.
5 Coalitions encourage consensus which is the result of compromise. That is, more voters get some of what they want and less of what they do not want.

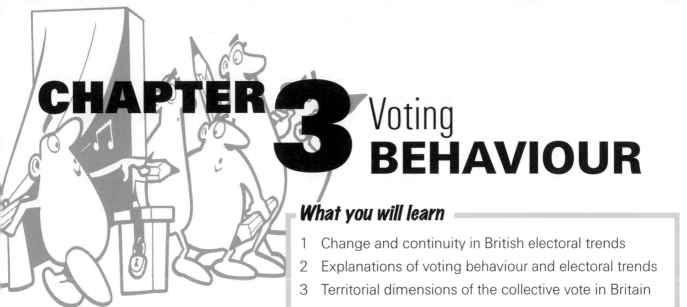

CHAPTER 3 Voting BEHAVIOUR

VOTING IS CONSTITUTIONALLY an individual action. In other words, the right to vote is given to individuals. However, elections are decided collectively when individual votes are counted and transformed into results by the electoral system described in Chapter 2. Elections and voting behaviour determine *who* governs us and to a large extent *what* they do in office.

CONTINUITY AND CHANGE

Election results over time constitute an important element of a wider British party system to be described in Chapter 4. British electoral patterns are characterised by a great deal of stability. The Conservative and Labour Parties have been the only two major parties in Britain for more than 60 years. The Conservatives won four elections in a row between 1979 and 1992, giving them control of the powers of government for 18 years. Labour has won a majority of Scottish seats in all 11 elections since 1959. Such continuities in election results are the product of a great deal of stability in individual voting behaviour over time. When a political party acquires or loses major party status, or loses an election as the Conservatives did in 1997, it does not win or lose all its supporters overnight. That is why minor parties such as the Liberal Democrats in Britain and the SNP in Scotland find it difficult to achieve major party status. It took Labour almost a quarter of a century to form its first administration, a minority government which lasted for only one year in 1923–24. By the mid-1930s Labour had replaced the Liberals as the second of two major parties, but it was not until 1945 that Labour formed its first majority government. Voters tend to acquire a loyalty to the party of their choice, a loyalty which is not easily or quickly overturned. However, one of the interesting questions about contemporary voting behav-iour is whether individual voters are less loyal to parties than they used to be, and if this is the case, why.

In every general election result we see a mixture of continuity and change. The study of voting behaviour is concerned with establishing and explaining both the continuities and the changes which determine ultimately what political parties attempt to do in office when they win elections. The principal continuities and changes in the collective decisions of the British electorate in the 15 elections since 1945 are illustrated on page 18.

Measuring Swing

Swing measures the 'net' movement of individual voters between the major parties.

Swing =[(rise in winning party's vote share) + (fall in losing party's vote share)] / 2.

Example: The 1964 Election brought 13 years of Conservative government to an end. To overcome the Conservative majority of 100, Labour needed more voters to change their allegiance than had been typical of postwar elections up to that point.

The degree of swing in 1964 can be measured using the statistics provided in Table 2.2.

Swing 1959–64 =[(Rise in Labour share of the vote) +(Fall in Conservative share)] / 2
=[(44.1-43.8) + (49.4-43.4)] / 2
= $^{6.3}/_2$ = 3.15%

3.15% was a relatively large swing at that point in British electoral history, but it gave Labour an overall majority of only three in the House of Commons.

CONTINUITY & CHANGE

Continuities

1 The British electorate has sustained a Conservative–Labour two-party system since 1945. Only once, in 1983, has the 'third' party come within 5% of the weaker of the two major parties.

2 The winning party usually wins over 40% of the popular vote, the only exceptions being the two closely fought elections of 1974.

3 The Conservatives have twice won more than two elections in a row (1951, 1955 and 1959, and 1979, 1983, 1987 and 1992), holding governmental office for 13 years and 18 years respectively. Labour has never won more than two successive elections, and indeed has yet to win two comfortable parliamentary majorities in a row. Prior to 1997 the Conservative Party had been the stronger of the two major parties in terms of both length of time in office and the margin of victory when parliamentary majorities were considered.

4 The performance of the principal 'third party' challenge to the two-party system in Britain divides neatly into two periods. From 1945 until 1970 the Liberals only once exceeded 10% of the vote. However, since February 1974 the 'liberal' challenge has attracted close to 20% support.

5 For most of the postwar period the degree of major party 'swing', ie. the relative changes in the Conservative and Labour shares of the popular vote, was within a range of 1–4%, suggesting that many individuals tended to remain loyal to one party'. In other words, Britain possessed a stable electorate. This was much lower than the degree of swing in American presidential elections during the same period.

Changes

1 Six of the 15 elections since 1945 have resulted in a change of government (1951, 1964, 1970, February 1974, 1979 and 1997).

2 The Conservative–Labour two-party system within the electorate has been considerably weaker since 1974. From 1945 to 1970 the two major parties averaged 91.2% of the popular vote. Their combined share has averaged only 75.6% since February 1974.

3 The 'third party' challenge has strengthened considerably since 1974. Since 1974 the 'third force' in British politics has averaged 19.4% of the vote. In the 1950s the Liberals stopped contesting every constituency because their share was falling drastically. However, by 1974 the Liberals and their successors were back to contesting the great majority of seats. In 1997 the Liberal Democrat share of seats more than doubled in spite of a slight decline in vote share because they successfully 'targeted' seats they thought they had a chance of winning.

4 The electorate has become much more volatile since 1979. Prior to the first Thatcher victory, the average gap between the votes of the two major parties was only 3.4%. Since 1979 that gap has averaged 10.7%. The Labour land-slide in 1997 was based on a large swing of 10%. Labour won a few seats which had been considered 'rock solid' for the Conservatives with a swing of 15%.

5 From 1950 to 1966, turnout never fell below 75%. (1945 was exceptional because wartime conditions made it impossible for many individuals on the electoral register to vote.) However, since 1970 turnout has fallen below 75% on three occasions. In 1997 turnout fell to its lowest point, 71.3%, in the postwar period.

6 Since the United Kingdom of Great Britain and Northern Ireland is both a unitary state constitutionally and a multi-national state historically, national and regional variations in voting behaviour are of special interest. Such variations have had significant political consequences, none more so than the electoral success of the SNP and Plaid Cmyru in 1974 which began the drive towards 'devolution' for Scotland and Wales. National differences in voting behaviour have also significantly influenced party policies and election outcomes. In 1950 and February 1974 Scottish and Welsh voters imposed a Labour Government on the English who returned more Conservative than Labour MPs.

1997 A 'Record' Election?

THE 1997 ELECTION was exceptional in several respects. The question arises whether the changes recorded signified a major change in voting behaviour which would have made this a 'critical' election, ie. an election in which new patterns of voting behaviour and election results were established. Commentators were quick to claim that the Conservatives were facing certain defeat in the next general election because of the scale and manner of the 1997 disaster.

The Conservatives

The Conservative share of the vote, 30.7%, was the lowest since 1832. Only twice before in the postwar period, in the two indecisive elections of 1974, had the Conservative share fallen beneath 40%. The Conservative presence in the House of Commons, 165 MPs out of a new total of 659, was the lowest since 1906. Labour had won 209 seats in 1983 when its share of the popular vote was only 28.3%. Seven Cabinet Ministers lost their seats, the second highest total ever. (In 1906 eight lost their seats including the Prime Minister.) For the first time ever no Conservatives MPs were returned from Scotland or Wales. In the words of one journalist the Conservatives were reduced to being "a party based almost entirely in the countryside and some suburbs". Conservative MPs were banished from Britain's cities, though a small rump of Conservative voters remained faithful. On Merseyside, with its 16 seats in Liverpool and its urban hinterland, the Conservatives won no seats and a mere 19.7% of the vote.

Labour

Labour's overall majority of 179 was its biggest ever, beating 146 in 1945 and 96 in 1966. Labour's margin of victory over the Conservatives in the popular vote was, at 13%, its biggest ever though its vote share in 1997 (44.4%) was smaller than in 1945 (47.8%) and 1966 (47.9%).

Liberal Democrats

1997 was the best 'liberal' performance in the postwar period. Their Commons delegation of 46 MPs was the highest total since the 59 seats won in 1929. The Liberal Democrat vote share was lower than the Liberal/SDP Alliance achieved in 1983 and 1987. However, the Liberal Democrats' campaign strategy was much more successful in 1997 when they 'targeted' (put more resources into) seats where they had a realistic chance of winning.

Swing

The degree of relative change in the major parties' shares of the vote in 1997 was 10%. This is the highest swing in the postwar period apart from 1945 when the 12% swing relative to 1935 was partly due to the ten-year interval between elections caused by the Second World War. The 10% swing in 1997 was almost double the Labour–Conservative swing of 5.2% in 1979, which was the highest recorded between 1950 and 1992. The large swing suggests that many more voters than usual changed their party allegiance and thus provoked the 'record' features of the 1997 Election. Why they changed will be examined below.

Turnout

The 71.3% of the registered electorate voting in 1997 was the lowest since 1945. The average turnout in the four Conservative victories between 1979 and 1992 was 75.4%. The relatively sharp fall in 1997 has provoked a debate about its significance. Conservatives argue that the fall was due to many Conservatives not voting rather than moving to support other parties. Such abstainers are more likely to return to the Conservative fold at the next election than those who did move over to the Labour camp. Another explanation offered for the low turnout was that the result was widely anticipated (the opinion poll predictions were accurate) because of the long-running problems experienced by the Major Government.

The 1997 Election also produced the lowest majority in an individual constituency since 1910. The Conservative Gerry Malone was defeated in Winchester by two votes—a result he was to contest in court. In 1910 a one vote victory was recorded.

'Tory-Free Zones'

In 1997, Scotland and Wales were proclaimed 'Tory-Free Zones' because no Conservative MPs were returned to Westminster.

EXPLAINING VOTING BEHAVIOUR AND ELECTION RESULTS

Students of voting behaviour have to explain both continuity and change, each of which may be short-term or long-term in nature. The fact that the Conservative–Labour two-party system has existed since 1945 is the principal example of long-term continuity which requires explanation. The four successive Conservative victories from 1979 to 1992 amount to a shorter term continuity which ended in 1997. The scale of the dramatic Conservative defeat in 1997 is the most recent example of a decisive short-term change which may or may not develop into a longer term continuity if Labour is re-elected in the first elections of the third millenium. The Conservative Party needs to know why it lost so decisively in order to consider reforms of policy and organisation which might lead to victory in the next election.

Table 3.1 illustrates the elements of continuity and change by comparing the 1992 and 1997 election results in two 'British' regions—Scotland with 72 constituencies and the South East of England (excluding Greater London) with 117 constituencies. Continuity is represented by the fact that Labour was the strongest party in Scotland and the Conservatives were the strongest party in the South East of England in both elections. There was very little change in the 'third' party shares of the votes between the two elections. Clearly, Scotland is a Labour stronghold and a Conservative political desert, while the South East is a Conservative stronghold (9% ahead of Labour in the popular vote) even in a disastrous election for the Party.

Nevertheless, there was change as well as continuity between the two elections. The most obvious is that the Conservative share of the vote fell drastically in both regions while Labour's share increased by almost as much as the Conservative vote fell. There were even more changes in terms of the distribution of seats. Although the 'third' party shares of the votes hardly changed at all, both the SNP and the Liberal Democrats gained seats in both regions. The South East was even more strongly Conservative than Scotland was Labour in 1992. By 1997 the two major parties were still dominant in terms of seats in their respective strongholds, but Labour had improved its share of seats in the South East of England and the Conservatives had been eliminated as a parliamentary force in Scotland. The Liberal Democrats gained 8 seats in the South East in spite of the slight fall in their share of the vote; no fewer than 21 of the

26 Liberal Democrat gains in 1997 are located in the three most southern regions of England.

Several questions arise from the above comparison. Why is Scotland so strongly Labour and the South East of England so strongly Conservative? What explains the Conservative decline in support and the Labour increase between the two elections? Why did the 'third' parties gain seats without much change in their vote shares?

Such questions may be answered by making use of two very general types of explanation of individual voting behaviour and collective voting trends. The first emphasises the specific sociological and even physical characteristics of individual voters. The second explanation focuses on the political background to particular elections such as the significant issues of the day which may influence individual voters and collective outcomes. Social explanations tend to explain long-term continuities and gradual changes in electoral trends. Issues tend to explain short-term changes such as Labour's defeat in 1979 which led to the Thatcherite era in British politics and the 'record'

Winchester By-Election

Gerry Malone

Repeated recounts at Winchester on the night of 1 May 1997 gave victory to Liberal Democrat candidate Mark Oaten over Conservative candidate Gerry Malone by two votes. After the result had been declared Mr Malone complained that the Returning Officer had incorrectly classified 55 ballot papers as 'invalid'. Mr Malone, with the full backing of the Conservative Party, felt that he had to pursue his claim in the courts. The High Court found in Mr Malone's favour and declared the 1 May result to be invalid. The by-election, held on 20 November 1997, produced a humiliating defeat for Mr Malone who lost by 21,450 votes to the Liberal Democrat, Mark Oaten. This massive victory margin was partly due to a 'tactical' campaign strategy by the Labour Party. The Labour candidate, who polled only 944 votes, fought a very low-key campaign and was not supported by any visiting Cabinet Ministers.

Continuity & CHANGE 1992–1997

	1992		1997	
	%Votes	Seats	%Votes	Seats
Scotland				
Labour	40.0	49	46.6	56
Conservative	26.0	11	17.5	0
SNP	22.0	3	22.0	6
Lib Dem	13.0	9	13.0	10
Total		*72*		*72*
South East England				
Labour	21.0	3	32.0	36
Conservative	54.0	106	41.0	73
Lib Dem	23.0	0	21.0	8
Total		*109*		*117*

Table 3.1

Market Research Definition of Social Class

Class	Categories		% in Category 1966	% in Category 1992
A	Higher Managerial	} A+B	12	19
B	Lower Managerial			
C1	Skilled Supervisors		22	24
C2	Skilled Manual		37	27
D	Unskilled Manual/Manual	} D+E	29	30
E	Residual/Unemployed/Poor			

Categories A, B, and C1 constitute the non-manual 'middle class' categories, while C2, D and E make up the manual 'working class'.

Table 3.2

characteristics of the 1997 result. Issues may also be related to long-term continuity in so far as they provide a motive for individual allegiances to a particular party which are then sustained over a long period of time.

CLASS AND VOTING

Social class dominated explanations of voting behaviour until the 1970s and is still considered to be influential today. The dominance of social class among the various influences on the decisions of the British electorate was dramatically expressed in 1967 in a celebrated claim by an Oxford political scientist:

> "Class is the basis of British panty politics; all else is embellishment and detail."

(PJ Pulzer, *Political Representation and Elections in Britain*, Allen and Unwin, 1967).

Pulzer's statement was widely accepted as an accurate description of the defining characteristic of such elements of British party politics as voting behaviour, party membership and party policies. Studies of voting behaviour were discovering that many people voted for the same party throughout their lives and that choice of party was strongly linked to 'social class'. Given its central position in explanations of British political behaviour, it is essential to define 'social class'.

A social class is generally taken to be a set of individuals who share certain social characteristics which collectively give them a similar attitude to life in general and to politics in particular. Individuals who are brought up in the same neighbourhood and who then live and work in similar conditions might be expected to develop similar views on politics (which party to support), sport (which team to support), religion (which church to attend), leisure activities (bingo or bridge) and so on. There are many social conditions which are included in lists of variables defining social classes: occupation, housing, education, income and wealth. Some individuals are born into poor families, others into wealthy families. The children of richer families tend to go to private fee-paying schools and on to higher education; the children of less wealthy families are more likely to go to comprehensive schools and are less likely to go on to higher education.

There has always been intense debate about the key features of social class and how to define it. Political scientists seeking to explain election results 50 years ago accepted the most widely used classification system of the time which was based on occupation and distinguished between the non-manual middle class and the manual working class. Occupation was strongly linked to income and to such social conditions as housing (owner occupier or council tenant) and education (private or state schooling). Such a broad dichotomy is not accurate enough for the purposes of political scientists who have tended make use of the social class categories employed by market research organisations in their efforts to find out why consumers buy certain products and not others. The market research definition of the British class structure uses 6 categories, namely A, B, C1, C2, D and E, which are based on a classification of occupations. These categories and their relative sizes are described in Table 3.2.

Table 3.2 illustrates a significant change in British social structure in the three decades between the late '60s and the early '90s. Britain is slowly becoming more middle class. In 1966 the gap between the two classes was 32; by 1992 it was down to 14. The two classes experiencing most change have been the upper middle class (A+B) which has increased in size, and the skilled manual class which has gone down. Before the 1997 Election this change in the relative sizes of the two principal social classes was considered to be a disadvantage for the Labour Party, contributing to the decision of Labour leaders after Michael Foot to redesign the policies, the image and the electoral strategies of the 'working-class party'.

The market research categories are employed by most polling organisations to produce data on voting behaviour linking social class to party support. Even though occupation is the sole criterion assigning individuals to particular class categories, the assumption is made that individuals in every social class category share many of the social features listed above with others in the same class category. They share a common 'life style' which differs from the other categories. The changing relationships between social class, as defined by the market research categories, and

party support/voting behaviour are illustrated in Tables 3.3–3.5.

Table 3.3 shows the relationship between social class and voting behaviour in two elections won by Labour. These are 1966 when Labour won its third largest majority and close to 50% of the popular vote, and the very close election of February 1974 when no party won a Commons majority and Labour won more seats but fewer votes than the outgoing Conservatives.

In both elections the links between social class and party support appear to be relatively strong. Conservative support increases with every step up the class scale from 26% in the unskilled/unemployed working class (DE) to 72% in the managerial upper middle class (AB). The same is true in reverse if we look at Labour support in class terms. The two ends of the class spectrum were particularly loyal in 1966 to the party associated with their class, with over 70% of AB voting Conservative and almost 66% of DE voting Labour. By February 1974 there had been a decline in support for the two major parties as the Liberal vote went up to almost 20%. This reduced the correlation between class and support for the two major parties.

The 1966 data is typical of the correlation between social class and party support in the heyday of the Conservative–Labour two-party system. Such data was interpreted as an indicator that social class was the most significant factor in determining how individual voting allegiances were formed and how continuities in election results over time were established. The working class was perceived as 'Labour' and the middle-class as 'Conservative'. The Labour Party was perceived as the 'natural party' of the working class and the Conservatives as the 'natural party' of the middle class.

Note the big gaps in party allegiance between the C1 and C2 categories, ie. at the class divide. Note also that Conservative support in the lowest class category, DE, was greater than Labour support within the upper middle class, category AB. The middle class was more loyal to its 'natural' class party than the working class was to its 'natural' party. There were more 'working-class Conservatives' than 'middle class radicals'. . Importantly, this was true in absolute terms—because the working class was considerably bigger than the middle class. Thus the class interpretation of British voting behaviour had to be qualified by exceptions to the general rule that class determined

SOCIAL CLASS & PARTY SUPPORT: 1966 & FEBRUARY 1974

Class	1966			February 1974		
	Con	Lab	Lib	Con	Lab	Lib
AB	72	16	11	67	10	20
C1	59	30	11	51	21	25
C2	32	59	8	30	47	20
DE	26	65	7	25	54	17
Total	41.4	48.7	8.6	38.7	38.0	19.8

Table 3.3 Sources: D Butler et al, The British General Elections of 1966 & February 1974

party support—without working-class support the Conservatives could not win elections.

In 1966, 64% of the electorate voted for their natural class party. Such statistical evidence was interpreted as indicating a strong class influence on individual voting behaviour. This interpretation was justified by other evidence that the Conservatives were middle class and Labour was working class. For example, very few Conservative candidates or MPs were working class. Most trade unions, the most influential working-class organisations, were affiliated to the Labour Party. Party policies were also linked to class in that Labour favoured a redistribution of wealth from rich to poor and the more capitalist minded Conservatives resisted such moves even though they also accepted a mixed economy (public and private enterprise) and the welfare state.

Table 3.3 shows how the social classes divided between the political parties. Nevertheless, we may also look at where the votes of the parties came from in class terms, ie. at how dependent each party was on its 'natural' class support. Because the working class is bigger than the middle-class and because the Conservative share of working-class votes was bigger than the Labour share of middle-class votes, the Conservative vote in 1966 was 52.4% middle class and 47.6% working class. The Labour vote was much less evenly divided between the classes, being 83% working class and only 17% middle class. The Conservatives used such evidence to claim that they were much more representative of all sections of the nation than the Labour Party, which relied on a much narrower social cross-section for its votes.

Table 3.4 shows the links between class and party support in 1983 and 1987, two elections won comfortably by the Conservative Party. At one level there was still a relationship between class and party support. In other words, Conservative and Labour support still increases as we look up or down the class scale. However, the proportions in each class voting for the natural class party fell compared to 1966 and 1974. Furthermore, Labour support in the working classes has fallen well below 50% because these two elections were Conservative landslides in which Labour support was low relative to 1966 in all sections of the electorate.

The historical class–party link (the working classes are more Labour than Conservative; the middle classes are more Conservative than Labour) was broken in 1983 in one critical area which was worrying for the Labour Party. For the first time more skilled working-class people voted Conservative (40%) than Labour (32%). Even the unskilled/unemployed working class (DE) were only 8% more Labour than Conservative in 1983. Labour narrowed the gap in the C2 category in 1987 but the Conservatives still led Labour by 4%.

Another interesting feature of Table 3.4 is that Liberal support appeared to be largely independent of class—a similar proportion voted Liberal in all four class categories. The considerable Liberal/Alliance vote and the large working-class support for the Conservatives in 1983 and 1987 reduced the proportion of the electorate supporting their natural class party to 44% in 1987.

In 1992 the Conservatives enjoyed their fourth consecutive victory, though this time their overall Commons majority was reduced to 21 and the gap in the popular vote between Conservative and Labour was reduced from 11.7% to 7.1%. An intriguing feature of the 1992 result was that the still large Conservative vote won fewer seats than was the case in 1983 and 1987. This was because Labour did much better in marginal constituencies and held on to or won seats which they would have lost if the swing had been uniform.

There was still a relationship between social class and party support in 1992 but it was much reduced. Although Labour regained its position as the strongest party in C2, the skilled working class, its lead was very small at 3%. There was still more working-class Conservative support than middle-class Labour support. The proportion of the electorate voting for the natural class party rose to 49%

SOCIAL CLASS & PARTY SUPPORT: 1983 & 1987

| Class | 1983 | | | 1987 | | |
	CON	LAB	LIB	CON	LAB	LIB
ABC1	55	16	28	54	18	26
C2	40	32	26	40	36	22
DE	33	41	24	30	48	20
Total	42.4	26.6	25.4	43.4	31.7	23.2

* Note: The 'middle class' figures for 1983 & 1987 combine A, B & C1

Table 3.4 Source: Butler & Kavanagh, *The British General Elections of 1983 & 1987*

SOCIAL CLASS & PARTY SUPPORT 1992 & 1997

| | 1992 | | | 1997 | | | |
	CON	LAB	LIB	CON	LAB	LIB	SWING
Class							
AB	56	20	22	42	31	21	12.5
C1	52	25	19	26	47	19	24.0
C2	38	41	17	25	54	13	13.0
DE	41	50	15	21	61	13	15.5
Tot.	42.3	35.2	18.3	31.4	44.4	17.2	10.1

Table 3.5 Source: Butler & Kavanagh *The British General Elections of 1992 and 1997*

in 1992. The Liberal Democrats had more of a class look to their support, the middle classes being several points more supportive than the working classes although the class connection remained much less pronounced than in the case of the two major parties.

Studies of voting behaviour in the twenty years prior to 1997 concentrated on Labour's electoral weakness. The changing class structure and the four successive Conservative victories suggested that Labour faced long-term difficulties which were not due to the particular circumstances of each election. Then in 1997 Labour was elected following the largest swing in support between the two major parties since 1945.

The 1997 Election has been described previously as a record-breaking election. The record-breaking theme may also be applied to the survey findings linking class to party support. For the first time ever the larger middle-class category, C1, gave more votes to Labour than to the Conservatives and by a wide margin (21%). Furthermore, the lower middle class 'swung' to Labour by an astounding 24%, twice the overall swing which was itself a record for the post-1945 period. The highest social class, AB, remained faithful to the Conservatives, but for the first time fewer than 50% of ABs voted Conservative. There were many more middle-class radicals (Labour voters among ABs and C1s) than working-class Conservatives (Conservative voters in C2/DE).

Residence
There is a strong correlation between form of housing tenure and vote. Indeed, evidence suggests that home owners of whatever class are more likely to vote Conservative than Labour. The rea-son for this may be that they perceive a Conservative vote as being in their own interests, or they may be influenced by the fact of living in a particular neighbourhood.

Gender
In the 1950s and 1960s a higher percentage of men than women voted Labour, while a higher percentage of women voted Conservative. By the 1980s this difference had virtually disappeared with a higher percentage of men than women voting Conservative in 1983. In 1987 and 1992 there was evidence of the traditional pattern reasserting itself but this was hardly conclusive. In 1997 the gender gap disappeared.

Age
Age does appear to be a factor in voting preference (see Table 3.6) but the reasons for this are not easy to identify. Different age groups may vote differently because they have had different experiences of life and of political history. In 1997 the Conservatives 'won' among the over-65s, in spite of pensions becoming a prominent issue during the campaign, but 'lost' elsewhere. These older voters hardly changed allegiance overall compared to 1992. Younger voters, including new voters, were particularly strong supporters of Labour.

Age hardly influenced the Liberal Democrat vote at all. The Party's ability to poll evenly across both class and age divisions suggests that its appeal is not dependent on social factors. This may limit its ability to develop its electoral base. Parties which achieve major party status usually depend on securing the allegiance of particular sections of society. Both the Liberal Democrats (or their predecessors) and the SNP have, in the past, made spectacular inroads into the electorate (the SNP in 1974, the Alliance in the 1980s) but have then

VOTING BY AGE, 1997

Age Group	CONSERVATIVE	LABOUR	LIB DEM
18–29	22	57	17
30–44	26	49	17
45–64	33	43	18
65+	44	34	16

Table 3.6 Source: *Sunday Times* May 1997, BBC/NOP exit poll

fallen back from a peak without disappearing into oblivion. The Liberal Democrat gains in 1997 were based on a successful campaign strategy, not on increasing their vote share.

Summary
There are some unbroken long-term trends in the relationships between social class and party support. The upper middle classes (A/B) always prefer the Conservatives although the margin slipped from 43% in 1987 to 11% in 1997. Similarly, the unskilled working class (D/E) always prefer Labour, though the margin has varied recently between 18% in 1987 and 40% in 1997. The class–party relationship looks strongest in the two classes at either end of the class spectrum.

The two intermediary classes (C1/C2—lower middle/skilled working) are the most interesting. Until 1983, in spite of variations from one election to another, there was one cast-iron consistency within the two largest social classes. Lower middle class C1 was always more Conservative than Labour and skilled working class C2 was always more Labour then Conservative. This expected relationship between social class and party support in the two largest class categories did not hold for the skilled working class in 1983 and 1987 nor for the lower middle class in 1997. The Conservatives won more votes than Labour in the skilled working class in 1987 but not in 1992 despite winning that election. In 1992 the Conservative lead over Labour in the middle-class categories was sufficiently greater than Labour's lead over the Conservatives in the larger working-class categories to ensure the Conservative victory. Put another way, in 1992 the working class was less loyal to its natural class party than the middle class and the Conservatives won accordingly.

The 1997 result is particularly interesting in view of the changes which have been taking place in British party politics in the 1990s. The Thatcherite domination of the policy agenda which covered four elections from 1979 to 1992 forced Labour to change its traditional policies and its party organisation. (See Chapter 4.) Labour had to accept the Conservative emphasis on allowing the 'market' to take more and more economic decisions and on attempting to slow down expenditure on state functions such as the health service, education and welfare. Labour reduced the role of trade unions within the Party's decision making processes without completely eliminating the Party–union links. Labour changed its electoral strategy to get rid of its 'tax and spend' image which may have cost it victory in 1992. The failure in government of the Conservatives under John Major and the apparently successful transformation of 'old Labour' into 'new Labour' was reflected in the 'record' Labour victory and especially in the large swing to Labour which occurred in the lower middle class.

The major British parties, even if accepted as class parties in the heyday of the two-party system, had to appeal for votes across the class divide. The Conservatives could not win without considerable, if minority, support from the working class, thereby focusing attention on the celebrated, or notorious, 'working-class Conservative'. Labour needed some counter-balancing support from the smaller middle class. In 1997, Labour put much more emphasis on its appeal to *all* class categories, especially to the two large categories in the centre areas of the class spectrum, the lower middle class who usually preferred the Conservatives by a comfortable margin, and the skilled working class who had preferred the Conservatives in 1983 and 1987. Battle was being waged for the allegiance of 'Middle Britain'.

'DEALIGNMENT' or 'TRENDLESS FLUCTUATION'
British society and British voting patterns have changed since Pulzer's claim that "class is the basis of British party politics". That claim has to be re–examined in the light of the changes in the links between social class and panty support illustrated in Tables 3.3–3.5 Two rival explanations have been offered, both focusing on the role of social class. One explanation is the 'dealignment thesis' put forward by Professor Ivor Crewe and others. The second explanation, put forward by Heath, Jowell and Curtice in *How Britain Votes* published in 1985, focuses attention on problems inherent in efforts to define social class meaningfully. They rejected the market research categories described in Table 3.2, redefining social class to produce categories which they claim are more appropriate to the connection between occupation and political allegiance. Both theories of British voting behaviour in the 1970s and 1980s reflected the dominant feature of elections during that period: Conservative success and Labour failure.

Dealignment means a weakening relationship between social class and party support—a decline in the class basis of British politics. The evidence supporting the dealignment thesis may be seen in the fall in the proportion of the electorate voting for their natural class party from 64% in 1966 to 44% in 1987. Crewe explained deal ignment by distinguishing between an 'old' and a 'new' working class. Members of the 'old' working class still shared such definitive characteristics as an unskilled manual occupation in a traditional 'heavy' industry, trade union membership and council housing. They were to be found in greater numbers in North Britain (North of England, Scotland and Wales) than in South Britain. Members of the 'new' working class were more likely to be skilled, owner occupiers, working in newer 'high tech' industries and located in the Southern half of England. Two sets of evidence supported Crewe's division of the working class into two parts.

- Several social and political indicators suggested a growing 'North-South' divide.
- In the 1980s the skilled working class had moved from the Labour camp to the Conservative camp.

Heath et al challenged the dealignment thesis. First they focused attention on the widely accepted market research class categories in such a way as to strengthen the links between class and voting behaviour. Their new class categories are:

☞ *Salariat* (27%): managerial, supervisory and professional 'workers' with secure employment, relatively high income and some authority and autonomy.

☞ *Routine non-manual* (24%): clerks, salespersons and secretaries; subordinate position in the workplace but still 'white collar'.

☞ *Petty bourgeoisie* (8%): farmers, small proprietors and self-employed manual workers; essentially individuals who work for themselves and who are not subordinate within the workplace.

☞ *Foremen and technicians* (7%): 'blue-collar' elite, supervisory positions in the workplace. working class(34%): rank-and-file skilled and semi-skilled manual occupations in industry and agriculture.

The principal consequence of this alternative scheme for dividing the electorate into social classes is to reduce even further the size of the core working class (which was declining according to the market research categories also) by taking 'foremen and technicians' and some members of the 'petty bourgeoisie' out of the 'working class'. The reason for doing so is that as individuals with some supervisory authority or some autonomy in the workplace their status is fundamentally different to that of the 'working class' who do not possess either authority or autonomy. The Heath et al 'working class' is therefore smaller than the C2DE working class categories of the market research scheme. Consequently, Labour's pool of natural class supporters is smaller in the Heath et al social class scheme. The 'salariat' and the 'routine non-manual' categories are very similar to the market research categories ABCl.

Heath et al argued that the voting behaviour of these redrawn class categories supported their view of social class in Britain. The most Conservative class between 1983 and 1992 was the 'petty bourgeoisie'. 'Foremen and technicians' were more evenly divided between the parties, moving from favouring the Conservatives in 1983 to favouring Labour in 1992. Both were more Conservative than the working class because their possession of some authority and autonomy allowed them to see themselves as closer to the 'salariat' in the workplace. Voting Conservative was partly a confirmation of their higher status.

If individuals leaning to the Conservatives and assigned to the working class by the market research classification are removed from the working class, two consequences follow. Firstly, the residual working class is smaller and therefore Labour's natural pool of class support is smaller. Secondly, those remaining in the working class will be more loyal to Labour. Heath et al concluded that there had not been a significant reduction in the links between social class and party support, that dealignment was not a satisfactory explanation of the data reported in Tables 3.2–3.5. Rather the variations in the links between class and party support evident in voting behaviour since the 1970s, including 1997 when Labour took over from the Conservatives as the dominant party, suggest that the circumstances of each election might explain the result. Hence they talked of 'trendless fluctuations' beyond the control of the parties and the government. It had so happened that circumstances had favoured the Conservatives from the 'winter of discontent' in 1978–79 , through Labour's profound internal divisions before the 1983 Election to the economic recovery in the years immediately before and after the 1987 Election.

Crewe's distinction between the 'old' and the 'new' working class and the Heath et al redefinition of social class categories focus attention on the nature of class in contemporary Britain and on its political ramifications. The string of Conservative victories from 1979 to 1992 suggested that there was some stability in the electorate which was favourable to the Conservatives. Both Crewe and Heath et al provide explanations of Conservative success, but the 1997 result suggests that other factors were at work which had little to do with social class. It is to such factors, above all to the influence of 'issues' that we now turn.

ISSUE VOTING

So far we have looked at sociological explanations of voting behaviour. In other words, we have considered consistent links between party support and social divisions based on class, age, gender and so on. Correlations are suggestive, which means that they stimulate explanations which, in turn, have to be justified by other evidence. The class connection which dominated explanations of voting behaviour made sense because the parties were associated in the public's mind with policies which appealed more to particular sections of society than to others. Thus Conservative tax policies appealed to the rich rather than to the less well off, because the rich believed that they were likely to pay more tax under Labour. Labour was considered more likely to commit resources to the health and welfare services which were needed more by the poorer than by the richer sections of British society.

Although socialisation processes encouraged voting based on class, the decision of how to vote was also rational because the parties adopted policies which were interpreted by many voters in class terms.

The change of political direction brought about by the decisive turn round in party strength in the 1997 Election stimulates a search for explanations which cannot be satisfied easily in sociological terms. The political change was too great to be explained by any sociological changes. This means that we have to look at other influences on individual voting behaviour, a search which automatically focuses on issues which can be settled by the electorate.

Election campaigns revolve round two themes—*who* will form the government and *what* will they do in office? The 'what' is usually defined in policy terms—what the parties stand for and what they say they will do. The 'who' are often perceived in terms of how well they have performed in office. American presidential elections have been described as 'referenda on incumbency', which sim-

ply means that the American electorate passes judgment on the performance of the incumbent President—the one whose term of office is just ending. If he is believed to have been successful, like Ronald Reagan in 1984, he will be re-elected. If he seems to have failed, like Jimmy Carter in 1980 and George Bush in 1992, then he will be rejected. Sometimes the judgment seems to be as much on the President's opponent as on the outgoing President. Thus Bill Clinton's re-election in 1996 was partly due to the Republicans not being able to find a strong candidate and partly to Clinton's own successes. Although Clinton was not successful in terms of his legislative achievements, the American economy was booming much more strongly than it had been in 1992 when Bush lost.

An election result might depend on the performance of the incumbent Prime Minister and Cabinet or on memories of the performance of the major party rival the last time it held office. Some voters may be swayed by what the parties say they will do if elected. The 1992 and 1997 Elections with their very different outcomes offer an opportunity to look at the impact of several types of issue.

It is difficult to work out the precise impact of particular issues or the collective impact of all the issues which appear to be influential in an election campaign. What matters is how many voters mention an issue as important to them and how these voters divide between the parties. One of the features of the 1987 and 1992 Elections which Labour lost was that Labour seemed to be winning the 'battle of the issues'.

Table 3.7 indicates that Labour was the preferred party on the Health Service, unemployment and education while the Conservatives were preferred

ISSUES & PREFERRED PARTY: 1987 & 1992

ISSUE	Mentioned as Important by % of sample		Preferred Party Lead	
	1987	1992	1987	1992
NHS	33	41	Lab +49	Lab +34
Unemployment	49	36	Lab +34	Lab +26
Education	19	23	Lab +15	Lab +23
Defence	33	3	Con +35	Con +86
Prices		11		Con +59
Taxation		10		Con +72

Table 3.7   Source: Denver, *Elections and Voting Behaviour in Britain*

27

on defence, prices and taxation. In 1987, such survey data on issues posed a problem because Labour would have won if everyone had voted for the party which they thought had the best policy on the issues which mattered most to them. This dilemma was solved by the claim that the Conservative victory was based on another type of issue influencing voters. They may have preferred Labour on the policy issues, but they thought that the Conservatives were more likely to 'deliver' prosperity even though they did not mention economic issues other than unemployment which in fact favoured Labour. In 1992 economic issues entered the picture. The large Conservative lead on prices and taxation counterbalanced issues favourable to Labour but by smaller margins than the pro-Conservative issues.

The anticipated performance of the major parties also influences voting behaviour. It is significant that one of the first actions of the new Conservative leader William Hague, after the 1997 Election disaster, was to set about reforming Conservative Party organisation in an effort to prevent the Party indiscipline, especially over Europe, which had harmed Conservative chances in the Election.

THE LESSONS OF 1997

Explanations of election results from 1979 to 1992 made depressing reading for Labour supporters. Labour seemed to be increasingly a party which had failed to react to social and political changes characteristic of 'post-industrial society'. Patterns of employment were changing as the old heavy manufacturing industries declined, to be replaced by 'silicone valleys' requiring fewer but more highly skilled workers. This, combined with a switch of jobs to the service and financial sectors, caused changes in the class structure which, in turn, affected the electoral prospects of the parties. It is true that by 1992 the Labour vote had recovered from the low point of 1983, but the Conservative vote managed to hold up at over 40% and was still 7% ahead of Labour.

Then along came '1997', a record Conservative defeat—the worst performance by a major party in the postwar era. The scale of the defeat was much greater in terms of seats lost than in terms of votes lost. Labour's 13% lead in the popular vote would, on past performances when voting was uniform across Britain, have produced a majority of about 120. When the Conservatives won 15% of the vote more than Labour in 1983 their parlia-

mentary majority was 30 lower than Labour's was in 1997.

The reasons for this Labour advantage emphasise the increase in electoral volatility in recent decades. Firstly, the swing against the Conservatives was greatest in marginal constituencies where changes in party allegiance were more likely to produce a change in the identity of the winning party. Labour had also benefited from this phenonemon in 1992, but in that year it reduced the scale of the Conservative victory rather than increasing the scale of the Conservative defeat. Secondly, tactical voting was encouraged by the electoral strategy of the Liberal Democrats who targeted seats where they had a chance of winning—often seats where they had come second in 1992.

Tactical voting had two consequences. Firstly, the Liberal Democrats won 46 seats with a lower share of the vote than the Liberal/SDP Alliance had achieved in 1983 and 1987. Secondly, in spite of considerable agreement on constitutional issues between the Labour and Liberal Democrat leadership elites, there was often bitter fighting in the campaign between the two parties challenging the Tories in seats where both felt they had a chance of victory. The Liberal Democrats had some victories which upset the Conservatives. For instance, they defeated Norman Lamont in Harrogate. However, the Liberal Democrats also campaigned less vigorously in many marginals where they felt they would not win. This left such seats open to the

LABOUR'S LEAD ON THE ISSUES, 1997

ISSUE	LABOUR LEAD
Unemployment	+38
NHS	+49
Education	+39
Pensions	+37
Law and Order	+22
Taxation	+6
Inflation	-2
Defence	-8
Relations with EU	+12
Law and Order	+22

Table 3.8   Source: D. Sanders,'Voting and the Electorate' in
P. Dunleavy et al,Developments in British Politics 5 (Macmillan, 1997)

possibility of a Labour gain which duly transpired. Labour won about 40 seats more than their most optimistic projections.

The 1997 result requires a re-evaluation of some of the conventional wisdom about British voting behaviour such as class voting, the two nations thesis, and the impact of issues. Why did Labour win so handsomely?

Table 3.10 suggests that the trend in 1997 was comprehensively to Labour from Conservative throughout British society (outside Northern Ireland). *The Sunday Times* (4 May 1997) caption 'New Labour's Conquest of Middle Britain' focused attention on the controversial links between class and party support. The old trend of greater middle-class party loyalty was broken as C1s deserted the Conservatives for the first time, and did so decisively. Labour also did particularly well among new voters. The gender gap disappeared as women moved more strongly than men to Labour. Home owners, once thought of as a bedrock of Conservative support, changed allegiance in accordance with the average swing. Only the over-65s resisted the move to Labour. The concept of 'Middle Britain' suggests that old class differences have been declining as differences in income and life style between the the lower middle class (C1) and the skilled working class (C2) have been eroded. In 1997 the major difference in voting behaviour between the C1s and the C2s was that the C1s were slightly more favourable to the Liberal Democrats and the C2s were slightly more favourable to Labour.

The 1997 result was widely expected. The Conservatives had trailed Labour in the opinion polls for most of the lifetime of the Major Government, which never really recovered from the 'bad news' associated with the withdrawal from the European Exchange Rate Mechanism and the effective devaluation of the pound in the autumn of 1992. An intense conflict within both the Conservative Party and the Government between Eurosceptics and Europhiles painted a picture of Conservative indiscipline and ineffectual leadership. The reform of the Labour Party under John Smith and Tony Blair established a media success around the concept of 'New Labour' and projected a different image for the Party. An important reform by the post-Kinnock leadership was to remove Clause IV, the commitment to 'common ownership' which had allowed the Conservatives to saddle Labour with a socialist image. The leadership also launched a publicity drive designed to persuade the electorate that Labour was no longer the 'tax and spend' party which would relieve workers of their hard-earned income.

The contribution of issues to the dramatic turnaround in 1997 is illustrated in Tables 3.8 and 3.9. Table 3.8 indicates that public opinion had changed decisively between 1992 and 1997 on the issue of which party would 'best handle' the various economic and social issues which would confront the new government. Labour maintained or extended its lead relative to 1987 and 1992 as the party which would 'best handle' the NHS, employment and education. More dramatically, the Conservative lead on issues such as inflation, law and order and taxation, which had long been considered Conservative issues, was either severely reduced or eliminated altogether. The Conservative lead on both defence and inflation was under 10% compared to the massive leads recorded in 1992.

The taxation issue which had proved costly for Labour in 1992 was neutralised as Labour achieved a small lead. The highly publicised Conservative campaign of 'New Labour, New Danger' did not work. About 60% of voters believed that both parties would raise taxes after the election despite mutual protestations to the contrary. Decisively, Labour was trusted more on tax than the Conservatives: ie. slightly more voters believed that Labour rather than the Conservatives would take the right decisions on tax.

The 1997 Election also challenged a conventional wisdom that the incumbent government's economic record is a decisive influence on voting behaviour. The Conservatives boasted that falling unemployment and low inflation had turned Britain into the strongest economy in Europe. The Chancellor of the Exchequer, Kenneth Clarke, the

IMAGES OF THE PARTIES, 1992–1996					
IMAGE		1992	1994	1995	1996
Moderation	CON	61	48	48	51
	LAB	61	72	76	74
Capable, strong government	CON	84	32	27	27
	LAB	35	60	67	62
Party unity	CON	67	10	8	9
	LAB	30	64	67	54

Table 3.9   Source: Table based on data derived from John Curtice, 'Anatomy of a Non-Landslide' in the Politics Review, September 1997.

man in charge of the economy, enjoyed a strong reputation as a successful Chancellor. Opinion polls found that 35% of voters in 1997 believed that the economy had improved since 1992, compared to 31% who thought it had declined. However, more voters, 38%, believed that their own standard of living had declined. Only 25% believed that they had benefited from the economic recovery. Labour enjoyed a 4:1 lead among voters who considered that their living standards had not improved.

Why did public perceptions of how the rival parties would handle decisive issues change? After all, Labour had been ahead on the issues before, though not nearly so decisively, and lost the Elections of 1987 and 1992. The answer to this question is suggested by the data reported in Table 3.9. John Curtice (University of Strathclyde) has analysed public opinion on how British voters perceived the parties in terms of images such as 'moderate', 'good for all classes', 'strong, capable government' and 'party unity'.

The striking conclusion to be drawn from Curtice's data is that there was a drastic change in public perceptions of the strengths and weaknesses of the Conservative Party sometime following the 1992 Election. The surveys were held in the spring and early summer of the years in question. In 1992, shortly after the closely contested General Election, the Conservative image was much more positive than Labour's on party unity and on whether the parties were likely to offer strong and capable government. The parties were equally rated on 'moderation' which suggested that Labour had by then lost its radical left-wing image. By 1994 the Conservative image had been severely tarnished on both party unity and the ability to provide strong government. In contrast, Labour's image improved so much that from 1994 onwards Labour was widely perceived as more moderate, more united and more likely to provide strong, capable government.

Curtice attributes this dramatic switch in public perceptions of the attributes of the two major parties to 'Black Wednesday' in September 1992 when the Conservative Government had to withdraw Britain from the European Exchange Rate Mechanism and accept devaluation of the pound. Conservative disunity on European issues was highlighted by Eurosceptics rebelling in Parliament on the passage of the Maastricht Treaty and later the issue of the single currency.

TERRITORIAL POLITICS: A NORTH-SOUTH DIVIDE?

Regional and national variations in voting behaviour and election results have become a major focus of interest in recent years. The government of the United Kingdom to emerge from general elections has occasionally reflected differences in how the parties fared in the four nations. The Conservatives lost their hold on the relatively few Northern Ireland seats when the Ulster Unionists formed their own parties (UUP and UDP) on whose support the Conservatives could not rely completely in the Commons. The Northern Ireland party system diverged from the British with religion and nationalism rather than social class providing the principal political tensions. The Labour Governments elected in 1950, 1964 and 1974 were dependent on winning a comfortable majority of Scottish and Welsh seats to overcome Conservative majorities in England(1950 and 1964) or to compensate for the failure to achieve an overall majority in England (both elections in 1974). Nationalist electoral successes in Scotland and Wales in 1974 appeared to pose a potential threat to Labour's favourable position outside England and so prompted Labour's conversion to devolution.

NEW LABOUR'S CONQUEST OF MIDDLE BRITAIN

1997 vote, % (change on 1992 in brackets)

	Conservative	Labour	LibDem
All Great Britain voters	31 (-12)	44 (+9)	17 (-1)
Men	31 (-8)	44 (+6)	17 (-1)
Women	32 (-11)	44 (+10)	17 (-1)
AB voters	42 (-11)	31 (+9)	21 (0)
C1	26 (-22)	47 (+19)	19 (-1)
C2	25 (-15)	54 (+15)	14 (-4)
DE	21 (-8)	61 (+9)	13 (0)
1st time voters	19 (-16)	57 (+17)	18 (-3)
All 18–29	22 (-18)	57 (+19)	17 (0)
30–44	26 (-11)	49 (+12)	17 (-3)
45–64	33 (-9)	43 (+9)	18 (-2)
65+	44 (-3)	34 (-2)	16 (+2)
Home owners	35 (-12)	41 (+11)	17 (-3)
Council tenants	13 (-6)	65 (+1)	15 (+5)
Trades union members	18 (-9)	57 (+7)	20 (+2)

Table 3.10 Source: 1992 data ITN/Harris exit poll, 1997 data BBC/NOP exit poll

After 1979 the combination of Labour dominance in Scotland and long-term Conservative government at Westminster raised the spectre of the 'Doomsday Scenario'. Liberal Democrat seats were concentrated in Scotland from 1983 until the 1997 breakthrough in England. Finally, there was increasing talk of a deepening North-South economic and political divide under Thatcherism. The Conservatives were much stronger electorally in the Southern half of England, including the English Midlands, than in Northern Britain including Scotland and Wales. The electoral division seemed to be accompanied by economic trends which saw lower unemployment and higher incomes in the South than in the North.

The features described above have stimulated many writers of textbooks on British politics to include a chapter on 'Territorial Politics' in order to describe and explain differences in electoral and party politics in different parts of the United Kingdom. Labour's introduction of legislative devolution for Scotland and Wales increases the chances that territorial politics will become even more pronounced. The first six months of Labour Government were accompanied by several expressions of unease on the part of politicians representing English regions who feared that they would lose out to Scotland and Wales in the competition to attract 'inward investment' from the 'tiger economies' of the Far East.

What, then, are the territorial dimensions to British elections and what explains them? *The British General Elections Studies* reports election results using 8 standard English regions, Scotland and Wales as shown in Figure 3.1.

Table 3.11 illustrates regional variations in voting behaviour in 1987 when the Conservatives won decisively and in 1997 when Labour won even more decisively. In 1987 the Conservatives were the dominant party in terms of both seats and votes in the South of England where Labour was desperately weak outside Inner London. The Conservatives almost monopolised seats in the South East and South West of England, winning all but 5 out of 156 seats on the basis of over 50% of the popular vote. Rural East Anglia was just as strongly Conservative. Inner London, where Labour won 20 out of 29 seats, was an exception to Conservative dominance in the South of England. The Conservatives were also the strongest party in Greater London and the Midlands where they won well over 40% of the vote and well over 60% of the seats.

Only in the northern regions of England did Labour win more seats than the Conservatives in 1987 though Labour's margin, 94 seats out of 161 in the North West (mainly Lancashire), Yorkshire and Humberside and Northern England (essentially the border region) was much smaller than the Conservative margin in its Southern stronghold. Scotland and Wales were even less sympathetic to the Conservatives than the North of England with their vote down below 30%. The North of England was electorally closer to Scotland and Wales.

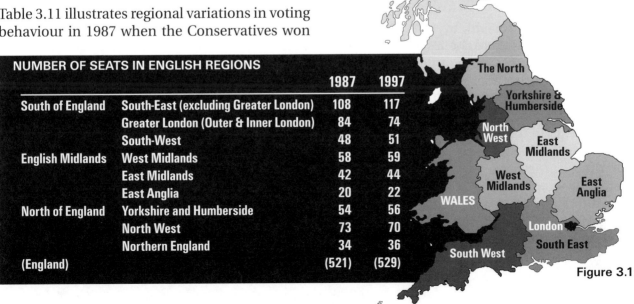

NUMBER OF SEATS IN ENGLISH REGIONS		1987	1997
South of England	South-East (excluding Greater London)	108	117
	Greater London (Outer & Inner London)	84	74
	South-West	48	51
English Midlands	West Midlands	58	59
	East Midlands	42	44
	East Anglia	20	22
North of England	Yorkshire and Humberside	54	56
	North West	73	70
	Northern England	34	36
(England)		(521)	(529)

Figure 3.1

The distribution of votes and seats in 1987 supported the concept of a 'North–South divide' in British politics and society. (See Table 3.12.) The Conservatives won over 80% of the 360 seats (55.6% of the Commons) in the South of England and the English Midlands combined. Labour won over 60% of the 271 seats in the North of England, Scotland and Wales. The 'South' side of the 'divide' could be sub-divided into two sections:

☛ the South East, not including Greater London, the South West and East Anglia where the Conservatives were supreme;
☛ Greater London and the English Midlands where the Conservatives held two-thirds of the seats.

The 'North' side of the 'divide' comprised Scotland and Wales where the Conservatives were extremely weak winning less than 20% of seats, and the three northern regions of England where Labour won more seats than their major party rivals but by much less convincing margins than in Scotland and Wales.

The 1997 Election produced similar territorial patterns though the fortunes of the parties have changed radically. There is now a Labour majority in the Commons and a comfortable Labour plurality in the popular vote. A North-South divide is still visible. The Conservative performance is still relatively in line with the regional patterns of support visible in 1987. The Conservative vote and share of seats falls the further north we go. The political centre of gravity of Britain has shifted decisively to Labour and it has moved northwards. Indeed the dividing line between North and South has shifted because Greater London and the English Midlands are now Labour territory.

The Conservatives remain, even in their worst electoral performance of the 20th century, the strongest party in the South of England outside London. Nonetheless, there are considerable territorial divisions in the South. Conservative strength is confined to the suburban and rural constituencies of the South East where they won 73 out of 117 seats. The only other region to favour the Conservatives was rural East Anglia where they won 14 out of 22 seats. In the South West of England the Conservatives are still the strongest party (36.7% of the vote and 22 seats) though they have lost seats to Labour(26% of the vote and 15 seats) and to the the Liberal Demo-

crats (31% of the vote and 14 seats). Thus the South West supports a three-party system with the Liberal Democrats challenging the two major parties. The South West, like Scotland and Wales, gives hope to the Liberal Democrats.

Outside Southern England and rural East Anglia Labour was dominant in 1997. Greater London became a Labour stronghold. The Conservatives lost three-quarters of their seats in the suburbs of Outer London. Labour is now the majority party in the English Midlands where Conservative losses were particularly heavy. Labour's superiority in North of England constituencies was dramatically extended and rivals the Labour lead in Scotland and Wales.

There are, then, two territorial features to the 1997 collective vote. There was a strong shift to Labour in every region of Great Britain. Labour actually picked up relatively more votes in the South than in the North, but the most significant dimension of the 1997 collective vote was the universal rejection by the voters of Great Britain of Conservative government. However, the territorial dimension remains within the nationwide move to Labour. The North-South divide, which has been developing for 30 years or more, remains in place, though the geographic boundary between 'North' and 'South' has changed with Labour's capture of Greater London and the English Midlands. Any Conservative recovery is likely to depend upon moving the North-South dividing line back to where it was in 1987, north rather than south of the English Midlands.

The territorial dimension in British voting may be explained in part by the class factor. The clue here is the presence of the Labour enclave of Inner London at the height of Conservative electoral dominance in the 1980s. Inner London remained true to Labour because there were enough working-class voters in its inner-city constituencies. Similarly Scotland, Wales and the North of England have more working-class constituencies than their Southern counterparts. However, the territorial divisions are not simply a mirror image of social divisions because the differences are greater than social factors alone would lead us to expect. Even here the explanation relies on class. It was established in the 1960s that the minority class in constituencies which were strongly working class or middle class crossed the party line to a greater

CONSERVATIVE STRENGTH BY REGION AND NATION: 1987 & 1997

Region	Conservative MPs		Conservative vote share(%)		Liberal MPs		Liberal vote share(%)	
	1987	1997	1987	1997	1987	1997	1987	1997
South-East England	107/108	73/117	55.6	41.4	0	8	27.2	21.4
Greater London	57/84	11/74	45.4	31.2	3	6	21.3	14.6
South-West England	44/48	22/51	50.6	36.7	3	14	33.0	31.3
West Midlands	36/58	14/59	48.6	33.6	0	1	20.8	13.8
East Midlands	31/42	14/44	45.5	34.9	0	0	20.9	13.6
East Anglia	19/20	14/22	52.1	38.7	0	6	25.7	17.9
North West England	34/73	7/70	38	26.4	3	2	20.2	14.3
Yorkshire & Humberside	21/54	7/56	37.4	28	0	2	21.6	16.0
North of England	8/34	3/36	32.3	22.4	1	0	21.0	13.3
[England	357/521	165/529		33.7	10	34	23.8	17.9]
Wales	8/38	0/40	29.5	19.6	3	2	17.9	12.4
Scotland	10/72	0/72	24	17.5	9	10	19.2	13.0
Great Britain		165		31.5	22	46	23.7	17.2

Table 3.11

extent than in constituencies where the classes were more evenly matched. Economic trends were also significant. The 'South' generally experienced less unemployment and attracted a higher proportion of the supervisory and skilled jobs in new industries based on technology. The 'North', where unemployment rates were higher, had more than its share of unskilled jobs in heavy industries which were dying out. Another clue lies in Crewe's 'old'-'new' working class distinction. Members of the new working class who were more inclined to vote Conservative than their older brethren were more likely to be found in the 'South' than in the 'North'. Scottish and Welsh support for Labour and hostility to the Conservatives is also explained by political issues such as devolution. Conservative intransigence on this issue in the face of support for devolution from the other parties added to the forces turning voters away from Tories.

THE NORTH SOUTH DIVIDE: CONSERVATIVE AND LABOUR SEATS (%), 1987 AND 1997

	1987		1997	
	CONSERVATIVE	LABOUR	CONSERVATIVE	LABOUR
The Conservative South (SE /SW) & East Anglia	96.6	1.7	57.4	31.1
Greater London and the English Midlands	66.7	30.4	22.0	74.0
North West & North East England	43.3	54.3	11.0	84.9
North of England, Scotland and Wales	17.8	70.6	2.0	81.2

Table 3.12

CHAPTER 4

Political PARTIES

What you will learn

1 The functions of political parties in a democracy
2 The changing ideological beliefs of the major parties
3 How the major parties are organised

THE ELECTORAL SYSTEM described in Chapter 2 ensures that Britain enjoys 'rep resentative democracy'. The voters, whose behaviour has been analysed in Chapter 3, have to be organised. The political institutions which have developed throughout the world to organise elections and voters are *political parties*.

THE BRITISH PARTY SYSTEM

Political parties contest elections, organise voters by giving them meaningful choices, represent them in the legislature, and organise the business of government once the electorate has ahd its say. The members and supporters of a political party share distinctive ideas and philosophies. It is this which provides the bond that in turn allows for the pursuit of agreed policies and objectives. This is not to say that political differences will not emerge within a party. Intra-party differences—conflicts over policy positions within individual parties—are often as significant as inter-party differences between rival parties. It could be argued that internal Conservative Party differences over the EU and a single European currency were the crucial factors in the heavy Conservative defeat in 1997.

Political parties represent the views of their members and supporters in Parliament. Parties compete in elections in the hope that they will win governmental office in order to implement agreed policies. In performing the functions of 'electioneering' and representation, political parties effectively organise the democratic process.

The range of parties in any country reflects its social composition, taking in class, religious, national and regional, linguisitic, ideological and other divisions. Countries with several major social divisions tend to generate several significant or major political parties. Countries with a limited number of social divisions generate fewer major parties. The number of major and minor parties is the product of the interaction between social divisions and the electoral system. As we saw in Chapter 2, proportional representation tends to give more parties representation in the legislature. Parties may be broadly or narrowly based. Comprehensive or 'catch all' parties, common to two-party systems, try to cover as wide a range of political beliefs and interests as possible to ensure a broad-based support capable of winning elections. Smaller parties, especially in multi-party systems which are encouraged by proportional representation, receive the support of such a limited social group that they cannot hope to form a government by themselves.

There are many commentators who argue that the political parties have become much too influential—particularly in the way in which the majority party dominates Parliamentary procedures and Parliamentary business. Nevertheless, although parties have become much more centralised and disciplined they still offer many ordinary people the opportunity to become involved in the political process.

Parties have remained the principal organisers of the political process in Britain even on the few occasions when elections have given way to referenda as the mechanism for achieving some popular control over major decisions. Interestingly, the resort to referenda in 1975, 1979 and 1997 led to parties temporarily renouncing strict party discipline as cross-party alliances emerged to campaign on one side or the other of the questions put to the electorate for decision. However, this was less true of the 1997 Scottish devolution referendum campaign.

There is much consistency and continuity in the names, the number, the functions and the policies of political parties in Britain. This enables us to talk of a 'party system' which may be defined by five dimensions.

1 *Number of major parties:* determines number of parties in the legislature and in the government.
2 *Parties in the electorate:* individual voters psychologically committed to one or other of the parties. (See Chapter 3.)
3 *Functions of parties:* what parties do for themselves and for society as a whole.
4 *Ideology or policy:* indicates the aims of parties and their committed supporters.
5 *Party organisation/structure:* internal distribution of power determining who controls the political parties.

THE NUMBER OF PARTIES: A TWO-PARTY SYSTEM?

The number of parties in any country with a parliamentary system has significant implications for the nature of government and also for the range of opinions represented in both government and in the legislature. The following points should be noted.

1 The fewer the number of major parties, the less likely it is that a country will have a coalition or minority government.
2 The greater the number of parties winning parliamentary seats, the stronger is the ability of every party to represent faithfully the views of its supporters in the electorate.

Historically, the British electorate has preferred a two-party system. The Labour and Conservative Parties have dominated political life since the 1930s. The last Liberal to hold Prime Ministerial office was David Lloyd George, 1916–22. Governmental office has been confined to Conservative and Labour since 1945. Only in one of the fifteen general elections since 1945 has one of the two major parties failed to win a parliamentary majority, though the governing party has lost its majority on occasion in between general elections. Nevertheless, many other parties do exist, some of which win seats in general elections. The situation in which a third party determines which major party should hold office after a general elec-

tion has arisen only once in fifty years. In February 1974, a minority Labour Government was formed after the Liberals decided to support Labour in the Commons rather than the Conservative Administration led by Edward Heath.

The possibility of the two-party mould being broken has been a frequent topic of speculation in the last quarter of the 20th century in response to such developments as:

1 The decline in the combined Conservative and Labour share of the popular vote (See Table 2.2.)
2 The formation of the Social Democratic Party (SDP) in 1981 by breakaway right-wing Labour politicians.
3 The realignment in the 1980s of the political centre when the Liberals and the SDP combined to form the Alliance and then the Liberal Democrat Party.
4 The hints in public opinion polls leading up to the 1992 Election that the result could be a 'Hung Parliament'. In the event, all five elections since 1979 have produced a government based on a single party with a working parliamentary majority, though the Major Government did lose its overall majority in the run-up to the 1997 Election.

The 1997 Election illustrates the arguments for and against the two-party label. The two major parties won their lowest combined share of parliamentary seats in the postwar period—88.6%. The Liberal Democrats won the largest number of seats (46) to go to a third party since 1945. No fewer than five parties won seats in Britain (England, Scotland and Wales). These were Labour, Conservative, Liberal Democrat, Scottish National Party and Welsh National Party (Plaid Cmyru). Six parties won seats in Northern Ireland: Ulster Unionist, Democratic Unionist, United Kingdom Unionist, Social Democrat and Labour Party (SDLP) and Sinn Fein. Nevertheless, the two major parties still won 73.9% of the popular vote. Furthermore, Labour won the biggest share of seats and the largest overall majority since 1945. The Conservative–Labour two-party system survived the 1997 Election in the United Kingdom as a whole.

There are national and regional variations in the strength of 'two-partyism'. Indeed, one could well argue that the 'British' two-party system is an English phenomenon only. It cannot be applied at all to Northern Ireland which has its own parties. In

Scotland the Conservatives won no seats at all in 1997 and they came third in the popular vote. The Scottish electorate, then, no longer supports a Conservative–Labour two-party system.

Scotland may be said to have a one-party dominant, four-party system. In 1997 the electoral system and the voters favoured Labour and the Liberal Democrats and penalised the Conservatives and the SNP. Labour was even more dominant in Wales, winning 55% of the popular vote and no fewer than 34 of the 40 Welsh seats. The Conservatives came second in the popular vote(20%) in Wales but won no seats. Plaid Cymru(10% of the vote) won four Welsh seats and the Liberal Democrats (12%) won two. The Conservative 'wipe out' in Scotland and Wales added a further dent to the two-party mould. The runner-up in terms of seats receives the prize of being designated Her Majesty's Official Opposition. Thus members of the Conservative Shadow Cabinet hold the right of first reply in parliamentary debates. However, the Conservatives have no Scottish or Welsh MPs and therefore have to appoint an MP from an English constituency to lead the debate on Scottish and Welsh issues. The Liberal Democrats suggested in vain after the election that one of their MPs should be the 'Shadow' Scottish Secretary of State.

In spite of these 'national' variations, the 1997 Election continued the 'norm' of the electoral system and the electorate interacting to produce 'majority party government'. This gives a Prime Minister and Cabinet from the one party enjoying a comfortable parliamentary majority. The biggest challenge to the two-party dimension in British politics came from the massive swing against the Conservative Party which won only 30.7% of the popular vote and 25% of parliamentary seats. Still, the long-term resilience of two-partyism is indicated by Labour's recovery from winning 27.6% of the vote and 32.2% of seats in 1983 to winning 43.2% of the vote and 63.6% of seats in 1997.

PARTY FUNCTIONS
Political parties fulfil a great many functions which can be summarised as follows.

1 *Candidate Selection or Political Recruitment:* Political parties select election candidates. Candidates at an election need the backup of a political party if they are to have any chance of being elected to Parliament. Voters tend to vote for a particular party rather than a particular

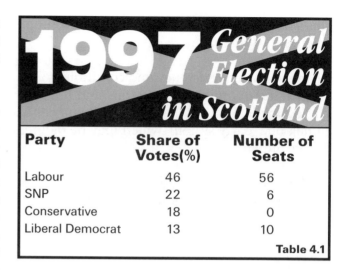

Party	Share of Votes(%)	Number of Seats
Labour	46	56
SNP	22	6
Conservative	18	0
Liberal Democrat	13	10

Table 4.1

candidate. Only one Independent was elected in 1997, the first since 1950. Martin Bell, who was a widely recognised BBC reporter, was elected as an anti-sleaze candidate in Tatton. This unusual Independent success was made possible by the tacit support of the Labour and Liberal Democrat Parties. Their candidates stood down in what had been considered to be a safe Conservative seat in order to secure the defeat of Neil Hamilton who had been accused of committing 'sleaze'.

2 *Electioneering:* Parties provide the money required for an election campaign. They publicise their policies and their candidates nationally and also locally where their members and supporters may canvass, deliver leaflets and so on.

3 *Policy Making:* Parties make elections meaningful by publicising their rival positions on the most important issues of the day. Most voters have a rough idea of what the different parties intend to do if elected. The parties encourage this awareness by publishing Election Manifestoes which state their policy programmes. This allows voters to choose a party whose policies are closest to their own point of view. American parties pay much less attention to policy making than to electioneering, whereas British parties focus strongly on the policy making function.

4 *Governing:* Government is organised by the winning party whose most senior MPs take control of Government Departments. This is why British government is frequently described as 'party government'.

5 *Organising the Parliamentary Process:* With the aid of the Whip System parties organise the

business of the House of Commons. This allows both government and opposition to be effective. As we shall see in Chapter 7 the British Constitution, in the shape of the conventions of ministerial responsibility to Parliament, encourages centralised and disciplined parliamentary parties.

The party functions listed so far describe what political parties do on their own behalf. Parties, however, also perform functions for the benefit of the political system and of society as a whole.

6 *Representation:* Parties represent the views and expectations of those who participate in politics. Through elections, parties ensure that Britain maintains a representative form of indirect democracy, although it should be noted that parties in office have been tempted, on occasion, in recent decades to resort to the more direct form of democracy provided by referenda. The people have been asked to state their collective view on such issues as membership of the European Community and devolution for Scotland and Wales. Parties contribute through the procedures of elections and referenda to ensuring that government is legitimate because it receives the consent of the people who are being governed.

7 *Limiting Polarisation:* The fringe groups which exist on the extreme wings of the political system do not enjoy much success in elections. This is due to the fact that voters can choose between different parties with different outlooks on various issues. In 1997 the British National Party, which blamed "immigration and multi-racialism" for "destroying our children's education, bringing mayhem to our towns and cities and making the British people second class citizens in their own land", came tenth and last with 188 votes in Glasgow Govan which elected Britain's first Muslim MP.

IDEOLOGY AND POLICY

Ideological and policy differences between British political parties have long been expressed in terms of a spectrum running from left to right. Thirty years ago Labour was thought of as left of centre, the Conservatives as right of centre and the Liberals as the centre party. For most of the fifty year period since the Second World War these ideological party images were defined in relation to economic issues and the role of the state in society. Ideologically Labour was a socialist party. It

General Election Results 1974 to 1997

Election	Results	Cons.	Labour	Libs.[2]	Others
February 1974	Votes (millions)	11.9	11.7	6.1	1.7
	Seats	296	301*	14	24
	% Vote	38.0	37.0	19.0	6.0
October 1974	Votes (millions)	10.4	11.5	5.3	1.9
	Seats	276	319*	13	27
	% Vote	36.0	39.0	18.0	7.0
1979	Votes (millions)	13.7	11.5	4.3	1.7
	Seats	339*	268	11	17
	% Vote	43.9	36.9	13.8	4.0
1983[1]	Votes (millions)	13.0	8.4	7.8	1.0
	Seats	397*	209	23	21
	% Vote	42.0	27.6	25.4	3.0
1987	Votes (millions)	13.7	10.0	7.3	1.4
	Seats	375*	229	22	23
	% vote	42.3	30.8	22.6	4.4
1992[1]	Votes (millions)	14	11.5	5.99	2.1
	Seats	336*	271	20	24
	% Vote	41.9	34.4	17.8	5.9
1997	Votes (millions)	9.6	13.5	5.2	
	Seats	165	419*	46	29
	% Vote	30.7	43.2	16.8	5.8

* Denotes Government

1 Number of seats increased to 650 in 1983, 651 in 1992 and 659 in 1997.

2 Liberal/SDP Alliance in 1983 and 1987; Liberal Democrats in 1992 and 1997.

Table 4.2

stood for a redistribution of wealth in society in order to reduce major disparities between the rich and the poor. Labour believed that the state should provide health and welfare for its citizens and control the economy to achieve its aims. Labour promised radical reforms of both society and economy.

The Conservative Party was opposed to socialism. It believed in leaving most economic decision making in the hands of the market economy while accepting the welfare state, the NHS and certain aspects of a mixed economy. Ideologically the Conservatives preferred gradual evolutionary change to radical reform. In spite of ideological differences and intense electoral competition from 1945 until the late 1970s, British politics were characterised as 'Consensus Politics'. There was a broad range of agreement over a number of key economic and social policies such as a mixed economy, the welfare state and the nationalisation of some, if not all, public utilities. Consensus was symbolised in the media by the term 'Butskellism' which suggested considerable policy and ideological agreement between a leading Conservative Butler and the Labour Leader Hugh Gaitskell.

The 1970s proved to be a decisive turning point in British politics. After the long period of Conservative government from 1951 to 1964, the electorate rejected Labour in 1970, the Conservatives in 1974 and Labour again in 1979. British governments during that period experienced major economic problems which troubled most Western capitalist countries. They were confronted by rising rates of inflation and found themselves having to choose between low inflation and low unemployment instead of being able to achieve both simultaneously. The humiliation of electoral defeat stimulated both parties to think out new policies in opposition. The 'Postwar Consensus' came to an end. It gave way to ideological polarisation, a divergence rather than a convergence in the ideological beliefs of the major parties.

Conservative defeats in the two 1974 Elections was followed by the right-wing Margaret Thatcher replacing the moderate Edward Heath as Leader in 1975 and by a radical policy rethink. Mrs Thatcher's name and her policies gave rise to the theme which was to dominate British politics for more than a decade after the Conservatives regained power in 1979. Her policy programme was summed up as 'Thatcherism'; her supporters were the 'Thatcherites'. 'Thatcherism' was considered to be radical and neo-liberal rather than conservative and evolutionary. It echoed Ronald Reagan's famous dictum that "Government is the problem, not the solution".

Electoral defeat in 1979 led to the Labour Party moving to the left because of discontent with the record of the Wilson and Callaghan governments.The left wing demanded, and temporarily achieved, a more socialist programme including a unilateralist defence policy and a commitment to withdraw from the EEC. However, successive electoral defeats in 1983, 1987 and 1992 forced Labour Leaders Neil Kinnock, John Smith and Tony Blair to bring Labour policies into the ideological centre ground. By 1997 the change was so dramatic and the left so marginalised that Labour was commonly referred to as: 'New Labour'. The Conservatives tried to remind voters of the

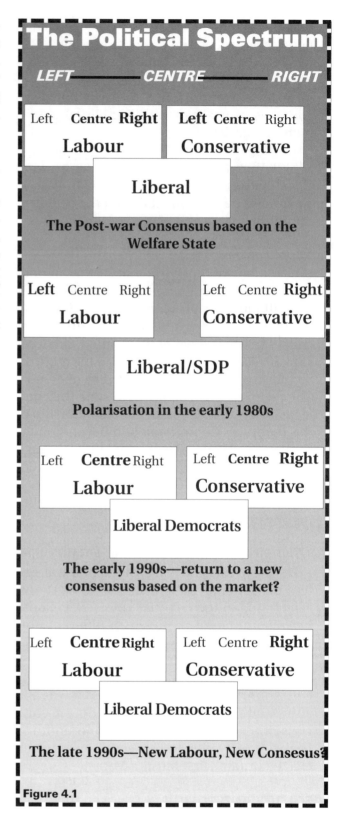

Figure 4.1

alleged deficiencies of the 'old' Labour Party by claiming 'New Labour, New Danger'.

The ideological and policy changes of both major parties are outlined below. The broad picture of the changing ideological spectrum of British politics can be seen by studying Figure 4.1. The left-right ideological spectrum retains some validity, especially because that is how the major parties prefer to see one another. Nevertheless, the left-right ideological dimension has to be qualified by three recent developments. Firstly, both major parties have been shifting their ideological position. The Conservative Party has moved to the right and the Labour Party has redefined its socialism as it moved to the centre. Secondly, a significant feature of recent British politics has been the dramatic impact of constitutional issues, such as devolution and Britain's membership of the European Union. Such issues have cut across traditional party rivalries. Thirdly, neither party is without internal disputes about where the party should stand on the main issues of the day.

Both major parties are themselves made up of competing groups or factions which disagree about policy and ideology. In spite of often bitter internal conflicts over policy British MPs rarely change their party allegiance. When a few do so this is an indication of ideological conflict within the party. In 1995 two Conservative MPs left to join rival parties. On 7 October Alan Howarth (Stratford upon Avon) made the long jump from Conservative to Labour. Howarth was found a safe Labour seat(Newport East) and rewarded after the 1997 Election with a ministerial post (Parliamentary Under-Secretary in the Department of Education and Employment) in the new Labour Government. On 29 December Emma Nicholson (Devon West and Torridge) left the Conservatives to join the Liberal Democrats. She did not contest the seat at the 1997 General Election and received a Life Peerage after the election.

The result of the 1997 election ensured that the defeated Conservative Party would be the one which, like Labour after 1979, would have to re-examine its central policies in the light of the electorate's disapproval.

THATCHERISM: ENDING THE CONSENSUS

From May 1979 until May 1997 British politics and government were dominated by the Conservative Party which won four elections in a row (1979,1983,1987 and 1992). For much of that period, until she was forced out of office in November 1990, the dominant figure was Britain's first female Prime Minister. 'Thatcherism', the decisive radical and neo-liberal policies associated with Mrs Thatcher and her supporters on the 'dry' wing of the Conservative Party, constituted a policy agenda which ended the 'postwar consensus' and changed the face of British politics. If 'conservatism' is associated primarily with preserving the status-quo, then Mrs Thatcher was clearly less 'conservative' than her predecessors Harold Macmillan and Edward Heath.

Mrs Thatcher was Conservative Leader and Prime Minister from May 1979 until November 1990. Under her leadership the Conservatives won three elections and enjoyed comfortable parliamentary majorities. Her policies were radical and not always popular, provoking internal opposition from more traditionally minded Tories who were dismissively known as the 'wets'. The main elements in the Thatcherite Agenda included:

- *Monetarism*
- *Trade Union Reform*
- *Community Charge (Poll Tax)*
- *Control of Inflation*
- *Reducing Income Tax*
- *Sale of Council Houses*
- *Consumer Choice*
- *Privatisation*
- *Greater Reliance on the Market*
- *Internal Markets applied to Education and the NHS*

Underlying these policies, which were implemented in stages as the 1980s unfolded, was a basic determination to reduce the role of government and to replace much of the public sector of the mixed economy with a reliance on market decision making. In two much publicised interviews Mrs Thatcher claimed that she intended to destroy socialism in Britain and to resist the interventionism of Conservatives such as Michael Heseltine whose policies "were more akin to Labour Party policies". Efforts to capture the essence of Thatcherism have used terms such as 'individualism', 'laissez-faire' and 'anti-statism'. Mrs Thatcher demanded that individuals be allowed to make their own choices whenever possible. Conservative educational reforms such as allowing schools to opt out of local authority control in favour of grant maintained status applied the principle of individual choice to education. The preference for market decision making over the bureaucratic alternative was behind the attempt to create a market within the NHS known as an 'internal market'. GPs became 'fundholders' who could 'shop around' for the best hospital treatment for their patients. Catering and cleaning services were put out to tender. Hospitals could apply for a status independent of regional hospital boards and become Hospital Trusts. Thatcher's ideological belief in the primacy of the market was clearly evident in the 'privatisation' of publicly owned utilities such as communications, electricity and water.

The pro-market and laissez-faire emphasis in policies such as privatisation and the internal market prompted the claim that Thatcherism was closer to 19th century liberalism than to 20th century conservatism of the type associated with Harold Macmillan and Edward Heath. Thatcherism sought to achieve limited government interference and a strong state. The state was to be strong, especially in its representation of British interests abroad, but at the same time, it was to be severely restricted in both its functions and its revenue-raising capacity. Tory 'wets', who lost influence progressively as the Thatcherite agenda unfolded, called for a return to 'One Nation Conservatism'. The Conservative Party had long claimed that it represented the interests of the whole nation, hence 'one nation', while accusing Labour of representing narrow class interests, basically trade union interests. A frequent criticism of Thatcherism was that its free market and 'anti-state' principles were enlarging the gap between rich and poor and so contributed to 'two nations'.

Thatcherism frequently combined ideological and political objectives. Council house sales were justified ideologically by references to the desirability of a property-owning democracy. However, they also reduced the role of local government, which was often Labour controlled in urban areas, and they increased the number of owner occupiers who were more likely than council house tenants to vote Conservative. Industrial relations reform could be justified for its own sake, but it could also be seen as weakening the powers of unions and their leaders who were strong supporters of the Labour Party. Legislation was introduced to force the unions towards greater internal democracy and to require ballots of union members before a strike could be called. Mrs Thatcher had a strong personal aversion towards 'corporatism' which is the practice of government consulting widely with interested parties, particularly both sides of industry, before taking decisions.

Running out of Steam
The Major Government elected in April 1992 ran into severe political trouble almost from the start. The issue which was to cause Major severe difficulties which he never quite overcame was the same issue which had stimulated the revolt against Thatcher (though not against all aspects of 'Thatcherism')—Europe. John Major and others had persuaded Mrs Thatcher, against her instincts, to take Britain into the Exchange Rate Mechanism, which allowed limited exchange rate

movements. It was argued at the time that the exchange rate was much too high, especially against the German mark. The drastic fall in stock market share prices which happened on 16 September 1992 (Black Wednesday) proved too much for the pound which was allowed to fall from 1.9 to 1.6 against the dollar. This was, in effect, a devaluation and Britain came out of the Exchange Rate Mechanism. Ironically, the devaluation of the pound made British exports relatively cheaper and imports dearer. This was to provide the foundations of an export-led economic recovery which established the solid reputation of Kenneth Clarke as Chancellor of the Exchequer(June 1993–May 1997). Unfortunately for Mr Major the next step on the horizon of European integration was to be the establishment of a common currency and a common monetary policy . The Conservatives were hopelessly divided internally between Eurosceptics on the right who argued that a common currency meant the end of the British state and more pragmatic Europhiles who believed that, given the right conditions, a common currency could be beneficial to the British economy. Major adopted a 'wait and see' policy as the 1997 Election approached. Opinion polls showing Labour with a large lead forced the Prime Minister to wait until almost the last minute before holding the election.

Willam Hague, a self-proclaimed Thatcherite

The Conservatives lost by a massive margin. John Major resigned as Conservative Party Leader to be succeeded by the youthful William Hague (36) who proclaimed himself a Thatcherite and received her support in the third ballot against Kenneth Clarke. The 1997 Election relegated the Conservatives to the opposition benches and gave the new leadership the opportunity to consider the organisational and policy reforms which many deemed essential if the Party was to regain office.

THE LABOUR PARTY: FROM 'OLD' TO 'NEW'

Labour was also beset by internal battles over ideology and organisation. In particular Labour faced the problem of what to do about its socialist commitment. The choices were to move more radically to the left in pursuit of socialism, or to redefine socialism by moving in the direction of less ideological social democratic parties. Such parties in Scandinavia maintained traditional socialist objectives of social justice and equality of opportunity while accepting a strongly market-oriented economic system.

The period following election defeat in 1979 was one of internal argument for Labour as left and right struggled for control of the Party against a background of failure in government in the 1970s. Labour's left-wing radicalism had been suspended in government because the struggle to control inflation took precedence over all other economic and political problems and frustrated parties which hoped to spend money on social reform. This was a period of electoral defeat for incumbent governments irrespective of political ideology. Conservatives took over government in Britain, Germany (Helmut Kohl) and the USA (Ronald Reagan) while the socialist François Mitterand won the French Presidency (1981).

In October 1980 James Callaghan resigned as Leader and was succeeded one month later by Michael Foot. At this time there was a significant ideological conflict between the 'left' and the 'right' of the Party. The 'left' preferred the radical socialist vision. The 'right' preferred the social democratic option. It was hoped that Foot would be able to bring together the Party's warring factions.

The battle between left, centre and right focused on two critical areas of the Labour Party Constitution. The first of these concerned Party rules relating to the leadership, the selection of parliamentary candidates and decisions about election manifestoes. The second area was that of Party policy, especially the Party's socialist commitment in the celebrated Clause IV.

In 1980–81 Labour's left wing achieved two significant organisational reforms and changed the Party's policy direction. An Electoral College was established which decentralised the process for selecting the Leader and Deputy Leader who, until then, had been elected by Labour MPs only. The Electoral College had three sections, illustrating the federal nature of the Labour Party: the trade unions with 40% of the vote, the PLP (the MPs) with 30% and the Constituency Labour Parties with 30%. For most of the postwar period the sections of the Labour Party outside Parliament had been much more left wing than Labour MPs and Labour governments who had to face the realities of power, especially the electoral realities. The right wing of the Party believed that left-wing leadership candidates would benefit from the Electoral College which gave the sections outside Parliament a say in the election of the Leader. The second organisational reform was mandatory reselection of MPs before every general election. Proposals that the Labour Manifesto should be decided by the National Executive Committee rather than by the Leader alone were not accepted.

The Labour left wing also won decisive policy battles when the Annual Conference reversed Labour Government policies of maintaining Britain's nuclear deterrent and remaining within the European Community. These organisational and policy victories for the left led to some leading right-wingers leaving the Party to set up the Social Democratic Party. The Gang of Four (Roy Jenkins, Shirley Williams, David Owen and Bill Rodgers) decided to continue the struggle for their beliefs outside rather than inside the Labour Party. The choice of name for the new party, whose aim was to 'break the mould' of British politics, was significant—social democratic rather than socialist.

Victory in the first round in the battle for Labour's ideological heart and soul seemed to have been secured by the left, but the right also had its successes. The right of centre Denis Healey, an effective Chancellor in the Wilson and Callaghan Governments, narrowly defeated Tony Benn for the post of Deputy Leader at the 1981 Annual Conference. Benn was the easy winner in the constituency section of the Electoral college which was being used for the first time but Healey won enough trade union and PLP votes to prevail. The battle between the hard left and the rest of the Party now centred on the role of the Militant Tendency, a Trotskyite group accused of attempting to gain control of the Party.

Labour's internal strife and Foot's allegedly weak leadership contributed to the re-election of the Thatcher Government in 1983. The first use of the Electoral College for the election of the Labour Leader led to the selection of Neil Kinnock from the centre-left of the Party. Kinnock won easily over Roy Hattersley who won the post of Deputy Leader almost as easily. Kinnock realised that Labour had to change its image if it was to have any chance of electoral success and he began the process of organisational and policy reform which took more than a decade, survived two more election defeats in 1987 and 1992 and culminated in the record-breaking electoral success of 1997.

The 1987 Conference agreed to a review of Party policy. The left wing of the Party, now on the defensive realising what was likely to emerge from the policy review, responded by challenging Kinnock's leadership. In the leadership election held at the 1988 Conference Neil Kinnock and Roy Hattersley easily saw off the left-wing challenge from Tony Benn and Eric Heffer. Benn received almost no support from the unions and only about 20% of constituency and PLP votes. The so-called 'dream ticket' of the 'soft left' Neil Kinnock and

the centre-right Roy Hattersley could now preside over major policy changes. The 1989 Conference agreed to several recommendations of the policy review process. Firstly, it abandoned unilateral nuclear disarmament. Secondly, it accepted most of the Conservatives' industrial relations legislation which reduced the power of union leaders. Thirdly, it commited the party not to undo the privatisations which had been a major feature of Thatcherism.

The Labour Party's change of direction seemed to be working when it went ahead of the Conservatives in the polls in 1990. The change in the Tory leadership as Thatcher gave way to Major marked the beginning of a Conservative revival. Nonetheless, Labour approached the 1992 election in a much more optimistic frame of mind.

The Arrival of New Labour
In the event, Labour did improve its share of both votes and seats in 1992 but the Conservatives were re-elected. Once again electoral defeat was followed by a change of leadership. Kinnock and Hattersley stood down. In the leadership election held on 18 July 1992 John Smith, MP for Monklands East and Shadow Chancellor, a clear centre right candidate, easily won in all three Party constituencies (Trade Unions, MPs and Constituency Labour Parties) against Bryan Gould. Margaret Beckett was elected Deputy Leader.

CLAUSE IV REVISED

Tony Blair was determined to change Labour's policy image

The new Clause IV is much longer than its predecessor. Its main points are summarised below.

1 Labour is proclaimed to be a democratic socialist party. This is an intriguing claim because in the early '80s, leaders of the Labour right defected to form the 'Social Democratic Party'. This term 'softens' the socialist commitment without jettisoning it altogether. It emphasises the democratic component which might have been obscured by charges of trade union dominance.

2 It also reflects the political philosophy associated with Blair— "communitarianism". In addition to calling for "power, wealth and opportunity" to be "in the hands of the many not the few", the new Clause IV also emphasises the "duties we owe" to the whole community. This community emphasis contrasts sharply with the individualism associated with Thatcherism.

3 Whereas the old Clause IV stressed "common ownership" and "popular administration and control of each industry or service", the new version refers to "a thriving private sector and high quality public services" and, unlike the old version, to "the enterprise of the market" and to the "rigour of competition".

4 Core values compatible with 'socialism' are retained: a "just society", an "open democracy", a "healthy environment".

5 The trade union link is not rejected. Labour is pledged to "work with trade unions and other affiliated organisations".

Smith continued the reform process, concentrating on organisational rules. He was particularly concerned to strengthen the Party's democratic credentials which suffered from a popular belief that the unions had too much power within the Labour Party. Smith persuaded the Party to accept the principle of 'One Member, One Vote' (OMOV) which required unions and CLPs to ballot individual members to decide who they would support in leadership elections. The three units in the leadership electoral college were made equal with unions, consituency parties and MPs each casting one-third of the votes.

Tragically, in 1994 John Smith died. In the ensuing leadership election the centre right of the Party, now popularly known as 'New Labour', won handsomely in the person of Tony Blair who defeated Margaret Beckett and John Prescott, winning over 50% of the vote in all three parts of the electoral college. John Prescott won the contest for Deputy Leader, defeating Margaret Beckett. Although Prescott represented 'Old' Labour through his working-class and trade union background, he was by no means on the Party's hard left.

Tony Blair set about implementing further reforms to ensure that Labour's past failures and image would not lead to a fifth Conservative victory. Blair was determined to change Labour's policy image. His principal achievement was the removal of the famous, or notorious, Clause IV from the Labour Party Constitution. Clause IV had stated that one of the major aims of the Party was: "To secure for the workers by hand or by brain the full fruits of their industry and the most equitable distribution thereof that may be possible upon the basis of the common ownership of the means of production, distribution and exchange, and the best obtainable system of popular administration and control of each industry or service".

Clause IV symbolised a commitment to socialism, to public ownership and to an interventionist state. It was an article of faith for the majority of Labour Party members for most of the 20th century and it was printed on every individual Party membership card. For the Conservatives Clause IV justified their claim, particularly evident during election campaigns, that Labour remained a socialist party. The post war Labour Government implemented Clause IV to some extent by nationalising certain 'heavy industries' such as steel, the railways and electricity. However, Labour Party members disagreed about the essentials of social-

ism and about how to achieve it, especially during long periods in opposition after 1951 and 1979. Right of centre Labour Party members believed that Clause IV was costing the Party votes. In the early 1960s the Labour Leader Hugh Gaitskell tried but failed to have the Clause removed from the Constitution. By the early 1990s the climate had changed sufficiently for Tony Blair to persuade the Party that Clause IV and the Party's socialist commitment should be redefined.

In April 1995 a special Party Conference voted by a two to one majority to replace totally Clause IV with a new statement of Labour's core values. Constituency Associations were particularly favourable suggesting that the left-wing activists who had been dominant there in the early 1980s had given way to enthusiastic supporters of the new Leader. The unions whose political ideology had been clear in the original Clause IV, supported the change by 55% to 45%.

The Labour Party of 1980 was hardly recognisable in the Party which won the 1997 Election so decisively. Indeed, the cartoonist's depiction of 'Tony' as 'Tory' Blair was merely a humorous way of stating a widespread belief that Labour had moved significantly to the right. Blair himself denied the cartoonist's view, preferring to emphasise that New Labour was attempting to establish a "Third Way" in between the socialism of Old Labour and the selfish individualism of Thatcherism. Many Labour supporters still believe in core values which they claim to be compatible with 'socialism' such as equality of opportunity, equity, and a more even distribution of wealth.

THE LIBERAL DEMOCRATS: REFORMING THE CENTRE

The Liberal Party, the forerunner of today's Liberal Democrats, has been classified as a 'minor' political party since the 1920s. It last won a parliamentary majority in 1906. It last won more seats than Labour in 1923 and its vote was reduced to less than 3% in the 1950s. The Liberals won only a handful of seats, usually less than ten, from 1945 until the 1970s when they enjoyed a 'revival' which suggested that the two-party system was weakening. However, the Liberals were the perennial 'victims' of the electoral system as their share of seats failed to match their share of votes. The party was electorally strongest in or near the 'Celtic fringes'. Its leadership has come from Scotland (Jo Grimond and David Steel) and South West England (Jeremy Thorpe and Paddy Ashdown).

The Liberals were perceived as the party of the centre—not socialist but not conservative either. The close election of February 1974 demonstrated that the Liberals were closer in spirit to Labour than to the Conservatives. The Liberals indicated that they would rather support a Labour Government than the continuation of Heath's Conservative Administration when neither of the two major parties won an overall majority in the Commons. When the Labour Government lost its overall majority in the Commons in 1976, it survived with the support of the Liberals who participated in an informal 'Lib-Lab Pact' which gave the Party some influence but no positions in the government. The Conservative victory in 1979 ended the period of Liberal influence.

The 1970s were thus a frustrating time for the centre party which was unable to achieve major party status. The political centre received a big boost when a number of right-wing Labour MPs left in order to establish the Social Democratic Party (SDP). Their stated intention was to "break the mould of British politics". The SDP was not socialist and its members had been long-term opponents of the Conservatives, so there were obvious similarities in policy orientation between the Liberals and the SDP. These similarities led to the formation of the Alliance between them which fought

the Elections of 1983 and 1987 with considerable success. The Alliance was essentially an electoral pact which allowed the two parties to maintain their separate identities and policy preferences. In 1883 the Alliance won 23 seats and a quarter of the popular vote, coming less than 3% behind Labour. However, the Conservatives increased their overall majority and thus deprived the Alliance of any hope of influencing the Government. In 1987 the Alliance fell back slightly and it was clear that neither the SDP nor the Alliance had 'broken the mould'.

Conservative electoral success effectively broke up the Alliance in the same way as it forced Labour into a major policy review. David Steel, the Liberal Leader, called for a complete merger of the two Alliance parties as the way forward. Steel's aim was to strengthen the political centre. His proposal received considerable support from both parties but there was opposition from influential minorities in both camps. David Owen, the charismatic SDP Leader, opposed the proposed merger and resigned his position. After negotiations a new party emerged in January 1988. This was the Social and Liberal Democratic Party (SDLP). About one-third of the SDP refused to join the new party and they continued to operate independently under Owen's leadership.

Under Paddy Ashdown the Liberal Democrats sought ways of redefining their old 'radical' image.

The SDLP had a short life. David Steel retired as Leader and Paddy Ashdown won the contest to replace him in July 1988. The SDLP performed poorly in the 1989 Euro-Elections, and there was considerable discontent with the new party's name. Old Liberals were unhappy even though they predominated within the SDLP; indeed the merger was described as "a Liberal takeover of the SDP". A postal ballot of the SDLP membership revealed strong support for 'Liberal Democrats' as a name consistent with the traditions of the 'old' Liberal Party and the aspirations of individuals who had opted for 'Social Democracy'. In June 1990 the SDP was disbanded though some of its MPs continued as independent Social Democrats until 1992 when David Owen decided not to seek re-election.

In 1992 the Liberal Democrats, in winning 18.3% of the vote and 20 seats, were clearly much stronger than the Liberals had ever been in the postwar period. Nevertheless, there was still an enormous gap between their support in the country and their representation in the House of Commons.

The Liberal Democrats, like Labour, had to adjust to Conservative electoral success. With Labour moving into the centre ground under Smith and Blair, the Liberal Democrats sought ways of redefining their old 'radical' image. Their chosen strategy was to stand aside from Labour's "we shall not raise income tax" platform. Instead, the Liberal Democrats took the bold step of promising to raise income tax by a penny in the pound in order to increase spending on education. The Liberal Democrats also retained their radical stance on constitutional issues, joining with Labour in the Scottish Constitutional Convention in support of devolution. In 1997 the Liberal Democrats benefited from a concentration of effort and resources in seats they had a realistic chance of winning. They enjoyed their most successful election of the post-1945 era, winning 46 seats—more than double their 1992 total— in spite of not raising their share of the popular vote. This was the most successful third party performance since 1929. Ironically, the size of Labour's majority meant that the new government would be unlikely to have any need of Liberal Democrat support in order to survive in office.

The Liberal Democrat gains were almost all from the Conservatives. The Liberal Democratic objective, which was established by the 1997 result, was to continue the process of replacing the Conservatives as the second major party. This objective was achieved in Scotland in 1997 at the parliamentary level.

THE IDEOLOGICAL COMPOSITION OF THE COMMONS

The electoral downfall of the Conservatives in 1997, especially its massive proportions, may be attributed in part to Party divisions—over Europe in particular. Labour divisions over devolution contributed to electoral defeat in 1979. Labour's massive 1997 victory focuses attention on intra-party conflict as potentially more dangerous to Labour than a weak Conservative Opposition. It is therefore worth considering the range of policy positions within the parties in the Commons elected in 1997.

Figure 4.2 illustrates Byron Criddle's view of the divisions or factions in the two major parties. Labour MPs are divided into four potential factions, with the great majority calculated to be loyal to the leadership under most forseeable circumstances. Only the 'public sector tax and spenders' and the 'old socialist Eurosceptics', a mere 20% of the PLP, are reminiscent of 'Old Labour' and potentially hostile to Labour's move to the centre ground of British politics. The remaining 80% of Labour MPs are divided into two equal groups. Two-fifths of the 418 Labour MPs are viewed as

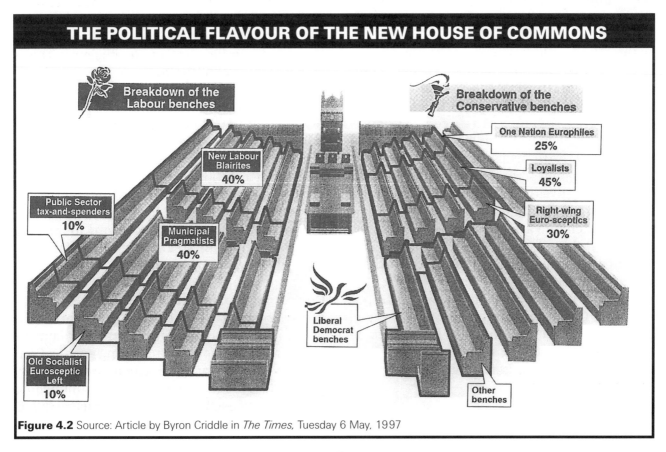

THE POLITICAL FLAVOUR OF THE NEW HOUSE OF COMMONS

Breakdown of the Labour benches

New Labour Blairites
40%

Public Sector tax-and-spenders
10%

Municipal Pragmatists
40%

Old Socialist Eurosceptic Left
10%

Breakdown of the Conservative benches

One Nation Europhiles
25%

Loyalists
45%

Right-wing Euro-sceptics
30%

Liberal Democrat benches

Other benches

Figure 4.2 Source: Article by Byron Criddle in *The Times*, Tuesday 6 May, 1997

'modernising Blairites', who are strong supporters of Blair's approach to politics. The other equally large group is described significantly as 'municipal pragmatists'. These are Labour MPs who developed politically as local government councillors during the period of severe Conservative constraints upon local government spending and initiative. This group could be described as 'Blairite' by necessity if not by inclination. If the forces of pragmatism are indeed stronger than the forces of left-wing ideological purity, then the Labour leadership should be able to rule effectively through the Party in Parliament.

Divisions in the Conservative presence of 165 MPs in the Commons are more acute. The centre is described as 'loyalist', which means that they are loyal to whoever is Leader. However, the centre and the Leader could be assailed from left and right. The old Tory 'wets', who were in the majority before the Thatcher era, are the smallest group. Their 'one nation' philosophy, which is opposed to the Thatcherite hostility towards the interventionist state, along with their sympathy towards the European Union puts them outside the contemporary Tory mainstream. Nevertheless, their influence could be considerable if the new Conservative leadership under William Hague decides that it must rethink Conservative policy and strategy in the light of the 1997 Election result. Their bitter opponents on the right of the Party, the Eurosceptics, are slightly more numerous.

In the 1997 Tory leadership contest, victory went to the centrist candidate William Hague, though he received, belatedly, Margaret Thatcher's backing. The Europhile Kenneth Clarke was defeated in spite of his reputation as a successful Chancellor of the Exchequer and his 'heavy hitter' reputation which arose from his political experience and effective debating perfomances in the Commons. The Conservatives in 1997 appeared to be right of centre and still committed to achieving even more of the Thatcherite agenda. It remains to be seen whether the need to win an election, which set Labour off on a long journey of ideological change, will exert an equally strong impact on the Conservatives. Many commentators wrote off the possibility of Conservative success in the next general election because of the sheer size of their defeat in 1997. It may take more than one election defeat to force the Conservatives to change.

THE ORGANISATION OF POLITICAL PARTIES

The study of party organisation focuses attention on where power lies within a political party. Who controls the major parties? This is a vital question because whoever controls the majority party also controls the government.

There are several levels of party organisation common to most major parties. Logically, one starts with individual dues-paying, card-carrying members. Individual members belong to and participate in the activities of local organisations which are formed around the basic electoral unit in Britain, the parliamentary constituency. In the case of the Labour Party one has to add 'affiliated organisations' to the membership list. These include trade unions, socialist societies, fabian societies and young socialists. Individual members, constituency associations and affiliated organisations constitute the grass roots of the party, sometimes known as the 'party in the country'. The main function of party members is to select the parliamentary candidate who will become the local MP if the party wins the constituency in the general election.

One might expect that the mass membership would be in charge of what a democratic political party does in terms of policy making and governing the country. However, that expectation ignores the need for 'organisation' both at the grass roots and in Parliament. In common with other large groups, political parties must be extremely well organised in order to promote efficiency. This is essential for any group whose members are drawn from all parts of Britain and is especially important for political parties whose members may disagree with each other over important political points. The need to be organised in the interests of efficiency extends to the party's successful parliamentary candidates. Thus the parliamentary parties are organised into leaders (the Cabinet and the Shadow Cabinet) and backbench supporters. Conservative backbench MPs belong to the 1922 Committee; Labour MPs are members of the Parliamentary Labour Party(PLP).

Constituency Organisation

What are the links between grass roots organisations in the country and the parties in parliament? At this point it is worth emphasising that the Conservative Party was established about seventy years before the Labour Party. The reasons behind the origins of each party were completely differ-

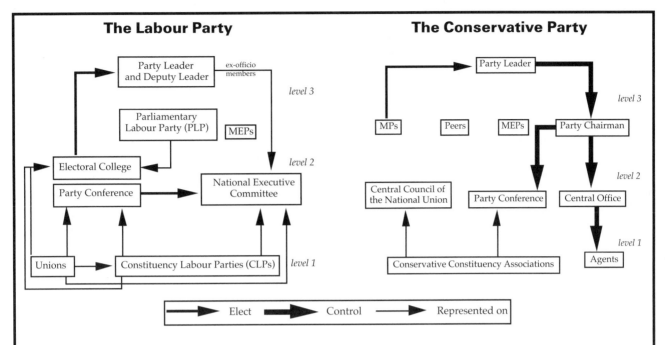

The Labour Party

Party Leader and Deputy Leader — ex-officio members

Parliamentary Labour Party (PLP)

MEPs

level 3

Electoral College

Party Conference

National Executive Committee

level 2

Unions → Constituency Labour Parties (CLPs)

level 1

The Conservative Party

Party Leader

MPs | Peers | MEPs | Party Chairman

level 3

Central Council of the National Union | Party Conference | Central Office

level 2

Conservative Constituency Associations

Agents

level 1

Elect ▬▶ Control ⟶ Represented on

Level 1 (Local)—CLPs composed of representatives from Party Branches, trade unions, Cooperative Party; selects candidates; picks representative for conference; organises local activities.

Level 2 (National)—Holds real power in terms of policy making; NEC suggests policy to conference; conference determines policy which PLP is expected to follow; conference elects NEC.

Level 3 (Parliamentary)—Leader and Deputy Leader elected by electoral college where MPs, CLPs & trade unions each have one-third of the votes. Argue for Party policy as determined by NEC & Conference.

Level 1—Registered members; select candidates; employ an agent to organise activities; pick representative for annual conference.

Level 2 (National)—Coordinates and links local associations; day-to-day administrative functions.

Level 3 (Parliamentary)—Leader appoints Party Chairman who runs Central Office; conference controlled by Leader through Central Office; MPs elect Leader.

Figure 4.3

ent and their contemporary organisation reflects these differences in origin. The Conservative Party proper, consisting of Conservative MPs only, can trace its origins back to the 1830s. Conservative MPs were organised within the House of Commons before the great 19th century reforms of the electoral system and the consequent extension of the franchise made it essential that parliamentary candidates be supported by party organisations in the country. Constituency parties were necessary to encourage the Party's supporters within the increasing number of voters to come out on polling day. Conservative Party Associations were created to serve the Parliamentary Party.

These Associations and their members now constitute the National Union of Conservative and Unionist Associations. The Conservative Central Office was established as long ago as 1871 to give some degree of coherence to Conservative electoral efforts across the country. Because the Constituency Associations and the Central Office were established to serve the Parliamentary Party before the onset of fully-fledged democracy, they have remained, for the most part, subservient to the Parliamentary Party. Conservative Party rules

assign effective power over most Party functions to level three (see Figure 4.3), especially to the Leader elected by the Parliamentary Party.

The Labour Party was established in 1900 as the Labour Representation Committee as a result of a Trades Union Council Resolution in 1899. In other words, it was organised by political forces outside Parliament. The objective was to ensure that the labour movement and the working class were represented in Parliament. At this time more and more working-class men were becoming eligible to vote. However, the two major parties, Conservative and Liberal, were middle-class parties. Labour Party membership could be acquired through individuals joining the Party directly or through membership of an affiliated trade union. These historical events explain why important Labour Party decisions are taken by MPs, CLPs and trade unions and also why Labour has a more complex and decentralised organisational structure than the Conservative Party. Power is spread through the various levels of the Labour Party unlike the Conservative Party in whose simpler, more centralised structure, power is concentrated at the top. (See Figure 4.3.)

In spite of profound differences in the origins of the two major parties, in their attitudes towards the role of government, and in their organisational structures, the widely accepted answer to the question 'Where does power lie within the major parties?' has been the same for both Conservative and Labour. Control of the party both inside *and* outside Parliament normally lies with the parliamentary leaders. The need for leadership and organisation at the parliamentary level and the broader constitutional rule of ministerial responsibility to Parliament (See Chapter 7) explain this central feature of British political parties.

British parties are celebrated for their centralisation and strict discipline, though these qualities are not without exception. The conventional wisdom has been that the Conservative Party is more centralised and easier to control than the Labour Party. Such a claim might have been true of the Conservative Party under Margaret Thatcher and the Labour Party under Michael Foot, yet few would claim that it accurately portrayed the Conservative Party under John Major and the Labour Party under Tony Blair.

Both major parties have a number of organisations and procedures which give the grass roots some say in decision making *and* allow the leaders to control the party as a whole most of the time. MPs are the most obvious links between the parties in the country and their party in Parliament. MPs tend to be loyal to the parliamentary leadership, partly because loyalty may lead to promotion and partly because disloyalty would weaken the party in the fight for political supremacy.

Party Conference

The next link is the national Party Conference which is common to all parties, major and minor. The major parties hold annual Party Conferences in the early autumn. These act as both a rally of the faithful and as decision making bodies. The Conservative Conference, which is heavily stage-managed, is usually devoted to demonstrating support for the Leader and for the policies decided by the Cabinet or Shadow Cabinet.

The Labour Party Conference is much less subject to control by the leaders. The Labour Constitution states that Party policies making up the Labour Programme should be approved by the Conference, subject to receiving two-thirds support. The election manifesto, which consists of policies from the programme, has to be agreed between the parliamentary leadership and the National Executive Committee of the Party. The Labour leadership submits its policy programme to the Conference and both CLPs and affiliated organisations may submit resolutions which may or may not agree with the leadership's point of view. Voting on resolutions is carried out by delegates from both CLPs and affiliated organisations such as trade unions who cast a number of votes determined by the size of their respective memberships. This means that the trade unions dominate voting as there are many more Labour members through trade union membership than through individual members joining the Party directly.

In 1992 there were over 600 CLPs, 280,000 individual members and 4.6 million trade union members from 38 affiliated unions. The trade union vote on conference resolutions is now limited to 70% of the votes cast, though in 1992 trade union membership amounted to 93% of the total membership. The most 'federal' element of Labour Party organisation is the National Executive Committee which oversees Party affairs in between Annual Conferences. The NEC has 29 members representing several levels of the Party. (See Table 4.5.)

The trade unions could elect a majority of the NEC membership if they voted together. However, NEC membership is mainly parliamentary in character because the members elected to represent the CLPs and women's sections of the Party are always MPs, as are some trade union members.

Labour retains a federal organisation in that despite the introduction of 'one member, one vote', voting is decided by electoral colleges of trade unions, constituency associations, MPs, and others. The federal organisation limits the power of Labour Leaders compared to their Conservative counterparts. Once elected, the Conservative

Labour's National Executive Committee

Section of the Party	Nᵒ·	Elected by
Leader and Deputy Leader	2	Ex Officio
Treasurer	1	Whole Conference
Trade Unions	12	Unions at Conference
CLPs	7	CLPs at Conference
Women	5	Whole Conference
Socialist, Cooperative & other affiliated organisations	1	These organisations at Conference
Young Socialists (YS)	1	The YS Conference

Table 4.3

Leader in Opposition has a free hand in relation to choosing the Shadow Cabinet and deciding Party policy.

The Labour Shadow Cabinet is selected by a vote of the PLP. Labour Prime Ministers are not subject to such limitations, since they select their own Cabinet colleagues. However, the organisational and policy reforms accomplished by Labour leaders since the mid-1980s strongly suggest that in the long run the parliamentary Party prevails over the Party in the country and the affiliated organisations.

SELECTING THE PARTY LEADERS

Differences in the location of formal decision making powers are illustrated by the ways in which the two major parties choose their leaders. Both parties have reformed the leadership selection process in recent times, the Conservatives in 1965 and Labour in 1981. Both parties allow for challenges to be made to the incumbent Leader. Leadership elections provide an indication of the degree of ideological or policy conflict within the major parties. They also provide, to an extent, a battleground for the resolution of conflicts between the different organisational elements of the parties, especially between the parliamentary and the extraparliamentary sections.

The Labour Party

The Labour leader used to be elected by the PLP only, a simple absolute majority being required for victory. Michael Foot was the last Labour Leader to be chosen only by MPs. He defeated Denis Healey in November 1980 in a contest which has been compared with the 1997 Tory leadership contest. Foot, a left-winger, defeated Healey who was regarded as the representative of the centre right

The 1994 Labour Leadership Contest

Candidate	Trade Unions	CLPs	MPs	Total
Tony Blair	52.3	58.2	60.5	57.0
John Prescott	28.4	24.4	19.6	24.1
Margaret Beckett	19.3	17.4	19.9	18.9

Table 4.4

leadership which had failed by losing the 1979 General Election.

The Labour leader is now chosen by an electoral college representing three elements of the Party inside and outside Parliament—Labour MPs, the membership organised in Constituency Parties, and members of trade unions affiliated to the Party. This reform was carried out in 1981 when the left wing of the Party, which was in favour of extra-parliamentary controls over the leadership in the House of Commons, was dominant. The CLPs and the unions, the Party outside Parliament, were each given a 'constituency' within a tripartite electoral college. MPs and the CLPs were each given 30% and the unions received 40% of the votes in the college. In 1992 the three electoral college constituencies were made equal. It was also decided at that time to make the leadership election process more democratic by requiring both CLPs and trade unions to consult with their individual memberships in accordance with the principle of 'one member, one vote' (OMOV). The operation of the electoral college may be explained by examining the result of the 1994 contest which established Tony Blair as the Leader.

Within the constituency section, every CLP has one vote which is assigned to the leadership candidate who wins the ballot of individual members. Within the trade union section, every affiliated union is assigned a share of the overall trade union vote (1/3 of the total electoral college) relative to its individual membership as a proportion of total trade union membership. Every affiliated union holds a postal ballot of its members and its electoral college votes are divided between the candidates according to their share of the postal ballot. Tony Blair won a majority in each section of the Party. John Prescott was the runner-up. His strongest support came from the trade union membership which reflected his own working-class and trade union background.

Blair's comprehensive victory symbolised the change in the Labour Party since electoral defeat in 1979. One commentator summed up the change thus: "The Labour Party has deliberately chosen a leader whose image and style appeal to a younger generation and whose association with class politics and fundamentalist socialism is almost non-existent." Three Labour Leaders, Neil Kinnock, John Smith and Tony Blair, have been elected by the electoral college in contests occasioned by the resignation after election defeat

(Foot and Kinnock) or death (Smith) of their predecessors. The leadership candidates must be MPs, which indicates that the House of Commons is the crucial political arena and gives the parliamentary leaders a significant advantage in battles for control of the Party. All three Leaders were elected in the first ballot by comfortable margins in all three parts of the electoral college. Only Neil Kinnock was challenged during his time in office. In 1988 Tony Benn stood as a representative of the old-style left against him but lost heavily throughout the electoral college.

The electoral college mechanism has not handed control of the Party over to either the Left or the Party outside Parliament. The long years in Opposition to Thatcherism convinced many Labour members that the Party had to be 'modernised' if it was to achieve electoral success. Both Kinnock and Smith had to fight long and hard to achieve organisational and policy reforms. Nevertheless, they succeeded and the prospect of election victory gave Blair and the parliamentary leadership effective control in the run-up to the 1997 election. However, Blair himself faced a difficult fight over rewriting Clause IV. Furthermore, the parliamentary leaders had to accommodate several policies recommended by Party sections outside Parliament such as minimum wage legislation and the unionisation of Cheltenham GCHQ.

The Conservative Party
The Conservative leadership election process has been much more competitive and controversial than Labour's in recent decades. The Conservative Leader has been elected only since 1965 when Edward Heath succeeded Sir Alec Douglas Home who stood down following Labour's victory in the 1964 General Election. Until then the Conservative Leader was said to 'evolve' from a consultation process held within the Party. However, the absence of a clear-cut electoral procedure led to difficulties in 1957 and 1963 when the Conservative Leader resigned while holding the office of Prime Minister. In controversial circumstances on both occasions, the leadership issue was settled when the Queen appointed the new Prime Minister. It was argued that the Conservative Party was unnecessarily involving the Monarch in the political process which was held to be contrary to constitutional principles.

The Conservatives adopted a complicated election procedure confined to MPs. In order to ensure that the elected leader would enjoy strong support after the election, a sizeable majority was required to win on the first ballot—an absolute majority plus 15% more of the vote than the runner-up. This majority has been accomplished only once in the five contests since 1965. This was in 1989 when Mrs Thatcher was opposed by a virtual unknown in what amounted to a protest against her leadership style. In 1990 Mrs Thatcher was forced out of office after failing by only a single vote to attract the 15% margin over Michael Heseltine. In the second ballot new candidates may enter the contest. At this stage an overall majority is required for victory. A third ballot may be held if necessary. This third ballot is confined to the leading three candidates in the second ballot. At this stage preferential voting is used if there are more than two candidates. A third ballot has been required only once, in 1997 when there were only two candidates.

Margaret Thatcher challenged and defeated Edward Heath in 1975. Thatcher herself was opposed by Sir Antony Meyer in 1989 and then forced out of office in 1990 as a result of the challenge from Michael Heseltine, though the winner was John Major who entered the contest after Mrs Thatcher's withdrawal. John Major resigned immediately after the 1997 Election defeat to be succeeded, after three ballots, by William Hague.

The 1997 contest took place within an environment dominated by electoral defeat and a Party badly divided by the issue of European integration, especially the single currency question. Four of the candidates had served under John Major until the Labour victory. John Redwood had resigned from the Cabinet to contest the leadership against Major in 1995. The policy divisions ran from Kenneth Clarke on the centre left of the Party to John Redwood on the right. Michael Howard and Peter Lilley were also regarded as right-wingers while the youngest candidate, William Hague, was considered to be the centrist candidate whose views were not as well known as those of the others.

The greatest divide was on 'Europe'. Clarke was the only 'Europhile', favourable to a common currency though open to persuasion about when Britain should join. Redwood was opposed to the common currency under any circumstances. Howard and Lilley were also opposed to a common monetary policy for the EU. Hague's view on the single currency was hostile, but less hostile than that of the three right-wingers. Clarke's disadvantage was

The 1997 Conservative Leadership Contest

Candidate	First 10 June	Second 17 June	Third 20 June
Kenneth Clarke	49	64	70
William Hague	41	62	92
Michael Howard	23		
Peter Lilley	24		
John Redwood	27	38	

Table 4.5

that the small number of Conservative MPs was more Eurosceptic than Europhile.

The contest turned on three issues: leadership, Party unity and the European question. Although Clarke was ahead on the first ballot, this was due to the right-wing vote being divided at least three ways. Hague did better than expected. It had been anticipated that Howard, Lilley and Redwood would unite behind whichever one of them did best in the first ballot. However, when this surprisingly turned out to be Redwood, who was the furthest to the right, Howard and Lilley withdrew and called for their supporters to vote for Hague as the best strategy to ensure the defeat of Clarke, the common enemy. In the second ballot Clarke was still ahead but narrowly. At that point the unexpected happened. Clarke and Redwood, the two furthest apart on most policy issues including Europe, reached an alliance which saw Redwood standing down in favour of the former Chancellor. Lady Thatcher then recommended Hague against Clarke who had advised Thatcher to withdraw after the first ballot in 1990. Clarke and Thatcher were poles apart on Europe.

Although virtually everyone pronounced the contest in the third ballot 'too close to call', Hague won by a surprisingly wide margin. He benefited from the belief that the Clarke–Redwood alliance was unnatural given their longstanding policy disagreements especially on Europe and that this issue would prevent Clarke from uniting the Party over crucial European matters. So Party unity and 'Europe' counted against Clarke. His strongest asset was leadership. Indeed, some right-wingers, who disagreed with him on policy, voted for Clarke

because he had a considerable reputation as a successful Chancellor of the Exchequer and as a tough political operator. A leading opponent who voted for him described Clarke as a "big hitter". Nonetheless, Clarke lost, essentially because his policy stance placed him on the minority left of centre in a Party which had been badly divided over the European issue which would not go away.

However, when Hague rather than Clarke was elected by Conservative MPs (none from Scotland and Wales because there were not any), there was considerable disquiet expressed by many Conservatives in the country concerning the limited electorate. The National Union took a poll of opinion in five sections of the Party: Conservative Peers, MEPs, Constituency Chairmen, Scottish Chairmen and Chairmen in European constituencies. Clarke won a clear majority in all five sections, reflecting his reputation as being a strong character who would put the Conservative case effectively in the House of Commons against the large Labour majority. Nevertheless, this support for Clarke was deemed to be 'elitist' because individual Party members were not asked for their views by many constituency chairmen. It seemed likely that the leadership election rules would be reformed before the next general election.

THE SELECTION OF CANDIDATES

British political parties tend to be run from the centre. The party leaders are drawn from the parliamentary wings of the parties and the leaders usually control the sections of the parties outside Parliament. The history of the Labour Party since Neil Kinnock's assumption of the leadership in 1983 illustrates the power of the centralising tendencies which are normally or eventually dominant in the two major parties. Conversely, the troubles confronting Labour in opposition in the early 1980s and the Conservatives in office in the 1990s indicate that the party leaders may rule uneasily if circumstances such as electoral defeat or intraparty ideological conflict stimulate opposition to the leadership in Parliament. One of the potential battlegrounds of intra-party conflict is the function of candidate selection. Whoever controls the selection of candidates, and the process of reselecting sitting MPs, could be expected to control the party.

The reason for this is that candidates represent the constituencies which elect them and democratic theory assumes that there should be an element of local control over who should be selected to represent both party and constituency.

There are elements of local and central control in the candidate selection procedures of the two major British parties. The Conservatives maintain a list of candidates approved by a committee under the control of the Party Leader. Would-be candidates are subjected to interview before they can get onto the approved list. They are then eligible to be selected by a constituency party. A short list of candidates is drawn up by committees before the full membership of a local Conservative Constituency Association meets to listen to the candidates and to select one in a vote of the individual members of the Party present.

Labour Party organisation at the constituency level is more complex than Conservative organisation. A CLP may include a number of branches based on local government wards and some affiliated organisations such as trade unions. Both the branches and the affiliated organisations may propose individuals as candidates. Labour Party headquarters in London does maintain lists of candidates who may be approached by CLPs. A short list is determined by the CLP's executive committee and the candidate is then chosen by a vote of the individual members of the constituency party.

The two major parties have experienced internal conflicts over candidate selection, especially at the stage of the reselection of sitting MPs. If an MP's general ideological position or his/her position on a particularly divisive policy issue is at odds with the majority of members in the constituency party then the MP may be in trouble. It was feared in the early 1980s when Labour required the mandatory reselection of sitting members that this would lead to the deselection of right-wing and centrist MPs out of step with left-wing majorities among the party activists who would turn up and vote at CLP meetings. In the event, though there have been a number of deselections, these fears were unrealised. Labour has acted to deselect left-wing Militant candidates who embarrassed the 'modernisation' of the party under John Smith and Tony Blair.

PARTY POLICIES

The comparison of the major policies of Conservative and Labour on page 53 is based on the Manifestoes published in the spring of 1997 in preparation for the election on 1 May. The manifestoes reflected the rival positions of the two major parties at that time. The Conservatives were at pains to defend a record based on 18 years in power, whereas Labour emphasised alleged deficiencies in that record and the alternative solutions offered by a party which had undergone an ideological and organisational transformation. Labour's policies are also of interest in so far as some accept elements of Thatcherism enacted after 1979.

The Conservatives emphasised Britain's economic progress from "sick man of Europe" to "its most successful economy". Conservative reforms had "rolled back the state" and "engage(d) the private sector in areas previously dependent on the public purse". The consequence is that the UK has become "the enterprise centre of Europe". Conservatives asserted the need to "protect our constitution and our unity as a nation".

Labour openly emphasised 'new Labour' whose policy programme belonged in "a new centre and centre-left politics" and was distinguished from both 'the old Left' and 'the Conservative Right'. 'New Labour' rejects both state control of industry and leaving "all to the market". It will not return to "the trade union law of the 1970s" and accepts "the global economy as a reality". Labour promised a "radical government" but a radicalism of "achievement" not of "doctrine".

CONSERVATIVE AND LABOUR PARTY POLICIES COMPARED

ISSUE	CONSERVATIVE	LABOUR
CONSTITUTIONAL CHANGE **1 Devolution**	Preference for evolutionary change which means giving more activities to the Scottish and Welsh Grand Committees but opposed to separate assemblies for Scotland and Wales which "could well pull apart the union". Following devolution referenda Hague stated that Conservatives will accept the wishes of the Scottish and Welsh people on this matter.	Commitment to establish a Scottish Parliament with law-making powers and limited financial powers which will "extend democratic control over the responsibilities currently exercised administratively by the Scottish Office". (Labour's manifesto commitments to Scotland and Wales were among the first major policies to be enacted by the new Labour Government. See Chapter 9).
2 House of Lords	Hardly mentioned; indication of opposition to Labour's proposed reforms.	Abolition of right of hereditary peers to sit and vote; legislative powers of Lords to remain unchanged. Appointment of life peers to reflect votes cast per party in the general election. Opposed to any one party enjoying a majority in the upper chamber. (See Chapter 6.)
3 European Union	Vision of EU as "a partnership of nations"; aim is to be in Europe but not to be "run by Europe". Totally opposed to a federal European state; diversity and flexibility preferred to rigidity. Social Chapter opt-out to be maintained and any new employment chapter in a revised Treaty to be resisted. Favourable to further enlargement and a strengthening of the Parliament. Commitment to a referendum on any proposals for a single European currency which a Conservative Government felt would be beneficial to Britain's interests.	Vision of EU as "an alliance of independent states"; opposition to a European federal state. Committed to reform including rapid completion of the single market, enlargement, urgent overhaul of the Common Agricultural Policy, retention of national veto over "key matters of national interest" and "Britain to sign the social chapter". The Cabinet, Parliament and the people in a referendum must all agree to Britain joining the single currency.
EDUCATION	National targets for school performance; parents to get full information of performance of child's school. Regular testing essential. More rigorous system for appraising teachers to be developed. Voucher scheme for 4-year-olds to be used in private or public sector according to parental wishes. Expansion of assisted places scheme. Grant maintained schools to be encouraged.	"…will be Labour's number one priority". Share of national income spent on education to be raised. Class size for 5–7-year-olds to be cut to below 30. Comprehensive schools to be modernised and "setting" to be introduced.
CRIME/LAW AND ORDER	Extend CCTV to town centres, villages and housing estates. Introduce voluntary identity card scheme. Parental Control Orders to encourage or require parents to take responsibility for unruly children.	"Tough on crime and tough on the causes of crime." (A new approach defining 'new' Labour and designed to make 'law and order' less of a Conservative issue.) Halve the time it takes to get persistent young offenders from arrest to sentencing. Decentralise the Crown Prosecution Service. Allow MPs a free vote on proposals to outlaw possession of handguns. "Zero tolerance" approach to "anti-social behaviour and crime on our streets".
NATIONAL HEALTH SERVICE	"Continue to increase real resources committed to NHS." Increase medical school intake. Encourage spread of GP fundholding.	"We will save the NHS." Raise spending in real terms every year. End the internal market in health care; spend on patient care rather than on the bureaucracy generated by the Conservatives' internal market. Introduce a food standards agency. End waiting for cancer surgery.
TAXATION AND SAVINGS	Aim of 20% standard rate of income tax; tax system to be made more favourable to families. Threshold for inheritance tax to be progressively increased. PEPs and TESSAs to be continued. State pension scheme to be "transformed" via 'personal pension funds' which will relieve the pension burden on future generations of taxpayers.	"No return to penal tax rates that existed under both Labour and Conservative governments in the 1970s". Labour will not raise the basic (23%) or top (40%) rates of income tax during the next Parliament, and will aim for a starting rate of 10% to help those at the lowest end of the earning scale. Introduction of 'individual savings accounts' (ISAs) to "extend the principle" of, but replace, PEPs & TESSAs: objective is to encourage poorer sections of society to save for their old age.
JOBS AND INDUSTRIAL RELATIONS	Priority will be to create jobs but "No Conservative government will introduce a new minimum wage". The EU's 'social chapter and minimum wage legislation criticised as 'the European social model' which Conservatives will continue to oppose because it breeds "red tape and regulation" and obstructs job creation.	Will introduce minimum wage legislation and a 'welfare to work budget'. "The key elements of the trade union legislation of the 1980s will stay-on ballots, picketing and industrial action".

CHAPTER 5 Members of PARLIAMENT

What you will learn

1   The role of MPs in British democracy

2   The gender and educational background of MPs

A GENERAL ELECTION is organised around individual candidates along with the voters in constituencies, which are geographically or territorially defined. The 1997 Election returned 659 men and women to the House of Commons to represent the various interests of the single member constituencies which preferred these candidates to their rivals. It used to be the case that only the names of the individual candidates were listed on the ballot paper. Now the candidates' parties are also listed. The power to elect MPs lies with voters in individual constituencies which vary enormously in terms of socio-economic composition, economic activity (how constituents make their living) and territorial extent. A constituency might be concentrated in a very small inner city area with a high population density (Glasgow Kelvin has 47.2 individuals per hectare) or spread across a vast rural territory running from one side of Scotland to the other (Ross Skye and Inverness West has a population density of 0.1 people per hectare). The individuals elected to represent the 659 localities are known by the name of the constituency which elects them—the Right Honourable Member for Glasgow Springburn or the Right Honourable Member for Edinburgh Pentlands. Single member constituencies and their MPs seem to emphasise an individualistic and local type of politics.

Representative Democracy

MPs are, above all, representatives. Britain is often called a 'representative democracy'. How do MPs carry out their representative function? How far can they go on behalf of their constituents? Members of Parliament have considerable powers. Collectively, through the right to vote in the House of Commons, they possess the powers to legislate and to hold the government to account. Once in the Commons it might appear natural that

each MP would decide how to vote according to the interests and wishes which are predominant among and sometimes unique to the voters who have returned him or her to Westminster.

However, MPs experience divided loyalties—to individual constituents, especially those who voted for them, to their local constituencies, to their party, to region and to nation, to individual conscience and to ideological beliefs. Predominant among these loyalties is the MP's political party. MPs do get the opportunity to be true to all of these loyalties but to vastly differing degrees. Elections and the House of Commons are organised by political parties, as we saw in Chapter 4. The Constitution, at least in the pre-devolution age, encourages centralisation and party discipline. Indeed, both major parties have been at pains to strengthen these characteristics because lack of unity and discipline cost Labour dearly in elections from 1979 to 1987 and helped to cause the Conservatives' downfall in 1997.

The proper role of the MP has long been the subject of debate. The classic case for allowing an MP to act primarily as an individual at Westminster was made in 1774 by Edmunde Burke, a celebrated political theorist. Burke had just been elected to the Commons as MP for Bristol. He informed the people who had returned him to Parliament that MPs should not be considered to be merely constituency delegates or agents. Rather, the MP should first be considered to be a Member of Parliament before being thought of as member of a particular constituency. In Parliament he (there were no female MPs until 1919) should represent the 'one interest' of the 'one nation' which he would define according to his own individual judgment of the issues to be decided by Parliament. Burke was the originator of 'One Nation

The role of the contemporary backbench MP includes:

1 **Supporting or opposing the government of the day.**
2 **Representing constituency interests.**
3 **Securing the redress of grievances on behalf of individual constituents.**
4 **Participating in the legislative process—usually as 'lobby fodder', though occasionally as the sponsor of a Private Member's Bill.**

Conservatism', the idea that the British nation as a whole has identifiable interests, which became a rallying cry of Conservatives opposed to Thatcherism on the grounds that it was dividing rather than unifying the country.

Burke was writing and acting in the 18th century when constituencies had few voters and many were 'rotten boroughs' under the control of the local landowning aristocrat. In the middle of the 19th century Parliament experienced a 'golden age' when MPs did indeed decide for themselves how to vote in pursuit of the national interest. However, beginning in 1832, the great Reform Acts of the 19th century gradually extended the right to vote to more and more males. 'Rotten boroughs' began to disappear and voters began to decide election results. With 'democratisation' came party organisation because it became essential to run election campaigns in order to attract votes. The Conservative Party in Parliament set up an organisation outside Parliament to run campaigns in the constituencies. The Liberals did likewise. The parliamentary sections of these parties quickly became dominant.

The formation of the Labour Party at the very beginning of the 20th century by organisations outside Parliament suggested that MPs should be subservient to the people and the interests which they represented. The widening franchise (the right to vote) and the resulting development of party organisation spelt the end of Burke's independent MP who had used his judgment to de-

cide what was best for the nation. Conservative Eurosceptics, who caused John Major so much grief after 1992, would no doubt claim that 'Europe' was an issue of such overwhelming importance that MPs were duty bound to adhere to Burke's concept of the independent MP. Nevertheless, such voting against the agreed party line had long since become the exception rather than the rule. MPs were expected to toe the party line.

MPs are still expected to represent their constituents and the nation, but there are strict limits on how far they may go as constituency representatives. MPs of the governing party are expected to support their party leaders in government so that their common objectives may be achieved. Opposition MPs are expected to unite behind their leaders who form an alternative government in waiting. Perceptions of party loyalty and unity may play a decisive role in determining general election results. Rebellious MPs are unlikely to advance through the ranks to hold governmental office.

The Roles of the Contemporary Backbencher

Members of Parliament are not equal in status in spite of their common representative function. There are two types of MP—frontbenchers and backbenchers. The seating arrangements in the Commons emphasise its partisan nature and also the presence within the legislature of the political executive, Prime Minister and Cabinet, which is a central feature of the parliamentary system. The two major parties sit confronting one another. Members of Her Majesty's Government and of Her Majesty's Opposition sit at the front and their supporters who do not hold office sit behind them. Thus each party has its frontbench leadership and its supporting backbenchers. Backbenchers are also known as Private Members.

The 1997 General Election returned 419 Labour MPs, including the Speaker, to Westminster. The new Government, the Labour frontbench, comprised 73 MPs (14 women), 15 members of the House of Lords (5 women), and one member of the executive who is not a member of either the Commons or the Lords (the Solicitor General for Scotland). Another 16 MPs (2 women) were appointed as Whips, and another 41 were appointed as parliamentary private secretaries (PPSs) to Ministers. The PPSs are on the fringe of government, hoping for promotion to ministerial status when the Prime Minister decides to reshuffle her/his

Parliamentary Timetable 1990-91

	% of Time
Government legislation	24.6
Government Motions and Debates	11.1
Opposition Motions	8.6
Ministerial Statements	8.3
Question Time	8.4
Backbenchers' Bills	4.2
Backbenchers' Motions and Debates	16.0
Miscellaneous (eg. debate on Queen's speech)	18.8

Table 5.1 Source: Bill Jones et al, *Politics UK* (Harvester Wheatsheaf, 1991) page 330.

government team. When Martin Chisolm resigned as Under Secretary of State at the Scottish Office, in protest at his government's proposed cuts in welfare benefits, he was replaced by Calum MᵃᶜDonald who was serving as PPS to the Secretary of State for Scotland, Donald Dewar. These government appointments left 290 Labour MPs on the backbenches. The Conservative frontbench in the Commons comprised 40 MPs; another 10 Conservatives were appointed Whips. This left just over 100 Conservative backbenchers. This chapter looks primarily at the role of backbenchers. Chapter 7 on the Executive analyses the role of frontbenchers.

The backbench 'class of '97' included 260 MPs new to the House of Commons, a postwar record. This was due to Labour's larger than expected majority and to a large number of retirements (117) prior to the Election. New MPs made up 44% of the Parliamentary Labour Party (PLP) and a majority (29 out of 46) of Liberal Democrat parliamentary representation. The size of the Labour majority and the large proportion of 'fresher' MPs stimulated speculation about how disciplined the new

intake would be. Large majorities are sometimes thought to encourage indiscipline because the government is very unlikely to be defeated if a few of its backbenchers defect or abstain on issues about which they feel strongly.

Representation, which is one of the central functions of the British Parliament and its members, may be looked at from two distinct perspectives. MPs 'represent' both their constituents and their constituencies. MPs are also representative of some sections of British society. To what extent are they representative of society as a whole, of all significant majorities and minorities? In other words, we are interested in *what* our Members of Parliament do and in *who* they are.

The first duty of the MP is discharged above all in the division lobbies of the Commons. MPs have little option but to toe the party line, especially if they are politically ambitious and hope one day to be part of the leadership of their party and thus be a member of the government. British parliamentary parties are strongly centralised and disciplined. Although slightly less so than they used to be, they are much more centralised and disciplined than, for example, their American counterparts in Congress. Thus MPs have frequently been disparagingly described as 'lobby fodder'— as mere supporters of their frontbench leaders who are expected to be like good children 'seen and not heard'. A government with a comfortable working parliamentary majority controls the business and the timetable of the Commons and allocates the great majority of the parliamentary timetable to enacting its own legislative policies and debating issues of its choosing.

Table 5.1 indicates the relative shares of frontbench (including Opposition frontbench) and backbench time in the 1990–91 parliamen-

Adjournment Debates in the House of Commons: Week of 2 June 1997

At the end of each parliamentary day a motion is put that 'this House do now adjourn'. A backbencher then speaks on an issue which he/she has chosen and a Government Minister replies. Backbenchers frequently select issues which are significant to their constituents, perhaps pointing out problems which their constituents believe are in need of attention. The range of topics which come up in Adjournment Debates is illustrated below.

	Backbench Sponsor	Topic of Debate
Monday 2 June	Hunter (Basingstoke), Conservative	Guardsmen sentenced to life imprisonment for shooting suspected terrorist in Ulster (victim was not a terrorist)
Tuesday 3 June	Galloway (Glasgow Hillhead), Labour	Human rights in Bahrain
Wednesday 4 June	Harris (Oxford West and Abingdon), Liberal Democrat	Road Safety
Thursday 5 June	Mackinlay (Thurrock), Labour	Loss of Accident and Emergency Unit from local hospital
Friday 6 June	Amess (Southend), Conservative	'Bed-blocking': hospital beds not being utilised **Table 5.2**

The Wild Mammals (Hunting with Dogs) Bill

ONE OF THE MOST hotly debated political issues in November 1997 was the Wild Mammals Bill, introduced into the Commons on Friday 27 November by Michael Foster, Labour MP for Worcester.

The focus of the Bill was foxhunting. Large majorities in public opinion polls both nationally and locally were found to be in favour of a ban. Backbench Labour MPs were enthusiastic supporters, but the issue raised one of the fundamental dilemmas of democracy: tension between the wishes of the majority and the rights of minorities. The minority in this case were people living in the countryside whose attitudes to fox-hunting differed from those of the urban majority opposed to it. Although the Bill was thought to possess unusually strong support, the attitude of the new Labour Government was lukewarm because of a fear that the Bill might use up valuable parliamentary time. Opposition MPs and Lords were considered to be capable of prolonging the time necessary to achieve passage of the Bill.

In the event, the Bill was given a second reading on a free vote by 411–151. The outcome was determined by the PLP's massive support for the proposed ban on fox-hunting—only two Labour MPs voted against. The Conservatives, now largely a rural-suburban party in the Commons, were almost equally united in opposition, though 8 Tories voted with the majority. The Liberal Democrats were the most divided— 3 Scottish Liberal Democrats voted for but 6 voted against. In contrast the SNP, representing similar constituencies with a strong rural element, joined Labour in favour of the proposed ban.

	For	Against	Not Voting
Labour	372	2	39
Conservative	8	126	26
Lib. Dems.	27	14	5
SNP	4	0	2
Others	0	9	13

tary timetable. Backbenchers are allocated about 20% of the timetable for their two major contributions to the work of the Commons: private members' legislation and debates on topical issues which they select. Backbenchers also play a leading role at Question Time, though the focus is more on how Ministers perform under the pressures of interrogation and the televising of parliamentary proceedings. MPs do participate in debates on government legislation and on issues selected by both front benches, though such debates are led by Government and Opposition spokespersons.

The most significant parliamentary procedures from the backbench perspective are adjournment debates, questions both oral and written, and Private Members' legislation. These procedures permit backbenchers to represent their constituents, to indulge in a little legislative creativity, and to compete for promotion to the front benches.

Backbenchers in the Legislative Process

Although the primary function of a legislature might appear to be to legislate, the legislative process in the Commons is dominated by the government of the day. Backbench MPs have very few opportunities to be creative legislators. Rather, they are expected to support or oppose the government's legislative programme which dominates the parliamentary timetable.

Backbenchers are given two procedures whereby they may introduce Bills which they have initiated themselves or put forward on behalf of the interests of their constituents or pressure groups to

The Class of 1997: MPs' Education & Occupation

	% of MPs who attended:	Labour	Conservative	Liberal Democrats
Education*	University	66	81	70
	Oxford & Cambridge	15	51	32
	Public School	16	66	41
Occupation*	Professions	45	37	50
	Business	9	39	24
	Manual Workers	13	1	2

*The educational and occupational categories are not exhaustive and so do not add up to 100%.

Table 5.3   Source: *Times Guide to the House of Commons*, May 1997

WOMEN CANDIDATES & MPs BY PARTY: 1997

Party	No. of Women Candidates	No. of Women Elected	Success Rate (%)	% of Party in Commons
Labour	159	102	64.0	24.4
Conservative	67	13	19.4	7.9
Liberal Democrat	142	3	2.1	6.5
Nationalist	23	2	8.7	20.0
Total	391	120	30.0	18.2

Table 5.4

which they are sympathetic—the Private Members' ballot and the 'ten minute' rule. Every parliamentary session a ballot is held which awards 20 backbenchers the opportunity to introduce Bills for which time is allocated on Fridays. The lucky MPs have a fair chance of seeing their proposals enacted—in 1990–91 ten of the Bills introduced in this way reached the statute book. MPs may also introduce Bills under the ten minute rule which permits an MP to explain the purpose of a Bill without any guarantee that space will be available in the parliamentary timetable to take the Bill through the full legislative process.

WHO THEY ARE

MPs represent, but how representative are they? Who are the MPs we elect in terms of their social characteristics? The conventional wisdom has long been that MPs have been predominantly 'male, middle class and white'. Nonetheless, there have been changes over the years and the 1997 General Election may be a significant landmark in gender representation. In the half century since the Commons elected in 1945, the Conservative Party in Parliament has become less elitist in educational terms and the Labour Party has become less working class and more middle class.

In 1945 a massive 83% of Conservative MPs had been educated at public schools, no fewer than 27% at Eton, and 65% had been to university, mainly to Oxford and Cambridge. The PLP was dominated by members of the working class until the 1930s.

MPs are highly educated individuals; no fewer than two-thirds of those elected in 1997 had been to university. The 165 Conservative MPs in the 'class of 97' were still distinctive in terms of educational background. Two-thirds had been to public school, though only 15 (9%) had been to Eton. Over 80% were university graduates, just over half having been to 'Oxbridge'. The proportion of Labour MPs with a university education had increased since 1974 from 53% to 66%. However, the PLP was less elitist than the Conservative Party in the Commons; only 15% had been to Oxford or Cambridge. Only one Labour MP had been educated at Eton though 64 (16%) had attended (lesser) public schools. The educational profile of Liberal Democrat MPs was almost mid-way between that of their major party rivals.

The occupational backgrounds of the parties in the Commons did differ but all three were almost exclusively middle class. Only 56 MPs, all but two of them Labour, came from manual occupations. The proportion of Labour MPs from manual occupations had fallen from 28% in October 1974 to 13% in 1997. The teaching profession were strongly represented in the PLP with no fewer than 111 having been employed in schools or higher education institutions. The PLP also contained representatives of other public sector workers such as civil servants, local government officers and social workers. Thirty Labour MPs and only 5 Conservative MPs had worked in the civil service or in local government. Conservative MPs were strongly representative of the professions, especially the law, and the business community. Over 50 Conservative MPs, compared to 16 Labour, were company directors or executives. The smaller Liberal Democrat representation in the Commons was closer to Labour in its number of MPs from the professions and closer to the Conservatives in its members from the business community.

Ethnic Representation

The number of candidates from an ethnic minority background almost doubled between 1992 (23) and 1997 (42). The Liberal Democrats led the way with 19 such candidates followed by Labour with 13 and the Conservatives with 10. Labour's ethnic minority representation increased from 5 in 1992

Number of Women MPs: Selected Elections 1945-1997

Election	Number of Women Candidates	Number Elected	% of House of Commons	Conservative	Labour	Liberal	Other
1945	87	24	3.8	1	21	1	1
1964	89	28	4.4	11	17	0	0
1970	97	26	4.1	15	10	0	1
1983	276	23	3.5	13	10	0	0
1987	327	41	6.3	17	21	2	1
1992	568	60	9.2	20	37	2	1
1997	NA	120	18.2	13	102	3	2

Table 5.5   Source: *Times Guide to the House of Commons* May 1997

to 9 in 1997. Glasgow Govan elected the first Muslim MP, Mohammed Sarwar. The only Conservative Asian MP, Nirj Deva, was defeated.

Gender Representation

The 1997 General Election may mark an important breakthrough in the representation of women in the British Parliament. The first woman to sit in the Commons was Nancy Astor in 1919. However, female representation at Westminster remained under 5% until the 1980s when it started to rise from a low point of only 10 in 1979.

There was very little change in female political participation as indicated by candidates selected by the political parties and by the number of women elected to Parliament between 1945 and 1970. The number of women candidates doubled between 1970 and 1979. By 1992 there were over 500 female candidates and the number elected jumped to 60 in 1992 and to 120 in 1997. Thus by 1997 almost one-fifth of MPs were women compared to 52% of the total population. Labour was well ahead of the other British parties (excluding the SNP) with women MPs making up almost a quarter of the Parliamentary Labour Party.

Table 5.4 emphasises Labour's huge lead in terms of getting women candidates elected to the Commons in 1997. There are two reasons for this achievement. Firstly, Labour's dramatic victory meant that the Party's overall success rate was high—419 candidates elected out of a total of 641 in Great Britain (Labour did not put up any candidates in Northern Ireland's 18 constituencies). Secondly, in spite of the eventual outlawing of women-only short lists in the selection process for candidates, Labour took positive steps to encourage Constituency Labour Parties (CLPs) to adopt

female candidates. The 1993 Conference set an objective of selecting women in at least half of the Labour held seats where the sitting MP intended to retire. Labour attempted to accelerate the process by encouraging women-only short lists. By early 1996, 35 CLPs had used this device. However, some disgruntled men complained to an Industrial Relations Tribunal that such lists ran foul of the Sex Discrimination Act. They argued that being an MP constitutes employment, that the selection of candidates amounts to competing in the job market and that therefore the Act outlawing sex discrimination in employment practices should apply. The Tribunal found in their favour in August 1996. Thereafter women-only short lists were not permitted but the candidates already selected by this method were allowed to stand.

SCOTLAND'S GENDER REPRESENTATIVES

Scotland's female representation (15%) lagged behind the overall Commons composition by gender (18.2%) except for the SNP's small group of 6 MPs, two of whom are women (Margaret Bain, Moray and Nairn,who is the Party's parliamentary leader, and Roseanna Cunninghame, Perth and Kinross). Almost 16% of Scotland's 56 Labour MPs were women compared to 24.4% for the Labour Party as a whole.

Scotland's Women Candidates & MPs by Party, 1997

	Nº. of Women Candidates	Nº. of Women Elected	Success Rate (%)	% of Women MPs in Scottish Party
Labour	15	8	53	15.7
Conservative	9	0	0	0
Lib. Dems.	16	1	6	10.0
SNP	15	2	1	33.3
Total	55	11		15

Table 5.6   Source *Times Guide to the House of Commons* 1997

CHAPTER 6 PARLIAMENT

PARLIAMENT IS the centrepiece of the British political system. It is in Parliament that the policies proposed by Her Majesty's government are debated and then transformed into the law of the land. It is in Parliament that Ministers of the Crown carry out their democratic responsibilities to the elected representatives of the British people. In other words, the British system of government is first and foremost a parliamentary system.

To most people the British 'Parliament' means the House of Commons. Indeed, this is where we see the major party leaders in action. The MPs we elect sit in the House of Commons. Nevertheless, 'Parliament' also includes the House of Lords and the Monarch. The British legislature's full formal title is the 'Queen in Parliament'. The Monarch and the

House of Lords are, under the constitution, still required to give their consent to legislative proposals passed by the Commons before they can become the law of the land as Acts of Parliament.

In recent years constitutional reform has developed into a significant issue on the political agenda. Both the Monarchy and the House of Lords have been subjected to calls for reform, though for different reasons. The cost of the Monarchy (eg. the debate in January 1997 about the financing of a replacement for the royal yacht *Britannia*) and the behaviour of the present Queen's children and their spouses have put the Monarchy on the front pages of the tabloids. Reform of the House of Lords, in particular reform of the way in which many of its members inherit, in an undemocratic way, the right to be a member, is some-

The business of Parliament ranges from highly ceremonial occasions such as the State Opening, when the Queen's Speech is read by the Monarch in the House of Lords, to present-day political dramas such as Prime Minister's Questions in the House of Commons when the leaders of the two major political parties indulge in the modern political equivalent of hand-to-hand combat. 'Parliament' therefore combines long-standing formal traditions associated with the celebrated evolutionary character of British political history and modern political dramas such as Sir Geoffrey Howe's speech in the Commons on 13 October 1990 which led to the resignation of the most powerful Prime Minister of modern times. (See page 83)

The BRITISH Constitution

A 'CONSTITUTION' is a set of rules which lay down the powers and duties of the institutions of government and establish the rights and liberties of citizens.

It is frequently claimed that the British Constitution is unwritten. This is misleading. What is true is that the British Constitution, unlike the American, does not consist of one comprehensive document most of which was laid down at one historical moment (such as 1787 in the case of the USA) and subsequently amended to meet changing circumstances. The American Constitution is to be found at the back of every textbook on American politics. It is impossible to produce a copy of the British Constitution which has 'evolved' over many centuries. Nevertheless, one can describe its major sources, which are Parliamentary Statutes, the common law and 'conventions'.

Acts of Parliament which are 'constitutional' in nature include the Act of Settlement of 1700 which requires that the Monarch is a member of the Church of England and the Parliament Act of 1911 which limited the legislative powers of the House of Lords. Various Representation of the People Acts lay down the law relating to who has and who does not have the right to vote. The controversial Police Powers Bill which passed into law immediately before the 1997 General Election enlarged the powers of the police in relation to arrest and search.

Many principles of the Constitution are to be found in the common law and not in parliamentary statutes. The 'common law' is to be found in judicial decisions many of which are centuries old. The formal powers of the Monarch are essentially common law powers. Individual rights are often to be found in the common law.

'Conventions' are the most difficult part of the British Constitution to define. 'Conventions' are accepted constitutional rules which do not have legal status (they are not enforceable by the courts) but which are obeyed because most people believe that they should be obeyed. The best way to explain 'conventions' is to give an example. It is now a constitutional rule that the Prime Minister must be a member of the House of Commons. The reason is that in a democratic age the chief executive politician should be accountable to the people's elected representatives. In the 19th century it was commonplace for Prime Ministers to be members of the House of Lords, but the last Prime Minister in the Lords was Lord Salisbury who left office in 1902. Now politically ambitious members of the House of Lords give up their peerage if they wish to compete for the highest political office in the land. Lord Home gave up his peerage in 1963 when the Conservatives selected him to succeed Harold Macmillan who had resigned as Prime Minister. Sir Alec Douglas-Home was, for a short time, Prime Minister without being a member of either House of Parliament. However, he entered the Commons by winning a by-election in Perthshire in a seat left vacant by an obliging Tory MP. No law was broken during the short period that Home was Prime Minister but not a member of the Commons. Nevertheless, the force of the convention was demonstrated by the Prime Minister quickly becoming an MP.

Some of the most important constitutional rules in Britain take the form of conventions as we shall see in the next chapter when we look at the rules determining the relationship between government and Parliament, eg. the conventions of ministerial responsibility. Conventions are also vital to the conduct of modern politics in that they dictate how some common law powers which have great historical significance, are applied in an age when they are no longer appropriate. This applies particularly to the prerogative powers of the Monarch.

thing Labour has been promising for years.

THE MONARCHY

It must be emphasised at the outset of any discussion about the Monarchy that the British parliamentary system includes a Constitutional Monarchy which has no effective political power. The royal prerogatives, ie. personal powers which the Monarch still holds such as the power to dissolve Parliament, are by convention (See 'The British Constitution') held by others such as the Prime Minister and other Ministers of the Crown. They are in turn responsible to an elected House of Commons. Therefore, although he or she carries out certain prerogative functions which suggest some royal influence over political decisions, there is, in practice, no choice available to the Monarch of the day. Indeed the modern Monarchy illustrates the role of 'conventions of the constitution'—constitutional rules which do not possess the force or status of law but which are obeyed because of their widespread acceptance. Conventions often dictate how traditional legal powers such as the royal prerogatives should be wielded in modern Britain.

In spite of its lack of real political power, the Monarchy's proper role in the British political system has become an emotive and widely debated issue in recent years. Often, people hold strong opin-

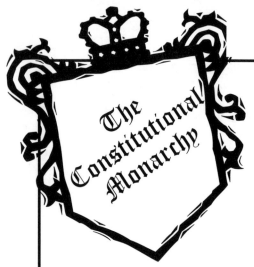

The Constitutional Monarchy

PREROGATIVE FUNCTIONS

Even at the end of the 20th century the British Monarch still holds some long-standing common law powers known as Royal Prerogatives. These play a very visible part in British politics even though the Monarch no longer wields such powers personally but must exercise them on the advice of members of the government.

The Opening of Parliament

The parliamentary year runs from the date when the Queen 'summons' (opens) Parliament until the date when it is 'progued' (closed). Parliament actually chooses these dates, the Monarchy simply having a ceremonial function. The reading of the 'Queens Speech' containing the government's major policy proposals marks the beginning of the parliamentary year.

Dissolution of Parliament

The maximum term of any Parliament is five years, at the end of which the Monarch declares that Parliament has terminated and gives the date of the general election which has been decided by the Prime Minister. When the Prime Minister decides to go to the country before the five years are up, he/she must request the Monarch to dissolve Parliament before a general election can be held. The Monarch also dissolves parliament when a government resigns after losing a vote of confidence in the House of Commons.

Appointing the Prime Minister

The Monarch still 'appoints' Ministers of the Crown, including the Prime Minister. By convention all Ministers other than the Prime Minister him or herself are effectively appointed by the Prime Minister who 'advises' the Monarch of his/her choices as Foreign Secretary, Chancellor of the Exchequer, Home Secretary etc. The Prime Minister is responsible for these appointments. However, a Prime Minister cannot choose his/her successor because he/she cannot be held responsible after leaving office. The possibility that the Monarch might have a real say in the appointment of the Prime Minister forced the Conservative Party in the 1960s to change its method of selecting its Leader to one of election by Conservative MPs. Labour elects its leader by means of an electoral college comprising MPs, trade unions and constituency associations.

The Monarch's choice of Prime Minister after an election and when the existing Prime Minister resigns or else dies in office is automatic provided that one party in the House of Commons has a majority. In such circumstances the Monarch 'appoints' the leader of the majority party. However, if there was no majority party in the Commons, the Monarch's choice of a new Prime Minister could be a difficult one. Should proportional representation (PR) be introduced at some future date (PR has become an issue on the constitutional agenda), elections might routinely fail to produce a majority party in the Commons. In such circumstances the selection of a Prime Minister supported by a Commons majority could become more difficult and a much more political process. It would be harder to abide by the constitutional principle that the Monarch must not be involved in politics.

The Royal Assent

A Bill which has passed through the required legislative process in the Houses of Parliament must still receive the Royal Assent before it becomes an Act of Parliament. By convention the Monarch grants such assent.

SYMBOLIC FUNCTIONS

Head of State

It is the Monarch rather than the Prime Minister who is the Head of State. Unlike France and the USA, the British Head of State is above party politics.

Head of the Commonwealth

The Monarch heads this multiracial 'Family of Nations' and in this capacity usually opens Commonwealth Conferences.

The Crown

The Monarch's role as Head of State is reinforced by the fact that Ambassadors, Judges, Government Ministers and so on all carry out their normal functions in the name of the Crown.

Awarding Honours

The Monarch can only personally award a few honours, for example the Order of Merit, the Garter and the Thistle. All other honours awarded by the Monarch are, in fact, decided by the government.

ions about the Monarchy, either feeling that it is doing a wonderful job or else questioning the need for it at all in a democratic society rapidly approaching the 21st century. Some critics have even questioned the fitness of Prince Charles as the heir apparent in the light of his 'going public' over his marital problems with Princess Diana. In January 1997 a poll organised by ITV as part of a television programme on the Monarchy found that two-thirds of the British people still supported the existence of a Monarchy. There were intriguing regional variations. Only in Scotland was there a majority supporting the view that the Monarchy had outlived its usefulness.

Do We Need the Monarchy?

Many people feel that the Monarchy should claim its place in history. Since we live in a democratic society where political power lies with our elected representatives rather than with the Monarch, the whole extended Royal Family is seen by many as a drain on the nation's resources. The Royal Family receives an annual sum of money (known as the Civil List) from Parliament, but in addition other expenses are incurred as palaces must be maintained. In 1997 the Conservative government announced that it would fund the building of a replacement for the ageing royal yacht *Britannia*. This sparked a political controversy. Labour said that it would not contribute public funds to such an enterprise in the first two years after the 1997 General Election which it expected to win. Supporters of replacing the royal yacht and of the Monarchy generally argued that its value to the nation must take into account the tourist income which arises from visitors to Britain who come partly in order to see the Monarch carry out her ceremonial duties such as the State Opening of Parliament and to visit the royal palaces. A new royal yacht was seen by its supporters as a permanent floating demonstration of British engineering skills which should be viewed more as an economic asset than as a means of conveying members of the Royal Family around the world. Labour won the 1997 Election and Britannia was decommissioned in December of that year.

There are those who argue that the Monarch's constitutional role is a more effective safeguard of British democracy than any replacement, such as an elected President, could be. The Monarch's reserve powers may encourage politicians to abide by the constitutional rules of the game.

THE HOUSE OF LORDS

The House of Lords, like the Monarchy, has survived the transition to democracy because its powers have been cut back to meet democratic expectations. The House of Lords has progressively lost powers during the 20th century. Its constitutional status is to be found in the Parliament Acts of 1911 and 1949. The first of these provides an example of what may happen when a constitutional convention is broken. During the 19th century a convention developed which required the non-elected upper house *not* to reject the Budget and other money Bills passed by the Commons. This convention developed as democracy became more acceptable. It was believed that finance was so vital that only elected representatives should decide the content of legislation which raised revenue or proposed public expenditure. The Lords still enjoyed an absolute veto over non-financial legislation which had to receive the consent of both Houses of Parliament.

In 1909 the Lords rejected the Liberal government's budget which had secured the consent of the Commons. The result of this was a constitutional crisis in which the government threatened to request the Monarch to create enough Peers to secure the passage of the budget. The crisis was resolved by the passage of the 1911 Parliament Act which changed the convention relating to financial procedure into the more powerful constitutional Statute. The Lords also lost their veto over non-financial legislation. The 1911 Parliament Act limited to a period of three parliamentary sessions the power of the Lords to reject Bills which had passed the Commons. If the Lords rejected a Bill which received the consent of the Commons in two consecutive parliamentary sessions, it would become law without the consent of the Lords once it passed the Commons in the third parliamentary session. This amounted to a delaying power of just over two years.

The 1911 Parliament Act ensured that the Lords would, in the future, be less important than the Commons. The delaying power of the Lords was reduced by the Labour Government elected in 1945. The 1949 Parliament Act, which itself passed under the terms of the 1911 Act against the wishes of the House of Lords, reduced the Lords' power to delay legislation to two parliamentary sessions, effectively one year. There is, however, one significant exception to the elimination of the Lords' legislative veto: the Lords can still veto any Bill which seeks to extend the life of a Parliament beyond the

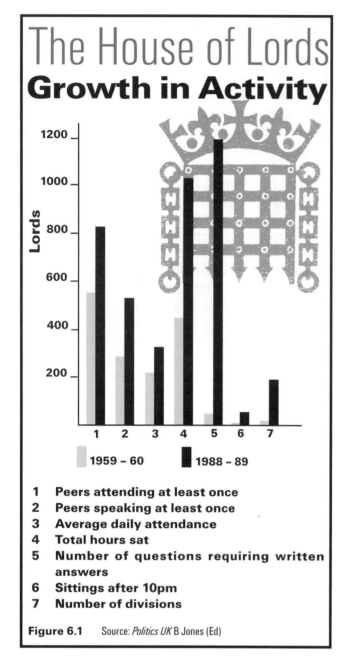

The House of Lords
Growth in Activity

Lords (y-axis: 200, 400, 600, 800, 1000, 1200)

Categories: 1 2 3 4 5 6 7

☐ 1959 – 60   ■ 1988 – 89

1 **Peers attending at least once**
2 **Peers speaking at least once**
3 **Average daily attendance**
4 **Total hours sat**
5 **Number of questions requiring written answers**
6 **Sittings after 10pm**
7 **Number of divisions**

Figure 6.1   Source: *Politics UK* B Jones (Ed)

The Composition of the Lords

The House of Lords consists of the Lords Spiritual, Hereditary Peers, Life Peers and the Law Lords. The Lords Spiritual are the 2 Archbishops (Canterbury and York) and 24 Bishops of the Church of England who represent the relationship between Church and State. The Lords Spiritual are only entitled to attend the House of Lords while they hold Church office. The Law Lords, 20 in 1996, enter the House by virtue of their appointment to high judicial office, though unlike the Lords Spiritual the Law Lords retain their seats until death. The Law Lords act as the highest court of appeal in Britain. There are almost 800 Hereditary Peers, of whom 16 were women in 1994. They have inherited their titles and will pass them on to the next generation.

The 1958 Life Peerages Act introduced the non-hereditary peerage. There are currently about 400 life peers of whom 60 or so are women. The titles of life peers, who are created by the Prime Minister, die with them.

Nowadays very few new hereditary peerages are created. Life peerages mean that the House of Lords is more politically and socially correct. This reform of the composition of the House of Lords, partly a response to demands for a more democratic upper chamber, has not removed the House of Lords from political controversy.

Functions of the House of Lords

Although the House of Lords usually gives way to the will of the House of Commons, many believe that it carries out a number of useful and indispensable functions which are listed below. There has been a significant growth in the number of Peers participating in the work of the House of Lords and in the work carried out. (See Figure 6.1.)

Legislation: Most Bills are passed by the Lords before becoming Law. However, Money Bills eg. the Finance Bill which contains the Budget, cannot be rejected by the House of Lords and other Bills may only be held up for about one year. If the House of Lords rejects a Bill which has been passed by the Commons in two consecutive parliamentary sessions, it automatically becomes law even if the Lords rejects it a second time.

In June 1990 the Lords rejected the government sponsored War Crimes Bill which intended to permit the prosecution of alleged Nazi war criminals living in Britain. The Lords do vote against legis-

five years currently permitted by Statute. This power, which has never been used in a negative fashion(the life of the Parliament which was in session when the Second World War started in 1939 was extended by agreement until 1945), provides a constitutional safeguard against a Commons majority which might be tempted to behave undemocratically.

In spite of its lower status there are still demands for further reform of the upper chamber. Indeed the House of Lords lies at the forefront of one of the key policy differences between the two major parties in the 1990s—constitutional reform. The Labour Party, which won the 1997 Election, has plans to reform the membership and the powers of the Lords which Labour regards as inappropriate in a modern democracy.

lation passed on by the Commons but rarely do so to the extent of triggering the procedures in the Parliament Acts. The War Crimes Bill had been approved in the Commons by 273 votes to 60 on a free vote. The Lords opposed the Bill as an example of 'retrospective legislation' which might have proved difficult to implement because it dealt with alleged crimes committed half a century ago. The Bill was reintroduced into the Commons in March 1991, rejected by the Lords again in April and received the Royal Assent under the Parliament Acts procedures in June 1991. This was only the fourth Bill to have been passed in this way. The Lords do not usually pursue their opposition to legislation passed by the Commons to this extent, partly because of the widespread belief that the elected House of Commons should prevail. The Lords hope to make the government and the Commons think again by amending Bills. Opposition in the Lords contributed to amendments which were made to the controversial Police Bill in 1997.

The bulk of the government's legislative programme is introduced in the Commons. Consequently, the legislative business of the Lords has to await the passage of Bills in the lower house. The government does introduce a few Bills in the Lords, usually, though not exclusively of the non-controversial variety. In session 1990–91, eighteen of the sixty eight Acts of Parliament passed began life in the upper house. The Lords acts as a cleaning up agency for the government which often introduces amendments in the Lords in response to improvements suggested as Bills pass through the legislative processes the Commons.

Public Debate: The more leisurely, less confrontational style of the upper chamber allows it to function as a debating chamber for issues which are of public interest. The Lords has the time to devote to such debates unlike the Commons. This also applies to the Lords 'tidying up' function in respect of government legislation. Consequently, the very existence of the Lords is often said to depend on its ability to perform useful tasks which cannot be fitted into the current organisation and timetable of the Commons.

Scrutiny: The primary function of a legislature in a system which is dominated by the executive branch is often said to be to find out and publicise what the government is doing. Thus the executive branch may be held to account for its actions by Parliament and ultimately by the electorate. The Lords possesses the various scrutiny

procedures available to the Commons such as Question Time, select committees and debate. The Lords make a special contribution through select committees in two areas: European Communities and Science and Technology. The Select Committees on these two topics in the Lords are acknowledged to be more expert than their parallel committees in the Commons.

Adjudication: the highest court of appeal in Britain is located in the House of Lords, though this function is performed only by the small band of Law Lords. About five to ten of the Law Lords form a judicial committee which considers appeals.

REFORMING THE LORDS
The constitutional debate over the House of Lords is centred around two key questions.
1 Does Britain really need a second legislative chamber?
2 If the answer is Yes, what should be the composition and the powers of the second chamber?

There are a few countries, for example New Zealand and Sweden, with unicameral legislatures, ie. only one legislative chamber. Most countries have bicameral legislatures although the relationship between the two legislative chambers varies. The upper house in the USA, the Senate, is as powerful as the House of Representatives because both are directly elected. As a result the legislative process in the American Congress is more difficult. In 1995–96 Democratic President Clinton faced a Republican Congress. However, the Republican Senate was much more moderate than the right-

The House of Lords
COMPOSITION

COMPOSITION		PARTY AFFILIATION	
Spiritual Lords	26	Conservative	481
Law Lords	21	Labour	116
Hereditary Peers (16 women)	762	Liberal Democrat	57
		Cross Bencher	320
Life Peers (65 women)	398	Others	111
TOTAL	1207		

Table 6.1   Source: Dods Parliamentary Companion December 1996

wing House of Representatives. The Senate often watered down more radical policies sponsored by Republicans in the House of Representatives, making life easier for Clinton.

In most countries the lower house is stronger than the upper house. The fact that almost every country in the world has a bicameral legislature explains why most commentators answer Yes to the first question above. Upper chambers, however they are set up, are useful. Firstly they can carry out essential tasks which the lower house has not the time to perform fully. Secondly, they can both debate themes of public interest and give representation to sections of public opinion. A third, more controversial, reason for an upper chamber is that it can act as a constitutional 'fail safe' device against a lower chamber which might be taken over by political extremists.

While there is general agreement that an upper chamber is useful and therefore desirable, there is much less agreement about its proper composition and powers. It has already been pointed out that the powers of the Lords have long since been cut back in order to meet the demands of the popular democracy which began to develop in Britain from the time of the Great Reform Act of 1832 which widened the franchise. When the Lords in effect challenged that democratisation in 1909 by breaking the convention about accepting money Bills passed by the lower house, its powers were promptly reduced by statute. Labour further reduced the delaying power of the Lords in the 1940s. The focus of constitutional debate in the 1990s about further reform of the Lords is on its composition. There have been significant reforms in this area which have watered down the hereditary nature of the Lords—the 1958 Life Peerages Act and the 1963 Peerages and Renunciation of Titles Act.

The Life Peerages Act 1958
This Act, introduced by a Conservative government, gave Prime Ministers the power to create peers whose titles die with them. Up to 1958 the Prime Minister could only appoint hereditary peers, a process which did not allow for a rapid change of membership of the Lords. The impact of life peerages has been to reduce the Conservative dominance of the Lords and to widen its social representation. Life Peerages are given to people who have achieved distinction in their careers. Individuals are selected from all walks of life, not just politics, so the composition of the House

of Lords shows more equality and is more socially representative compared to before 1958 when it was exclusively hereditary. In 1995, 29% of peers accepting the Conservative whip and 91% of peers accepting the Labour whip were Life Peers.

Peerages and Renunciation of Titles Act 1963
The passage of this Act belatedly confirmed the transfer of power from the Lords to the Commons, because it gave hereditary peers, who are not allowed to be members of the Commons, the right to renounce their peerage and stand for election to the lower house. The Labour MP, Tony Benn, campaigned for the right to renounce his peerage when he inherited it on the death of his father Viscount Stansgate. Since under the law at the time Benn, now Viscount Stansgate, was disqualified from sitting in the Commons, a by-election was held. Benn stood and won but was refused entry to the Commons. In the light of the publicity generated by Benn's crusade, the Conservative government introduced the 1963 Act. Coincidentally this legislation played a dramatic part in the Conservative leadership contest in 1963 following the resignation of the Prime Minister Harold Macmillan. Two Conservative Peers, Lord Home and Lord Hailsham, renounced their peerages to fight for the Conservative leadership. Home won and became Prime Minister as Sir Alec Douglas-Home. In 1994 Lord James Douglas Hamilton, MP for Edinburgh West and Minister of State at the Scottish Office, renounced his peerage when his father, the Duke of Hamilton, died. It was widely believed that his action was prompted by a fear that the Conservatives would lose the by-election which would have resulted if he had taken up his peerage. There has not been a great rush to renounce peerages; only the politically ambitious have been tempted to do so.

The composition of the Lords remains a controversial issue. At present all Peers, whether hereditary or Life Peers, are eligible to debate and vote in the Lords. The Conservatives see no great need for further reform. Labour attempted to reform the composition of the House of Lords in the 1960s when a Bill was drafted which would have enabled the Prime Minister to appoint the membership of a smaller House of Lords from the current peerage, including life peers. Labour's proposed reform would have removed the automatic right of hereditary peers to sit in the Lords and would have confined membership to those nominated by the Prime Minister, thus guaranteeing the government of the day a majority in the upper chamber. The Labour Government elected in 1997 proposed reforming the House of Lords in two stages. Firstly, Labour would abolish the voting rights of hereditary peers so that membership would be confined to those appointed by the Prime Minister. The second stage has yet to be finalised but might include an elected element. The Liberal Democrats propose a 300 strong House of Lords of whom 200 would be elected for six year terms and 100 appointed for 12 year terms. Direct election may appear an obvious solution to the problem of how to determine the composition of the upper chamber. However election, because it could give members of the upper chamber popular support, carries the risk of creating a more powerful upper chamber which might, on occasion, be tempted to take a major disagreement with the lower house to the electorate.

THE HOUSE OF COMMONS

The first function given to the Commons, sustaining a government, may appear to be out of place for an institution whose main activity is to legislate. However, the reality is that although the House of Commons does legislate and although the British Constitution assumes that the executive is responsible to the House of Commons (See Chapter 7) the impact of elections and party discipline has been to give the executive more power over the Commons than the other way round. The executive only has this power if the electorate returns a government with a comfortable working majority. Thus the first function of the Labour

1 *Maintaining and either supporting or opposing Her Majesty's government.*
2 *Legislating, ie. passing Bills sponsored by the government or by backbench MPs.*
3 *Scrutinising and publicising the work of government and thereby influencing what the government does.*
4 *Representing constituents and expressing the views of the country.*

THE MAJOR FUNCTIONS OF THE HOUSE OF COMMONS

majority returned in the May 1997 General Election was to maintain the Government of Prime Minister Tony Blair.

Supporting the executive is, of course, the primary function of the MPs of the majority party. The first function of MPs of other parties is to oppose the government. Unless there is a government with a very small majority or no majority at all, there are severe limits on the 'Power of Parliament'. Nevertheless, proceedings in the House of Commons above all provide the public with often dramatic information about the behaviour of government and opposition.

The Legislative Process

Legislative proposals (Bills) may be introduced in either the Commons or the Lords. However, the government introduces most of its legislation in the Commons. Government legislation expressing its policies take up most of the parliamentary timetable. A limited amount of time is made available for Private Members' legislation. There are six main stages in the legislative process.

- *White Paper*   A legislative proposal may begin as a 'White Paper' which contains the government's thinking on the issue in question. White Papers are really written to allow consultation. The government will consider comments from interested parties before firming up its policy by drafting a Bill to be introduced in Parliament.

- *First Reading*   The Bill is introduced by its title being read. There is no debate. The Bill is then printed in full and distributed to MPs.

- *Second Reading*   A debate is held on the floor of the House on the general principles of the Bill. The debate on government Bills may last from half a day to a two-day debate on major Bills such as the Bill to ratify the Maastricht Treaty in 1992. The debate commences with the government minister responsible for the Bill explaining and defending its contents. The opposition 'shadow' frontbencher then gives what is usually the case against the Bill. The critical moment is the vote at the end of the debate. If it is rejected, the Bill is withdrawn, although this has happened only three times in the 20th century. In 1986 the Conservative Government was defeated at the second reading stage of the Shops Bill (Sunday Trading). Usually the two major parties impose a 'three line Whip' to ensure maximum turnout and therefore victory for the majority governing party.

• *Committee Stage*   The Bill is now referred to a standing legislative committee for a detailed clause-by-clause examination. The committee stage of Bills of constitutional significance such as the European Communities (Amendment) Bill which led to acceptance of the Maastricht Treaty may be taken on the floor of the House of Commons. This is also where the committee stage of money Bills such as the Finance Bill (the budget) takes place, thus allowing all MPs to examine it in detail. Standing committees are made up for each Bill, with usually about 20 MPs sitting on the committee. The parties are represented according to their strength in the Commons as a whole, so the government normally has a majority. Amendments are made, many of which the government accepts because they will improve the proposed legislation.

• *Report Stage*   The Bill as amended by the committee is 'reported' back to the House when further amendments, often introduced by the government, are debated and put to the vote.

• *Third Reading*   Once again the principles of the Bill, now as amended, are debated. Usually the debate is shorter than it was on the second reading. If the Bill is approved by the Commons it then goes through a similar process in the House of Lords (unless it is a finance Bill) before receiving the Royal Assent. (The Monarch has not given the royal assent personally since the middle of the 19th century.) The Bill is now an Act of Parliament and enters the Statute Book as part of the law of the land.

The legislative process takes up about one-third of the time of the House of Commons, most of it on government Bills. In 1994–95, 54 Acts of Parliament were passed including 19 which were introduced in the House of Lords and 16 by backbench MPs. The most significant pieces of legislation included the Jobseekers Act, the Child Support Act, the Mental Health (Patients in the Community) Act and the South Africa Act which allowed South Africa back into the Commonwealth.

Scrutinising the Work of Government
As long as the government has a majority it will succeed in getting its legislative proposals accepted. It is often argued that even more important than legislation is subjecting the actions of the government to close examination so that the business of government is in the open. Scrutiny also allows interested voters to judge the perform-

---

Select Committee on Scottish Affairs

In session 1996–97 the Select Committee on Scottish Affairs was chaired by a Labour MP, William McKelvie (Kilmarnock). It had three English Conservative members to ensure a government majority. The 11 members were:

Conservative	Labour
Phil Gallie (Ayr)	William McKelvie (Kilmarnock)
Allan Stewart (Eastwood)	Bob Hughes (Aberdeen South)
Bill Walker (Tayside)	David Marshall (Glasgow Shettleston)
Tim Devlin (Stockton South)	
Peter Atkinson (Hexham)	
John Marshall (Hendon South)	

Liberal Democrat	SNP
Ray Michie (Argyll)	Andrew Welsh (Angus)

The Scottish Committee issued three reports in 1995–96: Closure of Psychiatric Hospitals in Scotland, Market Conditions in the Scottish Salmon Industry, and Operation of Enterprise Agencies. The Defence Select Committee was more active, issuing 13 reports. Issues covered included Gulf War Syndrome, Progress of the Trident Programme, and the Future of NATO.

The Scottish Select Committee appointed after Labour's victory in the 1997 Election included 7 Labour MPs, 2 Conservatives, one Liberal Democrat and one Scottish Nationalist. The two Conservatives had to be from English constituencies because of the 'Tory wipe-out' in Scotland. David Marshall (Labour, Shettleston) was elected chairman of the Select Committee which proceeded to conduct inquiries into the 'Welfare to Work' principle, which underlies New Labour's approach to social problems, and into the 'Operation of Multi-Layer Democracy', a topic which the establishment of the Scottish Parliament will bring to prominence in the next decade.

---

ance of the government on the basis of fact rather than guesswork. Such close study gives the House, in spite of its partisan framework, opportunities to 'influence' what the government does. Some commentators use the phrase 'control of the executive' to describe the impact of various scrutiny procedures though that may be going too far except when a government loses its majority or comes close to doing so.

The main scrutiny procedures are debates on the floor of the House, select committees and Question Time.

Debates
Debates include the second reading stage of the legislative process, adjournment debates, and substantive motions. Most debates involve the government having to explain, defend and justify

both its actions and its policies. The executive is forced to account for its actions to Parliament.

Formally the executive is accountable to Parliament. However, party politics and the electorate usually ensure that the government controls Parliament rather than the other way round. For this reason debates do not normally end up with the government being defeated. In the last three months of the Major government, when it lost its overall Commons majority, the opposition parties attempted to force a general election by bringing motions of confidence before the House. The government survived all of these motions because the Opposition parties could not unite. The Ulster Unionist parties frequently came to the government's rescue. The opposition parties are allowed 20 days per session (17 for the major opposition party and 3 for the third largest party) when they can choose the issues to be debated. Thus Labour selected the BSE crisis as the topic to be debated on 17 February 1997 in the hope of moving a vote of no confidence against the Agriculture Minister Douglas Hogg. This tactic failed, even though the government no longer had a majority in the House, because Ulster Unionist MPs refused to join in the attempt to bring down the government.

Backbench MPs are given the opportunity to force the government to explain and defend its policies through the procedure of adjournment debates which are held at the close of each parliamentary day. The issues which are chosen for debate by backbenchers often concern matters of interest to their constituents. On 17 December 1996, Mr Peter Kilfoyle (Labour, Liverpool Walton) used the adjournment debate procedure to seek a reopening of the inquiry into the Hillsborough Tragedy in which scores of Liverpool football fans died. The Home Secretary, Michael Howard, replied to the debate and promised to consider all the issues brought up before reaching a decision. On 4 February 1997 Jim Wallace (Liberal Democrat, Orkney and Shetland) used the procedure to focus attention on the problem of rural housing in Scotland. Mr Wallace pointed out that even though rural areas contain only 29% of housing stock, 39% of all Scottish houses judged to be below 'tolerable standards' were to be found in such areas.

Select Committees

Debates on the floor of the House of Commons are grand occasions which, through television and the press may catch the public eye and influence public opinion. A less dramatic but more detailed scrutiny of government is provided by a comprehensive select committee system covering the major government departments. This system has been in place in its present form since 1979. These committees have an investigative or supervisory function, ie. they were set up "to examine the expenditure, administration and policy of individual departments". They can look into how public policy is worked out or formulated and also how it is implemented or put into practice. The committees have the power to request the presence of both government Ministers and civil servants for questioning and representatives of outside bodies may also be asked to give evidence.

The purpose of the scrutiny function of the select committees is twofold: to keep government departments on their toes and to make sure that government is open to the public eye. The parties are represented according to their strength in the House as a whole. The committees have about 11 members.

There are currently 17 departmental select committees including one each for Scottish, Welsh and Northern Ireland Affairs. When the Select Committee on Northern Ireland Affairs was established in 1994, it was claimed that the decision was influenced by the government's need to retain the votes of Ulster Unionist MPs when it was in danger of losing the support of Eurosceptic Conservative MPs. It was also claimed that the committee's existence was insensitive at a time when the relationship between Britain and Northern Ireland was part of the 'Irish Problem'.

Committee proceedings often generate publicity which influences decision making. On 26 February 1997 the Defence Select Committee interviewed Nicholas Soames, the Armed Forces Minister, about Gulf War Syndrome. About 1200 British soldiers who had fought in the Gulf War in 1990–91 subsequently experienced a wide range of illnesses. Claims were made that their ailments were the result of the use of organo-phosphate pesticides to combat the effects of insect borne disease and the possibility of Iraq using germ warfare. Government spokespeople, including Mr Soames in the House of Commons, denied that organo-phosphates had been used. This denial turned out to be untrue. Soames had to explain to the Defence Select Committee that gross errors had been made by civil servants in a particular section of the Ministry of Defence. Labour called for Soames's resignation amid claims that the

Minister should have known the facts in spite of misleading advice from civil servants and army doctors. A key participant in the proceedings of the Defence Committee interview with Soames was a Conservative MP who expressed the opinion that he smelt a cover-up. Soames claimed that there had been "major errors" but no cover-up. The Select Committees often take a bipartisan line in their investigations.

Question Time

Question Time begins the business of the Commons four days a week. It lasts for about thirty minutes and now plays a dramatic part (proceedings are often televised) in securing the redress of constituents' grievances, representing the people and ensuring the responsibility of the executive to Parliament.

Question Time allows MPs to 'grill' Ministers about their policies and actions. MPs must put questions (of which Ministers are informed in advance); they must not attempt to debate. Questions may be designed to elicit information to embarrass the government (if the question is put by an Opposition MP), or to allow a government Minister to release a particularly favourable piece of information (if the question is put by a government back-bencher). Ministerial reputations can be made or lost at Question Time.

One of the first parliamentary actions of the new Labour Government in 1997 was to reform 'Prime Minister's Questions'. The Prime Minister had, since 1960, been present to answer questions for 15 minutes on Tuesdays and Thursdays. Labour decided to schedule 'Prime Minister's Questions' on Wednesdays for the full 30 minutes. Such a move was justified on the grounds that it would permit more in-depth questioning of the Prime Minister and that it would thus improve the ability of the Commons to hold the country's most powerful politician responsible for his/her own actions and also his/her government's actions. Others argued that the reform merely added to the cult of the personality and to the forces making for 'Prime Ministerial government' at the expense of 'Cabinet government'.

Question Time allows MPs to 'grill' Ministers about their policies and actions.

CHAPTER 7 The EXECUTIVE

What you will learn

1 The organisation and relative powers of the Prime Minister, Cabinet and civil service
2 The conventions of Ministerial responsibility
3 The limits on executive power

TRADITIONAL POLITICAL THEORY assumed three institutions of government:

➡ a legislature to pass laws

➡ an executive to implement these laws

➡ a judiciary to interpret the meaning of the laws passed by the legislature.

Such a view of government, which puts the legislature at the front of the political process, has long been inaccurate as a description of the policy making process. It is certainly true that the executive branch has the responsibility of implementing the laws passed by Parliament and that Parliament must give its consent. But in most countries the executive branch of government has become the most powerful source of the policies which are to be debated and passed or rejected by the legislature. In Britain, the executive branch led by the Prime Minister and Cabinet formulates the major policies which affect our lives, such as the decision to establish a Scottish Parliament. These policies are presented to Parliament for its consent. The executive branch then implements or 'executes' the laws passed by Parliament. The British Executive thus formulates policy proposals, presents them to Parliament and puts them into effect.

For most of the 20th century the British executive, through strong party discipline and loyalty together with working majorities in Parliament, has exercised strict control over the whole policy making process including the legislative process. The radical reforms achieved by the postwar Labour Government,1945–51, and by the Thatcher Governments in the 1980s illustrate the considerable strength of the British executive. The electoral defeats sustained by Labour in 1979 and by the Conservatives in 1997, which followed periods of weak government and the erosion of supporting majorities in Parliament, emphasise that the executive branch does not always dominate the policy process. There are two major areas of study in relation to the role of the executive in British politics. Firstly, how is power organised and distributed within the executive branch itself? The main issue here is whether Britain has Cabinet or Prime Ministerial government. Secondly, what are the constitutional and political relationships between the executive and legislative branches. This question focuses attention on the constitutional conventions of ministerial responsibility?

The British Executive, headed by the Prime Minister, formulates policy proposals, presents them to Parliament and puts them into effect.

71

THE PRIME MINISTER

The British executive branch divides into three parts: the Prime Minister, the Cabinet and the civil service. The Prime Minister and Cabinet are politically partisan whereas the civil service is politically neutral and performs administrative tasks. The Prime Minister, unlike most of his/her Cabinet colleagues, does not head a government department but is given the formal title of First Lord of the Treasury. The modern Prime Minister possesses three principal powers:

● the power of appointment commonly known as 'patronage',

● majority party leader,

● chairman/woman of the Cabinet.

Power of Appointment

The Prime Minister's power to appoint the members of the Cabinet and a long list of non-Cabinet Ministers is his/her most powerful weapon within the executive branch. The Prime Minister, in taking over the office, decides which politicians to include in the Cabinet and which subsequently to demote or promote. The power to 'hire and fire' includes the right to 'reshuffle' the membership of the Cabinet and government at any time and for whatever reason. The Prime Minister also decides the size of the Cabinet. Prime Ministers are strongly tempted to exercise such powers when their government is doing badly in the opinion polls and is believed therefore to be in need of a little 'freshening up'.

The power to appoint is known as 'patronage' and extends far beyond the 'hiring and firing' of members of the government. The Prime Minister has the final say in the appointment of Life Peers, of Archbishops and bishops in the Church of England and members of the judiciary. In exercising appointment powers the Prime Minister is essentially the heir to the personal prerogative powers of the Monarch who now has no influence over appointments, although newly selected Ministers still have to go to Buckingham Palace to be formally ushered into office by the Monarch of the day.

Party Leader

The Prime Minister reaches the top political position in British government by virtue of his/her leadership of the majority party in the House of Commons. Formally the Monarch appoints the Prime Minister. It is the one governmental office

The Structure of Government 1997

The following diagram describes the several layers of seniority within the Labour Government appointed after the General Election in 1997.

PRIME MINISTER AND CABINET (22)
(17 men; 5 Women: 20 MPs; 2 Lords)
Almost all are heads of individual government departments
eg. John Prescott, Deputy Prime Minister and Secretary of State for the Environment, Transport and the Regions (largest department)

MINISTERS OF STATE (31)
(25 MEN; 6 WOMEN: 26 MPS; 5 LORDS)
eg. 3 Ministers of State within 'Environment and Transport'
Michael Meacher: Minister for the Environment
Hilary Armstrong: Minister for Local Government and Housing
Richard Caborn: Minister of the Regions, Regeneration and Planning

LAW OFFICERS (4)

UNITED KINGDOM	SCOTLAND
Attorney General (MP)	Lord Advocate (House of Lords)
Solicitor General (House of Lords)	Solicitor General (not in Parliament)

JUNIOR MINISTERS (32)
(Parliamentary Secretaries and Under-Secretaries)
(24 men; 8 women: 26 MPs; 6 Lords)
eg. 4 Under-Secretaries within 'Environment and Transport'
Glenda Jackson: Minister for Transport in London
Nick Raynsford: Minister for London and Construction
Baroness Hayman: Minister for Roads (Lords)
Angela Eagle: Minister for the Environment and the Regions

PARLIAMENTARY PRIVATE SECRETARIES (41 MPS)
(Serve as personal assistants to Government Ministers)
(33 men; 8 women)

GOVERNMENT WHIPS
[House of Commons (16) House of Lords (7)]
Government Chief Whip: Nick Brown MP, Parliamentary Secretary to the Treasury

[130 Labour MPs are Government Ministers of various degrees of seniority or on the fringes of government as whips or parliamentary private secretaries, which leaves about 290 Labour MPs on the backbenches.]

Figure 7.1

to which the Prime Minister cannot make the appointment. The Monarch has no discretion. The choice is automatic as long as there is a majority party in the Commons. The belief that the Monarch should not have a choice led the Conservative Party to change its method of selecting its Leader in Parliament to one of election by its MPs. All the parties have made it clear that the Monarch should send for their elected leader when the opportunity to appoint a Prime Minister arises. In effect, then, it is the majority party which chooses the Prime Minister when it elects its leader. Such

The Labour Cabinet, 1997

elections may take place when the party is in office (John Major was elected to replace Margaret Thatcher in November 1990) or in opposition (Tony Blair was elected leader of the Labour Party when John Smith died in 1994).

As leader of the majority party, the Prime Minister enjoys the support of Parliament. As long as there is a working majority in support of the Prime Minister and Cabinet in the Commons, the Prime Minister can rely on Parliament to adopt the policies of his/her government. The loss of such a majority and dissension within the governing party can weaken the power of Prime Minister and government as the Major Administration discovered in the run-up to the 1997 Election. John Major had to devote much more time than Margaret Thatcher to the business of party management because of a smaller parliamentary majority.

Cabinet Chairperson

The Prime Minister chairs Cabinet meetings and is the political head of the civil service. As Chairperson of the Cabinet the Prime Minister may, in practice, dominate Cabinet meetings. The Prime Minister usually controls the agenda, leads the discussion and sums up the 'sense' of the meeting. The Prime Minister is the one member of the Cabinet with a 'global' view of the business of government. Cabinet Ministers who are in charge of large government departments are too busy with their own departmental responsibilities to be concerned with the work of other departments. The Prime Minister is a member of the most important Cabinet Committees which do much of the work of the Cabinet. However, there other powerful Cabinet members who may be able to limit the power of the Prime Minister. It was widely believed that the Chancellor of the Exchequer, Kenneth Clarke, a supporter of monetary union within the European Union, prevented John Major adopting a more 'Eurosceptic' position in discussions about whether and when, if ever, Britain should accept a common European currency.

THE CABINET

British government used to be labelled 'Cabinet government'. The Prime Minister's position relative to the Cabinet was described by a famous phrase, 'primus inter pares'—first among equals. This suggested that in spite of the Prime Minister enjoying powers denied to other Cabinet Ministers, such as the power of patronage and appointment, the Cabinet reached its decisions on a majority basis, even though the Prime Minister summed up the sense of the meeting. The phrase suggested that the Prime Minister's status as First Minister was of a formal nature with little extra power attached. During the course of the twentieth century, however, the Prime Minister has become more powerful so the holder of this office is no longer just 'first among equals'. Indeed, many commentators claim that British government should now be labelled 'Prime Ministerial government' to indicate where the decisive policy making power lies.

After Sir Anthony Eden, Conservative Prime Minister 1955–57, resigned in the wake of the 1956–57 Suez Crisis, he famously declared: "A Prime Minister is still normally 'primus inter pares', but in fact his authority is stronger than that. The right to choose his colleagues, to ask for a dissolution of Parliament and, if he is a Conservative, to appoint the Chairman of the Party Organisation, add up to a formidable total of power."

Prime Ministerial power is a variable which depends on three things. First of all, different Prime Ministers have different objectives. Also, there are variations in the political environments in which each Prime Minister must operate. Finally, there will always be differences in the ability of each individual to use the formal powers which are available to *all* holders of the office.

A Prime Minister's power to appoint his/her Cabinet, combined with the manner in which the Cabinet actually carries out its business, add up to quite significant power invested in one individual. Cabinet meetings only last for a few hours on one or two occasions each week which really does not allow enough time for discussion before important policy decisions are made. However, before the Cabinet meets to make these decisions, the policies have been closely examined and amended until agreement can be reached in various Cabinet committees which were set up by the Prime Minister. The full Cabinet often can do little more than formally approve the decisions of Cabinet Committees which are composed of the 'expert' Ministers on the subject matter dealt with by each committee. In 1994 there were 25 Cabinet Committees and sub-Committees. The Prime Minister sits on the most important of these but not on all of them. The increasing use of such committees led one former Cabinet Minister to describe British government as 'partial Cabinet government' since the full Cabinet is frequently faced with saying Yes or No to committee decisions which have been agreed by the Ministers most relevant to a particular subject area.

The Prime Minister's position may also be strengthened by the emergence of an 'Inner Cabinet' which may be formal or informal. This 'Inner Cabinet' may be no more than the leading Departmental Ministers among whom there is an acknowledged 'pecking order'. The Foreign Secretary and the Chancellor of the Exchequer are the two most most prestigious offices after the Prime Minister. The Deputy Prime Minister may or may not be significant. Mrs Thatcher reluctantly appointed Geoffrey Howe as Leader of the House of Commons *and* Deputy Prime Minister in 1989 but 'froze' him out of important decision making because they disagreed on the European issue. John Major appointed Mr Heseltine as Deputy Prime Minister in 1995 in order to secure the support of a senior Cabinet member. Michael Heseltine and Kenneth Clarke were in a pro-European Union minority in the Cabinet towards the end of the Major Administration when they limited the Prime Minister's options in this policy area which was tearing the Conservative Party apart.

Cabinet Ministers are, in theory, bound by the convention of collective ministerial responsibility. Every Minister is considered to have agreed to Cabinet decisions, even those which are not unanimous. Cabinet Ministers and all other members of the government not of Cabinet rank are bound by collective responsibility to support the agreed policies in public, even if they voted against the decision. If they publicly disagree with the decision, they must resign. In 1986 Michael Heseltine, then Secretary of State for Defence in the Thatcher Administration, resigned when he disagreed with the Government's policy on the 'Westland Affair'. Mrs Thatcher refused to allow a decision reached by a Cabinet Committee, with which Heseltine disagreed, to be discussed in the full Cabinet. Heseltine resigned because he would not support the decision in public and because he objected to the Prime Minister's handling of the matter in Cabinet. Although Mrs Thatcher 'won' in the Cabinet in 1986 she was to pay a price in 1990 when Heseltine and another Cabinet Minister who had fallen foul of the Prime Minister's powers, Geoffrey Howe, challenged Mrs Thatcher's leadership. The Prime Minister was forced into an election for the leadership of the Conservative Party in November 1990. Failing to win outright in the first ballot, Mrs Thatcher resigned as Party Leader and as Prime Minister. Not every Cabinet Minister who refuses to be bound by the convention of collective responsibility brings down a Prime Minister!

A civil service department called the Cabinet Office or Cabinet Secretariat takes responsibility for organising the agenda for all meetings relating to the Cabinet, keeping the minutes of such meetings and ensuring that the work of the Cabinet is carried out smoothly. The Prime Minister can call upon the the Cabinet Office for help at any time. Indeed, the Head of the Cabinet Office is a senior civil servant who is, essentially, the Prime Minister's Permanent Secretary. The Press Office also provides important assistance to the Prime Minister as do his/her personal 'political advisers' who cannot be Cabinet Ministers as they are not MPs or members of the House of Lords.

The Prime Minister enjoys other powers over the the Cabinet and his/her party. The Prime Minister alone decides when to ask the Monarch to dissolve Parliament and, consequently, to decide the date of the general election. The Prime Minister is, by convention, exercising one of the prerogative powers of the Monarch and it can be used to hold general elections whenever opinion polls suggest that the government will be re-elected. For this reason Mrs Thatcher successfully called general elections in 1983 and 1987 with one year of the five-year Parliament still to run. Mr Major had to wait out the full five-year term before holding

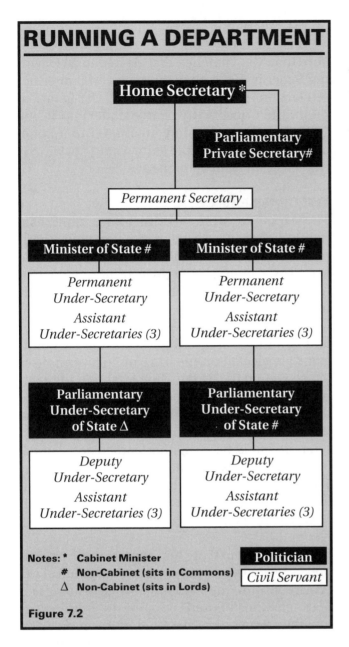

RUNNING A DEPARTMENT

Home Secretary *

Parliamentary Private Secretary#

Permanent Secretary

Minister of State #

Minister of State #

Permanent Under-Secretary

Assistant Under-Secretaries (3)

Permanent Under-Secretary

Assistant Under-Secretaries (3)

Parliamentary Under-Secretary of State Δ

Parliamentary Under-Secretary of State #

Deputy Under-Secretary

Assistant Under-Secretaries (3)

Deputy Under-Secretary

Assistant Under-Secretaries (3)

Notes: * **Cabinet Minister**
Non-Cabinet (sits in Commons)
Δ **Non-Cabinet (sits in Lords)**

Politician
Civil Servant

Figure 7.2

---

elections in 1992 and 1997. James Callaghan, Labour Prime Minister from 1977 to 1979 was criticised for not calling a general election in the autumn of 1978 when Labour might have won. Instead Callaghan waited in the expectation that Labour would do even better in the spring or summer of 1979. However, the 'winter of discontent' intervened and Labour was forced into an election in June 1979 which produced the first of three Conservative election victories under the leadership of Margaret Thatcher.

The power to dissolve Parliament is regarded by some as a weapon which may be used to discipline rebellious elements within the ranks of the governing party. However, the threat to call an election may not be credible if the government is behind in the opinion polls. Not long after the 1992 election, when the Conservative Party was trailing behind Labour in the opinion polls, John Major threatened to call a general election if the Tories did not back his stance on the Maastricht Treaty. This threat could obviously not be carried out and merely served to make Mr Major look weak, especially when he had to withdraw the threat, stating that he had been misunderstood. The last two years of Mr Major's reign as Prime Minister and as Tory Leader were plagued by internal Party dissension and criticism of his leadership. In 1995, in an effort to reassert his control over the Party, Major resigned as Party Leader but not as Prime Minister. He could not call an election because the polls suggested that the Conservative Government would be badly defeated. Major was opposed by John Redwood, who had been Secretary of State for Wales until he resigned to fight for the leadership of the Conservative Party. Major won the election by 218 votes to 89. This result was interpreted as both a vote of confidence in Major and as an indication that the right wing of the Party was unhappy with Major's leadership and his stance on European Union issues. The power to dissolve Parliament lies within the personal prerogative of the Prime Minister, but it appears that there are severe limitations on its use as a weapon against the governing party if opinion polls are unfavourable.

Technological progress has also added to the powers of the Prime Minister. Television and the tabloid press keep the spotlight on the Prime Minister and the Leader of the Opposition. A popular Prime Minister will meet fewer challenges to his/her leadership of party and government. The media encourages a 'personality cult' through which the Prime Minister personifies the government in the minds of the electorate. However, as John Major discovered a 'bad press' may encourage opposition within the governing party.

LIMITING THE PRIME MINISTER'S POWER
During the twentieth century, Prime Ministers have gradually acquired more influence over the decisions which are made by the government. However, the Prime Minister's powers are controlled in various ways.

Party Support Without party backing, the Prime Minister would not be party leader and therefore not Prime Minister. Party leaders are subject to re-election annually, though challengers have been thin on the ground. Mrs Thatcher became Conservative Leader by challenging and defeating Edward Heath in 1975 after the Party had lost the October 1974 General Election. She was challenged on two occasions during her 16 years as Conservative Party Leader. The first challenge in 1988 did not pose a serious threat to her leadership, but the second challenge in 1990 led to her stepping down as Leader and as Prime Minister.(See page 83.)

Powerful Colleagues The Prime Minister's power in the Cabinet is limited by certain considerations. Theoretically a Prime Minister can promote to Ministerial rank whichever MPs he/she chooses. However, those who display the greatest ability really must be included in the government, even though some of them may represent views to the right or the left of the Prime Minister's own ideological position. Senior party members are more or less guaranteed a Cabinet place, though the Prime Minister may not always give them the government post each desires. It is generally assumed that it is safer for the Prime Minister to include potential rivals in the Cabinet rather than to leave them on the backbenches where they could become the focus of opposition if and when public opinion turns against the government. The convention of collective responsibility forces Cabinet Ministers to support all government policies in public and prohibits the voicing of dissent.

The Power of the Media Media coverage may strengthen or weaken the Prime Minister's position. The Prime Minister's personal popularity often protects the chief executive from his/her leading rivals. In spite of critical press comment, John Major remained more popular in the opinion polls than his party as a whole. Media comments suggested that his most dangerous rival was Kenneth Clarke, the Chancellor of the Exchequer. However, Clarke was even more unpopular than Major with the Tory right wing because the Chancellor was perceived as being a Europhile rather than a Eurosceptic.

The Power of the Electorate The electorate also exercises some control over the Prime Minister whose party must seek re-election at least every five years. An unpopular party will not be re-elected. Prime Ministers who lose general elections may resign as party leader shortly afterwards (Home in 1964, Callaghan in 1979 and Major in 1997) or they might, (like Heath after the 1974 Elections) lose a party leadership election. Wilson, on the other hand, survived Labour's loss in the 1970 General Election. Most commentators believe that Mrs Thatcher, first elected to 10 Downing Street in 1979, grew more powerful after her re-election in both 1983 and 1987. Her failure to retain the Conservative Party leadership in the 1990 contest was widely attributed to a belief among Tory MPs that the Party would not win the next election if she remained as Leader.

THE CIVIL SERVICE
The executive branch in Britain comprises a political element, elected politicians, and a non-political or neutral administrative element, civil servants. Theoretically government Ministers make the policy decisions and civil servants administer these decisions. Constitutionally, Ministers are responsible to Parliament for the policies and administration of their departments. Politicians are elected on the basis of policy promises which should determine their aims and their approach to the policy issues and problems arising during their term in political office. Civil servants, who are permanent appointees, are expected to be anonymous, being neither 'named nor blamed' in public for departmental successes and failures. They provide for Ministers the advice they need to formulate and to supervise the administration of policy decisions.

Just as the theory of the separation of powers breaks down in practice because the political executive controls the legislature, so the dividing line between Ministers and civil servants is difficult to maintain in practice. Devotees of the popular TV situation comedy *Yes Minister* were treated weekly to the sight of the clever senior civil servant controlling the politician rather than the Minister commanding the civil servant to do his will. Civil servants may remain in the same department for many years whereas Ministers on average rarely serve more than two years in one department. Accordingly, civil servants acquire an expertise in the type of problems confronting the Minister which may give the bureaucrat considerable influence in the departmental decision making process.

Historically, fears have been expressed that the civil service could frustrate the will of both individual ministers and whole governments. Senior civil servants are likely to have been educated at Oxford or Cambridge, and they constitute a social elite in strategic positions within government.

Such fears have not been realised. The radical policy reforms introduced by the 1945–51 Labour Government and by the Conservative Governments of the 1980s suggest strongly that a determined government should have little difficulty in binding the civil service to its will. The same is true of many individual Ministers.

Reform of the civil service has been a consistent governmental objective since the 1960s. Britain's weak economic performance relative to many international competitors stimulated the view that the efficiency of the government machine could and should be improved. One reform introduced by Labour after their 1964 and 1974 Election victories, in spite of opposition from within the civil service, was the appointment as advisers to Ministers of experts in relevant fields of research and administration beyond the civil service in Whitehall. It was hoped that this reform would broaden and improve the quality of advice by weakening the bureaucratic tendency to protect the 'departmental interest' at all costs. It broke down the traditional 'anonymous but permanent' character of the civil service because these temporary appointees were often political supporters brought into government in order to strengthen the political and partisan dimensions in the advice given to the Ministers who take the final decisions. This practice was continued and extended by the Conservatives after 1979.

The most profound modern reforms of the civil service were introduced after 1979 when the principles of 'Thatcherism' were applied to government administration. The Thatcherite principle that as much decision making as possible should be taken by the market or according to market principles and the Thatcherite prejudice against the public sector stimulated several major changes in the size, organisation and functions of the civil service. The first step in the reform process was called the Financial Management Initiative (FMI). The objective was to cut public expenditure by improving the financial management of government departments. How was improvement to be measured, though? The FMI's emphasis on measurement suggested that market criteria could be used to measure the efficiency of public servants and departments.

In 1988 a reform known as Next Steps was introduced. It distinguished between the policy making and the managerial functions of civil servants.

Policy making means formulating policy, deciding on solutions to the problems faced by government, eg. what to do about traffic congestion. Implementing the chosen policy solution, eg. ensuring that roads are built cost effectively, is regarded as managerial. Civil service functions deemed to be 'managerial' in character were transferred to 'agencies' such as the Benefits Agency and the Employment Service Agency. There were almost 750,000 civil servants in the mid-1970s. About half of all civil servants were employed in departments dealing with social security, taxation and defence. By 1994 the number of civil servants had been reduced to just over half a million.

GOVERNMENT AND PARLIAMENT

The study of democracy poses both theoretical and practical questions. The key theoretical question is: what should be the central elements in a democratic political system? Most people would specify majority rule and the protection of individual and minority rights. The practical questions concern how to achieve what is theoretically desirable and how to eliminate threats to the achievement of democracy. The most widely accepted definitions of democracy are based on some form of representative government, ie. government is entrusted to elected representatives. Such indirect democracy, however, contains the possibility that the elected few become too powerful at the expense of the vast majority who elect them.

Over 250 years ago a Frenchman named Montesquieu, a political philosopher, studied the problem of how to ensure that representative democracy does not concentrate too much power in too few hands. His theoretical conclusions provided the basis for practical attempts to establish democratic constitutions and democratic politics. Montesquieu argued for 'The Separation of Powers' principle as the answer to the problem of too much power being concentrated in too few hands. Montesquieu's solution was based on his observation that government seemed to fall naturally into three functions: the legislative, the executive and the judicial. Montesquieu argued that as long as the institutions charged with the implementation of these three functions are separate from one another in terms of powers and personnel, then too great a concentration of power in one institution will be avoided. Furthermore, since each has distinct functions, each branch will be able to put a degree of restraint on the other two.

O N 26 February 1996, the Conservative government survived by a single vote a motion on the Scott Inquiry Report into allegations that the government knew about and encouraged sales of military equipment to Iran and Iraq in the 1980s. Three executives of a British firm, Matrix Churchill, had been charged with deceiving the government into granting it export licences for materials which could be used to construct weapons. These materials were to be exported to Iraq. The case against the three defendants was dropped when it became clear that their defence would be based on the claim that some government Ministers were aware of the type of materials for which the export licences were sought and indeed encouraged such firms to apply in such a way as to disguise the nature of the exports. Since this affair hit the headlines after the outbreak of the Gulf War against Iraq, the Scott Inquiry was widely believed to be political dynamite threatening certain Ministers and possibly the Government as a whole.

The Scott Report was really an evaluation of exactly what was meant by Ministerial responsibility in relation to sensitive defence and foreign policy issues. There were two questions raised by the Report. Firstly, were individual Ministers guilty of a breach of the convention of individual Ministerial responsibility? Secondly, would the House of Commons be able to enforce the sanctions (punishments) which are understood to exist in the constitutional conventions of individual *and* collective responsibility? The final sanction is that the House of Commons can force a Minister to resign. The opposition called for the resignations of two Ministers whom

Arms Sales to Iraq: The Scott Report

William Waldegrave stated that the Report found him not guilty of lying to Parliament and of intending to mislead the public.

they accused of misleading the House on the true nature of the government's policy on arms sales to Iraq and Iran.

The government was accused of 'running scared'. When the Report was published on 15 February 1996, government Ministers and civil servants were given three days in which to prepare for the inevitable debate in the House of Commons. Opposition MPs were given three hours in which to read the Report's 1806 pages!

The Report did not lead to the resignation of any Government Ministers. One of the Ministers most at risk, Mr William Waldegrave, stated that the Report found him not guilty of lying to Parliament and of intending to mislead the public. Scott did indeed clear Ministers of any "duplicitous intent" and of the charge of conspiracy to deny the Matrix Churchill defendants a fair trial. However, the Report was critical of the way in which the Executive

used the convention of ministerial responsibility. "Throughout the period that the Inquiry has had to examine there is found to be a consistent undervaluing by Government of the public interest that full information should be made available to Parliament. In circumstances where disclosure might be politically or administratively inconvenient, the balance struck by Government comes down, time and time again, against full disclosure." Scott also concluded that the Government had misled both Parliament and the public into believing that "a stricter policy towards non-lethal defence and dual-use exports to Iraq was being applied than was the case".

The Government's single vote victory in the House of Commons emphasises the crucial fact that partisan tensions (Conservative government against Labour opposition) usually outweigh executive v legislative tensions. Party interests are more powerful than parliamentary interests for the great majority of MPs most of the time. Only very occasionally do MPs desert their parties' interests in pursuit of the interests of Parliament. Consequently, the sanctions or punishment elements in the conventions of Ministerial responsibility are weak as long as a government enjoys a majority, even if it is only one, in the Commons.

The vote on the Scott Report also illustrated the difficulties which face a British government whose parliamentary majority is progressively eroded during the lifetime of a five-year Parliament. The Ulster Unionists voted against the Government on the Scott Report as did two Conservative MPs and an Independent Conservative who had resigned the Tory Whip.

American and British governments, which are distinguished by different degrees of constitutional separation, offer a modern test of Montesquieu's theory.

The American Constitution: Separation

In 1787 the Founding Fathers of the newly established United States of America wrote a constitution which is still the best illustration of a faithful implementation of Montesquieu's 'separation of powers' principle. The Constitution of the USA contains some extremely well-planned 'checks and balances' along with almost complete separation of the institutions of government. With one minor exception (the Vice President is President of the Senate), no member of the executive branch is allowed to be a member of the legislature (Congress). Conversely, members of Congress are not allowed to hold executive office. The party to which the President belongs need not be the majority party in the legislature because Congress cannot bring down the President unless it resorts to the impeachment process, which has been attempted only twice in more than two hundred years. The judiciary, headed by the Supreme Court which is appointed for life, is independent of both President and Congress. The Supreme Court has the power to invalidate any actions of both the President and Congress, including Acts of Congress signed by the President, which it decides are unconstitutional, ie. in conflict with the 'supreme law of the land' as laid down in the Constitution. The Supreme Court may be thought of as the 'Guardian of the Constitution'.

The separation of powers in the American Constitution has contributed to a decentralised political system in which the President's policies are frequently defeated in Congress without the President losing office. The separation is emphasised by a complex electoral system in which many institutions (President *and* the House of Representatives *and* the Senate)are subject to frequent election. Thus President Clinton was elected to office in 1992 along with a Democratic Congress but he lost his Democratic majority in Congress in 1994 and did not regain it in 1996.

The British Constitution: Fusion

The British Constitution differs from the American in several ways. It is only partly written in the form of Acts of Parliament which relate to significant constitutional matters such as the right to vote, the royal succession and the powers of the House of Lords. Unlike the American Constitution which is comprehensive in scope and constitutes the 'supreme law of the land', the British Constitution gradually evolved over several hundred years instead of being thought out and written on one occasion. Indeed much of the British Constitution does not enjoy legal status but is rather a matter of conventions, ie. rules which are obeyed because it is widely agreed that they should be. One significant convention is that the Prime Minister must be a member of the House of Commons. This is not a legal requirement but is accepted as appropriate in a democratic age. The British Constitution, unlike the American, does not include a detailed separation of powers. Rather there is a 'fusion' of powers and institutions which, according to some commentators permits too great a concentration of power in too few hands. A key question is whether the combination of fusion, rather than separation, and relatively few and infrequent elections compared to the USA weakens British democracy.

The 'fusion' in the British Constitution means that certain members of one branch of government are also members of another branch. The Monarch is a member of all three branches, being the constitutional head (figurehead) of the legislature, the executive and the judiciary. The Cabinet and government, which together make up the executive, must be made up of members of the legislature and include leading judicial officers such as the Lord Chancellor and the Solicitor General. Although he is not an elected official of any of the branches, the Lord Chancellor is a member of the executive, the legislature and the judiciary. He heads the judiciary, is the government's chief law officer which makes him a Cabinet Minister and thus a senior member of the executive and, as President of the House of Lords (roughly equivalent to the Speaker of the House of Commons) is a member of the legislature. The Prime Minister leads the executive, is chief adviser to the Monarch, is a Member of Parliament, is leader of the political party which holds a majority of seats in the House of Commons and he or she makes appointments to the judiciary, although this is done in the name of the Monarch.

The British version of democracy does not have the distinct separation of powers or institutions shown in the American version. Indeed the legislative, executive and judicial powers are shared among the interacting institutions of government. Some commentators argue that Montesquieu's aim of preventing too great a concentration of

ON Wednesday 11 December 1996 David Willetts, MP for Havant, and widely regarded as one of the rising stars of the Conservative Party, resigned as Paymaster General in John Major's Government. Willetts had been harshly criticised in a report unanimously approved by the prestigious Standards and Privileges Committee and published the previous day. Willetts was the third Ministerial resignation to emerge from a 'cash for questions' scandal which had come to light in 1994 when Willetts was a Conservative Whip. Willetts was not directly implicated in the scandal, but his behaviour as a junior Whip in trying to lessen the potential damage to the Conservative Party was deemed to be unacceptable. The resignations linked to the 'cash for questions' scandal are all examples of the convention of individual Ministerial responsibility being played out to the full. However, the reasons for the various resignations all relate to issues of the personal behaviour of the offending individuals rather than to alleged failures of departmental policy.

Willetts himself had not been accused of accepting cash in return for asking parliamentary questions on behalf of interested parties outside Parliament. Rather, he stood accused of attempting to influence the conduct of the Members' Inter-

CASE STUDY

The Resignation of David Willetts

ests Committee which was investigating such charges against other MPs. Although the two MPs in question, Tim Smith and Neil Hamilton, had already resigned as junior members of the Government, their behaviour as MPs was under investigation by the influential Members' Interests Committee.

Such an attempt was considered to be unacceptable because it amounted to inexcusable interference by a member of the executive branch into the affairs of the legislature. Willetts's standing was further damaged when he was judged to have been "inaccurate" in his evidence to the Standards and Privileges Committee when it investigated his behaviour as a

Conservative Whip. The crucial role in the questioning of Willetts by the Standards and Privileges Committee was attributed to a Conservative backbencher, Quentin Davies, MP for Stamford. The Committee was chaired by a Cabinet Minister, Tony Newton who was Leader of the House of Commons. Newton's membership illustrates clearly the fusion of executive-legislative institutions in the British parliamentary system. A member of the Conservative Cabinet chaired a Commons Committee which severely criticised a junior Conservative Minister. The Committee stopped short of recommending any punishment. Willetts resigned while proclaiming that he had told the truth in spite of the charge of "inaccuracy" by the Committee. The Prime Minister would have preferred Willetts to have stayed but accepted his resignation.

One conclusion which the Standards and Privileges Committee did reach was that in future MPs should be interviewed under oath to ensure that "inaccuracies" would be avoided. The Committee's unanimity and Willetts's resignation indicated that the publicity given to allegations of 'sleaze' against MPs had reached such a level that it was necessary to show that the House of Commons was putting its own house in order.

power is, nonetheless, achieved by a system of checks and balances. Although it is the duty of the courts to uphold laws passed by Parliament, their decisions cannot be swayed by whichever government happens to be in power at any given time. Furthermore, Parliament is not allowed to discuss anything which is sub judice (being considered by a court of law or a judge). It is absolutely essential that in any democracy the judiciary is independent and is able to act as a check on any government which tried to abuse its power. The Courts ruled unlawful several decisions of the Home Secretary Michael Howard in the early

1990s. However, the Courts are limited to judging Ministerial actions against the content of legislation passed by Parliament. Unlike the American Supreme Court, the British Judiciary cannot invalidate Acts of Parliament because of clashes with the law of the Constitution.

There is a view that the judiciary has become a more effective check on the powerful British executive than Parliament. This has occurred partly because EU membership has introduced more rights to be defined by the courts and partly because Parliament can do little if the government

INDIVIDUAL MINISTERIAL RESIGNATIONS 1992–97

MINISTER	DATE OF RESIGNATION	DEPARTMENT
David Mellor	September 1992	National Heritage
Michael Mates	June 1993	Northern Ireland
Tim Yeo	January 1994	Environment
Lord Caithness	January 1994	Transport
Tim Smith	October 1994	Northern Ireland
Neil Hamilton	October 1994	Trade and Industry
Jonathon Aitken	July 1995	Chief Secretary to Treasury
David Willetts	December 1996	Paymaster General

All of these Ministers resigned because of personal misdemeanours committed in and out of Parliament. Only two, Mellor and Aitken, were of Cabinet rank. Mellor, Mates, Yeo and Lord Caithness resigned because of embarrassing personal actions which had nothing to do with parliamentary business. The others got caught up one way or another in the 'cash for questions' scandal in which it was alleged that MPs accepted cash in return for asking questions in Parliament on behalf of outside parties. In some cases the Prime Minister accepted the resignation with regret, in others he was clearly glad to see the back of an embarrassment to his government. The 'cash for questions' scandal is a clear example of conflict between the executive and legislative branches in which partisan competition was to some extent put aside in defence of the interests of Parliament as an institution independent of the dominant executive branch.

enjoys a comfortable majority in the Commons.

The Monarch has no effective political power over the legislative process. The Royal Assent to legislation has not been denied since Queen Anne did so in 1707. Nevertheless, both the Monarch and the House of Lords could, in theory, act as check on the power of the elected Commons if it attempted to act undemocratically—for instance, if it tried to do away with the requirement of periodic elections. This is a power of last resort. The loss of effective political power by both the Monarchy and the House of Lords means that British democracy depends upon the conventions of Ministerial responsibility, by which the executive is responsible to the House of Commons, and on elections which ensure that every five years at least the executive's actions can be judged by the electorate.

The Conventions of Ministerial Responsibility
The language of Parliament suggests that effective power over the executive lies with the legislature. Anyone watching the televising of parliamentary business quickly becomes aware that Ministers are constantly respectful of the traditions and formalities of the Houses of Parliament. One of the most significant constitutional rules defining the relationship between the executive and the legislature declares that it is the executive which is responsible to and therefore dependent on the legislature. There are two conventions of ministerial responsibility: collective and individual. What limitations do these conventions impose on British government?

The convention of collective responsibility has two elements. The first relates to the executive branch. Members of the government, no matter how low they are in the pecking order, for instance parliamentary private secretaries, must support publicly the policies arrived at in Cabinet or else they must resign. The second element relates to the links between the executive and legislature by requiring that the executive resigns if it is defeated on a motion of confidence in the House of Commons. This is the constitutional rule which defines a parliamentary system unlike a presidential system where such responsibility does not apply.

However, the practical significance of the rule depends largely on election results. A majority party in the legislature usually supports faithfully its leadership who occupy the executive offices of the state. Only when the majority disappears does the sanction of resignation become a possibility. During the last nine months of the Conservative Government elected in 1992 there were frequent claims that the Government would lose its majority and be forced to resign. The Government had some narrow squeaks on issues such as the Scott Report, (See page 78) but survived to call an election in May 1997.

The convention of collective responsibility would play a much greater role in British politics should the two-party system, in which Conservative and Labour have been winning more than 90% of seats in the legislature, give way to a multi-party system with no majority party in the Commons. The threat of defeat and resignation seldom becomes a reality. The government's collective responsibility is limited to having to explain its policies to the legislature and to receiving its consent.

Ministers are also individually responsible to Parliament for their own actions and for the work of their departments. This entails giving Parliament full information about the policies and actions of the executive branch eg. at Question Time and during debates. Over the years the extent of individual responsibility has been narrowed as it has become clear that Ministers are personally acquainted with only a small proportion of departmental decisions and actions. Ministers remain responsible for the major policies of their departments although collective responsibility may take over in order to shield Ministers who are under attack. When Lord Carrington resigned as Foreign Secretary over the events leading up to the Falklands War, Mrs Thatcher tried to persuade him to carry on. The Prime Minister was prepared to protect her Foreign Secretary by, in effect, assuming that the entire Cabinet was responsible for those events.

If a government enjoys a clear working majority in the Commons it will win all the motions of confidence it is likely to face and most of the important votes on its policies. Responsibility, therefore, which contains the threat of defeat and resignation, is usually confined to 'answerability', ie. the government is expected to answer questions in Parliament and to explain and defend its policies. This does not mean that Ministers and governments are never forced to resign. Individual ministerial resignations are quite common, although they are usually the result of personal 'misdemeanours' rather than the result of departmental legislative or administrative failures, and very seldom the consequence of votes in the House. (See page 81 *Individual Ministerial Resignations 1992–1997.*)

The conventions of ministerial responsibility have a crucial impact on British politics. Because a government could be forced to resign if defeated on a major issue in the House of Commons, the government's backbenchers will normally be loyal in the voting lobbies in order to prevent the opposition from taking over the powers of government. Similarly, opposition MPs usually toe the party line in order to put maximum pressure on the government. As a consequence, the constitutional rules of Ministerial responsibility tend to produce centralised and disciplined political parties, especially when two parties predominate. Political parties do, however, diverge from the centralised, disciplined model from time to time. The Labour Party in the early 1980s appeared to be decentralised and undisciplined, but successive electoral defeats allowed its leaders—Neil Kinnock, John Smith and Tony Blair—to change both the organisation of the Party and its policies in order to construct a credible alternative to the Conservatives who were eventually defeated after winning four elections in a row.

The conventions of executive responsibility to Parliament and the certainty of periodic elections usually ensure a strong British executive by encouraging party loyalty. Nonetheless, a government may be weakened by its own backbenchers if the governing party is deeply divided by an emotive issue such as 'Europe' and electoral defeat seems likely. Mr Major's term as Prime Minister was made difficult by the issue of Britain's membership of the European Union and in particular right-wing fears about what the future political character of the EU might mean for Britain.

A DOMINANT EXECUTIVE?

For much of the second half of the 20th century, critics of British government have claimed that the Prime Minister and Cabinet, the executive branch, have enjoyed too much power over the legislature. Party loyalty and party discipline along with the electorate's tendency to return one party with a comfortable working majority to the Commons have ensured that British governments usually secured the consent of Parliament for their major policy proposals. British government enjoyed a reputation for strength and stability which was the envy of other nations. In 1958 when the French were writing a new Constitution for the Fifth Republic they looked at the British system for hints on how to strengthen the executive branch against

The Downfall of Margaret Thatcher

THE resignation of Mrs Thatcher on 28 November 1990 after over 11 years in office indicates that there can be limits to the tenure of even the most powerful of Prime Ministers. Her downfall was caused by a combination of factors:

✘ She had made enemies in the Conservative Party, particularly Sir Geoffrey Howe and Michael Heseltine.

✘ The provision of a constitutional mechanism for challenging party leaders.

✘ The belief of many Conservative MPs that they would not be re-elected if Mrs Thatcher remained as Leader.

✘ The highly emotive influence of the European issue within the Conservative Party.

The crucial element in the story of Mrs Thatcher's exit was provided by Sir Geoffrey Howe, Leader of the House of Commons and Deputy Prime Minister. Howe resigned from the Cabinet on 1 November 1990 because of personal and policy factors. Howe may have been Thatcher's most senior Cabinet colleague, but he had, in effect, been demoted when Thatcher moved him against his wishes from the Foreign Office to be Leader of the House of Commons in 1989. Although on economic issues Howe was perceived as almost more 'Thatcherite' than the Prime Minister herself, the two disagreed vehemently over issues of European integration and Britain's relationship with the European Union. In October 1990 Mrs Thatcher accepted without enthusiasm Britain's membership of the EU Exchange Rate Mechanism. At the Rome Summit in late October Mrs Thatcher was at odds with most other European leaders. On her return she declared in the House of Commons that "we have surrendered enough" to the European Community. Mrs Thatcher's abrasive approach to European issues was too much for Howe who resigned.

Howe's departure from the Cabinet was not immediately perceived as a fatal blow to the Prime Minister. Few believed that Geoffery Howe could defeat Margaret Thatcher in a leadership election. *The Times* leader on 2 November ruled out a leadership contest claiming that Thatcher's leadership was "robust, undaunted and unchallenged". One day later Michael Heseltine hinted that he might be prepared to stand against the Prime Minister for the leadership of the Conservative Party. Heseltine had resigned from the Government in 1986 as a protest against Thatcher's handling of the Westland Affair and her allegedly autocratic control of the Cabinet. Heseltine believed that Mrs Thatcher had replaced Cabinet Government with Prime Ministerial Government.

The next crucial step was Howe's resignation speech in the House of Commons on 13 November. Howe argued that the Thatcher style of abrasive diplomacy would result in Britain, which had joined 14 years after the foundation of the European Community, "being once again shut out" when the Community made vital decisions.

Howe's dramatic speech, which was televised and which dominated the newspaper headlines the following day, gave Heseltine his chance. He announced his candidacy for the Conservative leadership on 14 November. The first ballot was held on 19 November. The Prime Minister, who was in Paris, 'won' by 204 votes to 152 with 16 Conservative MPs not voting. The margin of victory was 52:14.6% of those voting (abstentions not counting). The election rules required a *15%* margin: 54 votes out of the 356 voting. So Mrs Thatcher would have won in the first ballot if two abstainers had voted for her or if one Heseltine supporter had voted for the Prime Minister instead.

In the second ballot an overall majority was required. Heseltine was certainly going to stand. Who would be running against him? The Prime Minister immediately announced her intention to stand. On 22 November came the dramatic announcement that Mrs Thatcher was withdrawing from the contest. Why did she take the decision which brought her 'reign' to an end? The explanation of her actions lies in the first ballot which was interpreted in conflicting ways. Thatcher's supporters emphasised how close she was to winning. Her opponents emphasised that the 152 MPs who voted for Heseltine were voicing a profound vote of no confidence in her leadership of the Party and the country.

Mrs Thatcher consulted with her Cabinet colleagues. If they had been unanimous in encouraging her to contest the second ballot she would have done so, but most of them told her she would lose to Heseltine in the second ballot. This advice proved crucial. Ironically, the collective decision making model of Cabinet government prevailed; the Prime Minister gave way to the majority view. She stood down, releasing Major and Hurd to take part in the contest. On 2 December Major won by 185 votes to Heseltine's 131 and Hurd's 56 votes. Heseltine did not force a third ballot, preferring to stand down and guarantee himself an important post in the Major Cabinet.

Mr Major's victory was based on several factors:

● Major was Thatcher's preference among the contenders because he was closest to her on policy. Major appealed to many Conservatives because he was perceived as being 'Thatcherite' in policy but not in style. Many Conservatives voting against the Prime Minister were rejecting Thatcher the individual but not the policy side of 'Thatcherism'.

● Major attracted more support than his rivals from the Thatcher Cabinet, and from the many Conservative constituency associations which had not been in favour of Heseltine's challenge to the Prime Minister. Thatcher might have survived if the constituency associations had had a vote in the leadership contest.

● Unlike Heseltine, Major did not suffer from the disadvantage of having divided the party. Consequently Major was much more likely to be able to unite the Party in time to fight the next election.

the legislature which had been all too successful in bringing down governments in the Fourth Republic (1946–58). At the same time British critics were calling for reforms to strengthen the House of Commons against an executive which they believed had become too powerful. Out of these criticisms were to come reforms of the committee system in the House of Commons with the introduction in 1979 of a specialised select committee system to scrutinise the policy formulation and policy implementation of individual government departments.

Not all British governments have been strong. There are limits to the power of even the strongest governments and weak governments often go down to electoral defeat. Mrs Thatcher could not make the Poll Tax popular and her successor John Major had to withdraw it. The Major Government ran into severe difficulties over the European issue in its various forms though these difficulties were to be found mainly within the Conservative Party itself which was badly divided over 'Europe'. As we saw in Chapter 3, one of the main reasons for the electorate's rejection of the Conservative Government in 1997 was that its reputation for strength and unity was dealt a savage blow by the currency crisis known as 'Black Wednesday' in September 1992. The Major Government in its latter stages did not appear to conform to the image of 'strong government' because its overall majority of 30 had been whittled away by by-election defeats and by the rebellions of the Eurosceptics.

The 'strength' of government is a variable in Britain dependent upon how several factors combine:

1 the size of the government's parliamentary majority

2 trends in public opinion including voting intentions

3 party unity or the lack of it

4 the efficiency of opposition parties

5 global economic trends beyond the influence of the British executive.

The elections of 1979, 1983 and 1987 produced comfortable majorities which enabled the Conservatives to enact much of the radical Thatcherite agenda. However, the prospect of a fourth Conservative victory under Mrs Thatcher's leadership was threatened by a fall in the Government's popularity in 1990 which coincided with the leadership crisis when Geoffery Howe resigned. Mrs Thatcher lost her position but the Conservatives went on to win a somewhat surprising victory in 1992. The string of Conservative victories was made easier by a badly divided Labour Party which was challenged for second place in the 1980s by a regrouping of the political centre and the formation of the Alliance and then the Liberal Democratic Party. Labour's organisational and ideological regeneration under Kinnock, Smith and Blair gradually established it as a viable alternative to the Conservatives as a credible party of government. The Conservatives lost in 1997 because the electorate had lost faith in their ability to govern effectively. The ultimate check on the executive is the electorate.

CHAPTER 8 Pressures and INFLUENCES

What you will learn

1 The role of pressure groups as representative institutions
2 The differences between pressure groups and political parties
3 The targets and strategies of groups trying to influence government decisions

LET US IMAGINE that your American cousin has arrived in Britain for a holiday just as you have finished reading the first seven chapters of this book. Your cousin is fascinated by British politics but is also confused because of the profound differences between British and American politics at all levels—the party political, the electoral, the constitutional and so on. The American asks you to summarise the essential characteristics of British and Scottish politics so that she can understand what is really happening as the new Labour Government sets about attempting to enact its major campaign promises. Since you have been revising for an exam on British politics you set about the task with great enthusiasm. A number of very well-known phrases trip off your tongue: 'Parliamentary System'; 'Cabinet or maybe Prime Ministerial Government'; 'Representative Government'; 'Party Discipline'; 'Unitary State'; 'Devolution, not Federalism' and so on. Above all you say that Britain is a 'democracy', 'the oldest democracy in the western world'.

As you go through the list, believing that you are really well prepared for the approaching exam, you notice that your cousin looks a bit puzzled. Each phrase you have offered captures an essential element of the British political system. You describe with great clarity reform of the House of Lords and the establishment of a Scottish Parliament. Power is to be placed even more firmly in the 'hands of the people'. Nevertheless, your cousin is not convinced. In your enthusiasm to explain all things British you have forgotten about the European Union and elections to the European Parliament—after all you have not yet read Chapter 10. It is not surprising that your cousin notices that there are very few elections compared to the American system. Above all, she is amazed by the fact that the Chief Executive is not directly

elected by the people and by your failure to mention 'the Lobby'.

"It does not look to me as if there is much representation in the 'oldest democracy in the western world'; we elect every political official from the President down to the local sheriff. If your wonderful political parties are so centralised and disciplined, how on earth do you influence what the government does in between elections? If your executive, be it Prime Minister or Cabinet, is so much stronger than the American President, why is Labour meeting so much opposition to its proposals for welfare reform? I live in a pluralist society which is more democratic than yours because our people have more opportunities to influence what the government does. We can stop the government doing what it wants to do just as we rejected President Clinton's plans for reform of health care in 1994."

Now it is your turn to be puzzled. 'Pluralism'? 'The Lobby'? What do these terms mean? You realise that the story is not complete. You need to know more about the political process in your own country; you need to go beyond elections and parties, beyond manifestos and campaigns. What is missing from your description of Britain's 'Representative Democracy'?

The answers to these questions are given in this chapter in which the 'representative system' is extended to include pressure groups and interest groups, civil servants in Whitehall, and the increasing role of public opinion. This can be expressed in protest demonstrations against such issues as benefit cuts and fox-hunting and in the polls on every imaginable political issue which are published weekly in the media.

PRESSURE GROUPS

All textbooks on British politics have a chapter on 'pressure groups' and 'interest groups'. This is because political parties and elections are not the only ways in which individuals participate in politics. Political parties are the most obvious representative institutions because they dominate both the electoral process and the organisation of Parliament and government. However, political parties, especially in a two-party system, can represent only the broadest of the common interests of the individuals who join or vote for each party. The Conservative and Labour parties both constitute a 'broad church' because they need to attract as much support as possible in order to achieve their first objective which is to win elections. People who join a political party have to compromise in order to gain power and to influence what the government does. Members of a political party, including the governing party, will not all agree with all the details of all the policies decided by the leadership. Labour's 'honeymoon' period ended in the winter of 1997 when rumours began to spread about the likely targets of its review of the 'welfare state' and the expensive benefits it provides for various sections of the population. Labour Party members and supporters were among the most critical opponents of potential change even before the government had announced the full range of proposed changes. The tensions generated by the need to compromise give rise on occasion to the ideological or policy conflicts which have made intra-party conflict a decisive feature of British party politics in recent decades. (See Chapter 4.) In other words, party leaders cannot satisfy all sections of their parties all of the time.

The government will not be too concerned about satisfying the policy aims of the people who did not vote for it. Also, people who have little interest in party politics will sometimes be provoked into political action by an issue which affects them intimately. Consequently, many people have specific interests or political objectives which may be threatened by or are unlikely to be satisfied by the government of the day. So individuals seeking to achieve political objectives often have to go beyond party politics to achieve their aims.

Other avenues of political participation and representation are available. One of the most famous political sayings is Aristotle's ancient dictum "Man is by nature a social animal". Society breeds organisations. Sport, religion, work, leisure, 'good causes', 'social problems' and personal problems all stimulate the existence of organisations such as the Scottish Football Association, the Church of Scotland and the Roman Catholic Church, the Transport and General Workers Union, the Ramblers Association, the Salvation Army, the Howard League for Penal Reform and Alcoholics Anonymous. The list seems endless.

When government decisions seem likely to affect their members adversely, social organisations will enter the political process to advance or protect the interests of their members. In seeking to influence government decisions they will put pressure on the government to behave or *not* to behave in certain ways—hence the term pressure group. Pressure groups are social organisations rather than political parties and seek to influence governmental decision making in favour of their members. Most social organisations are created for reasons which have nothing to do with politics. Some organisations are explicitly political and others are established to promote a view on a single issue which may be only temporary in duration. All social organisations are potential pressure groups.

Groups become involved in politics, some on a temporary basis, others more permanently. Religion provides one source of pressure group activity. In the 1997 Election campaign one of the few adverse moments for the Labour Party in Scotland occurred when Archbishop Winning reprimanded the Party for its refusal to take a pro-life stand on the abortion issue. The General Assembly of the Church of Scotland makes known its views on a wide range of issues. Legislative proposals either by the government or by backbenchers often stimulate pressure group responses. After the 1997 Election a Private Members' Bill to introduce a ban on fox-hunting stimulated many organisations to campaign for or against the proposed legislation—the League Against Cruel Sports supported the Bill while the Countryside Alliance opposed it. These organisations were in existence long before the Bill was introduced in the Autumn of 1997.

Types of Pressure Group

There are two basic types of pressure groups: interest groups and promotional or 'cause' groups. Interest groups are so called because they represent the economic interests of their members. Their distinguishing feature is *who* they represent. Promotional groups are defined by the cause they represent—by *what* they stand for. The Howard

League for Penal Reform promotes a particular view of prison policy (what prison should be for; conditions of inmates). Membership of promotional groups is open-ended; anyone who believes in the cause can join.

The best known interest groups, and the biggest, are trade unions and employers' federations. Trade unions were created and still exist primarily to defend and improve the wages and working conditions of their members. Their principal adversaries are the firms employing their members and whose main activity is to compete in the marketplace and make profits. Interest groups have closed memberships. In other words, individuals have to work in a particular industry or possess a particular skill in order to join the union which represents workers in that industry or with that particular skill.

The two sides of industry are represented by the most powerful pressure groups in Britain. Trade unions individually and collectively represent millions of workers. In 1992, six unions had over half a million members each. The biggest union, the Transport and General Workers Union (TGWU), had over one million members. By the end of the 1970s there were over 13 million trade unionists, though the number had fallen to 9 million by 1993. Collectively, unions are organised into the Trades Union Congress (TUC) which acts as an 'umbrella' organisation for the union movement. TUC leaders and the leaders of individual unions are frequently consulted by the government because their approval may make the difference between success and failure in respect of many economic and industrial policies.

The political role of British trade unions has been a central issue in recent years for two reasons. Firstly, the role of unions within the Labour Party raised questions about their political power. Many people believed that the unions possessed too much power. Secondly, trade union power and organisation was one of the major targets of 'Thatcherism' in the 1980s. There was much trade union reform which has, for the most part, been accepted by New Labour. Conservative governments in the 1980s reformed industrial relations and weakened the political power of trade unions. Secondary picketing was made unlawful. Ballots were required both for the election of union executives and before strike action could be taken. The unions which had prevented the implementation of Edward Heath's 1972 Industrial Relations

Act and frustrated Labour's efforts to enforce an incomes' policy in the late 1970s (leading to the famed 'winter of discontent' which contributed to the Conservative election victory in 1979) were unable to prevent Mrs Thatcher from introducing these detested reforms.

The titanic struggle between the Conservative Government and the miners in 1985 was won by the Government. Unemployment strengthened the hand of the Government in the battle with the unions. Conservative success encouraged Labour in opposition to speak about reforming its constitutional links with the unions which had created the Party at the beginning of the 20th century.

The links between the 'other side' of industry, companies who are the employers, and the Conservative Party are much less formal than the links between Labour and the unions. There is no equivalent of trade union affiliation to the Labour Party. The most obvious connection between business interests and the Conservative Party is financial. Many companies contribute large sums of money to the Conservatives. Industries form their own federations to make representations to the government when necessary, for instance the Engineering Employers Federation. The top business pressure group is the Confederation of British Industry (the CBI) which is the TUC's counterpart. Other umbrella associations on the business side are the British Chambers of Commerce, the Small Business Association and the Institute of Directors.

Many groups combine 'interests' and 'cause'. In December 1997 there were rumours that Labour's review of the welfare system would result in cuts in various types of benefit and in some benefits being made conditional on going to work. Several groups receiving benefit reacted by protesting outside the gates of Downing Street, throwing paint on the gates and chaining themselves to the railings. One protest was organised by the Disabled People's Direct Action Network which feared that disabled people would lose benefit which in some cases paid for goods or medicine 'which they could not otherwise afford'. Other disabled groups such as Radar (Royal Association for Disability and Rehabilitation) and Scope supported the action. These groups see the fight to safeguard the economic interests of disabled people and to safeguard their benefits as a cause since the disabled need special protection.

Pressure groups may be ad hoc and temporary in character. Such groups are established in order to fight for a particular objective and are disbanded once the fight is over, whether it is successful or not. A British government decision to permit the construction of an electricity power line between Scotland and Northern Ireland led to protests and the establishment of a pressure group in Southern Scotland. This pressure group, known as STOP opposed the venture because it necessitated a line of pylons, principally in Ayrshire, to convey the electricity to the undersea power line. STOP represents those who believe that the pylons will be unsightly, spoiling the beauty of the countryside. Other factors have changed since the original British government decision to sanction the venture, leading to a reopening of the whole issue of whether the power line should go ahead. Once a decision is taken and the power line is either built or abandoned, STOP is likely to be wound up.

PARTIES AND PRESSURE GROUPS: WHAT IS THE DIFFERENCE BETWEEN THEM?
Political parties and pressure groups are both representative institutions. They both have memberships to satisfy. What are the differences between them?

Firstly, parties and groups are not independent of one another. Some of the most powerful interest groups are strongly linked to a particular political party. Everyone knows that trade unionists are more likely to vote Labour than Conservative and that the great majority of trade unions not only support the Labour Party financially but are actually affiliated to the Labour Party. Most people are aware that businesses have been strong supporters of the Conservative Party and have demonstrated that support by making financial contributions to the Party. So many pressure groups, especially those of the economic interest variety, are strongly connected to particular parties.

The main differences between parties and pressure groups are related to the range of interests and aims each possesses. Groups are much more specific in their interests and aims, most being too small to contemplate an existence as a political party. The first-past-the-post electoral system and the huge costs of competing in elections do not encourage parties which would represent a narrow social section such as individuals opposed to fox-hunting or abortion or a party to represent doctors or welders or football players.

Occasionally people feel so strongly about an issue that they resort to ignoring the existing parties and competing in elections to make their point even though they have no hope of winning a seat or even of saving their £500 deposit. All parliamentary candidates are described on the ballot paper as belonging to a political party. In 1997 at least 150 'parties' competed, many putting up candidates in only one or two constituencies. Some of these were nonsense parties, the most famous of which is the Monster Raving Loony Party. Such parties are not serious in that they have no hope of winning any seats at all and their aims are essentially weird. Other parties are more serious in that they have a full range of policies and would like to influence government policy. The British National Party, the far right party opposed to immigration, put up 57 candidates(only three saved their deposit) and won 35,833 votes. The influence of such a party does not depend on winning any seats because that is unlikely to happen but on winning enough votes to frighten one of the major parties into taking up some of their policy recommendations. It has been claimed that the Conservative Government elected in 1979 moved to the right on immigration issues for that reason.

In 1995, opponents of developments in the European Union formed the Referendum Party which campaigned for a referendum which would ask the people if they wanted Britain to be part of a federal Europe. The Party founders promised to disband it as soon as a referendum was held. It was a single issue party, though the European issue is one of the most significant in recent British political history. Its main aim was to force the other parties to put the European issue to the voters. The Referendum Party, financed by the multimillionaire Jimmy Goldsmith, put up 547 candidates (504 lost their deposit) and won 2.6% of the vote but no seats. The Referendum Party may have cost the Conservatives about 4 seats.

Other 'parties' to appear on the ballot paper in 1997 were closer to pressure groups in character. The Pro-life Alliance campaigned for a ban on all abortions except those essential for saving the mother's life. The Pro-life Alliance brought together many groups which campaigned as pressure groups against abortion. Pro-life put up 53 candidates all of whom lost their deposit. They won 118,545 votes averaging 0.7% in the seats they contested. Other pressure groups fought the election at a much more local level. 'Bypass' put up a

DIFFERENCES BETWEEN POLITICAL PARTIES & PRESSURE GROUPS

POLITICAL PARTIES

Principal Objectives
Winning elections
Forming government
Implementation of broad policy platforms

Membership
Open-ended: anyone may join

Methods
Putting up candidates in elections
Putting MPs into government

Figure 8.1

PRESSURE GROUPS

Principal Objectives
Protecting specific economic interests or
promoting a specific cause
Influencing government

Membership
Interest Groups (closed): confined to members
Cause Groups (open-ended): anyone may join

Methods
Persuasion
Protest
Campaigns to influence public opinion
Sponsoring parliamentary candidates

candidate against the Newbury by-pass. 'Scrapit' opposed the proposed Avon ring road.

PRESSURE GROUP TARGETS

Pressure groups 'target' elements of the political system which will help them to achieve their objectives. The most obvious targets are:

1 the executive branch (Ministers and civil servants)
2 the legislature (backbench MPs)
3 party factions (left, centre and right wings of the major parties) sympathetic to specific pressure group interests or causes
4 public opinion and voters

The strategy and tactics of pressure groups in any country depend to a large extent on how the power of the policy making process is structured. In the USA the Constitution sets up several competing centres of power, including the Administration (the Presidency and Government Departments), the Congress (Senate and House of Representatives), and the governments in each of the 50 states. The American Constitution established more institutional access points of which modern pressure groups can take advantage.

In particular, the separate election of the executive (the President) and the legislature (the Congress) in the United States has meant that the British tendency towards a dominant political executive has not been repeated across the Atlantic. Members of Congress are much less likely than

British MPs to toe the party line because the tenure (political survival) of the executive is not dependent on votes in the legislature. Members of Congress are freer than British MPs when they vote in the legislature.

In Britain decision making is much more narrowly concentrated than in the USA. The focus of most pressure group activity has traditionally been Whitehall. Policy making in Britain, once the general election is over, concentrates on government departments which means on government Ministers or the civil servants advising them. A government which has just been elected, especially if it has replaced a government of the rival major party, will have certain policy objectives from which it is unlikely to be diverted. The scope for influencing policy will not be great when a government transforms its manifesto proposals, such as devolution, into legislative form. On the other hand, the government will also have to cope with problems which arise unexpectedly. In these cases the government may be open to suggestions from 'interested parties'.

In contrast to American Senators and Representatives, British MPs have long been considered to be much less useful to pressure groups because voting in the legislature in Britain is determined much more by party loyalty and discipline enforced by the whips. In the USA the votes of many individual members of Congress cannot be taken for granted. Therefore pressure groups find it profitable to attempt to influence members in their favour before the vote takes place. Congressmen and women are strongly inclined to vote in accordance with the wishes of their constituents, and of the pressure groups which are important to these constituents, because they depend on them for reselection as party candidates in primary elections. Most British MPs, on the other hand, feel compelled to vote with the party majority most of the time unless they feel very strongly about an issue. For this reason, although MPs may be useful to pressure groups as far as publicity is concerned, they do not usually cross party lines to vote in accordance with these objectives when party interests clash with pressure group interests.

BRITISH PRESSURE GROUPS IN ACTION: FROM PERSUASION TO PROTEST

Pressure group participation in politics takes various forms. The larger economic interest groups, which are often consulted as of right when the government is formulating policy, will try to 'persuade' the government to grant their wishes or demands. Promotional groups are more likely to resort to aggressive though non-violent protests against policy decisions which have been taken or are thought likely to be taken.

Pressure group actions vary according to the nature of the groups involved and the stages of the government decision making process. The principal decision making stages are:

1 formulation of policy where the emphasis is on consultation and persuasion for groups who have access to the government
2 legislative stages where the emphasis is on the publicity generated by MPs speaking in support of group interests or causes
3 implementation where the emphasis may be on protest on behalf of those who have lost out when decisions were taken.

Consultation

Often the government will invite groups and organisations to comment on policy proposals which have been published in the preliminary form of a White or Green Paper. At this stage the government is still open to persuasion. In the Autumn of 1997 the Labour Government invited the public to respond to its proposals to encourage saving which involved replacing TESSAs and PEPs with Individual Savings Allowances (ISAs).

The consultative access granted to many, but not all, pressure groups as representative institutions has long been accepted as a necessary and legitimate part of the democratic process. Politicians and civil servants spend much time and effort listening to pressure group demands. This is done in order to persuade public opinion of the validity of the government's policy and to facilitate implementation of that policy once it has entered the Statute Book. Groups in turn realise that they need to persuade the government to give them some of what they want from government. A process of consultation has therefore emerged in which representatives of groups and interests are in frequent contact with the policy makers (government Ministers and civil servants), in Whitehall. This is particularly important when the government is formulating policy to be enshrined in Bills to be placed before Parliament. Groups also need publicity for their aims in order to move public opinion in their favour, and MPs may be useful to them if they speak out on their behalf.

The process of consultation between groups and government developed much earlier and is much more pronounced in the USA where it has become known as 'lobbying'. Pressure groups are known collectively in the USA as the 'Lobby' because their representatives lie in wait for important policy makers in the corridors in the Congress buildings (Capitol Hill) and in government departments. The profession of 'political consultant' developed in the USA as groups looked for professional advice in their efforts to make contact with and to persuade the government to take decisions in their favour. Political consultants were often former politicians who had left the service of government or who had lost their seats in congressional or state elections. For many years 'lobbying' and 'lobbyists' were regarded with suspicion in Britain because they were associated with giving undue influence to a limited number of groups and with corruption because it seemed that votes were for sale in Congress where party discipline is much weaker than in the House of Commons. However, in recent years the business of political consultants has developed significantly in Britain and accusations of 'sleaze' against some consultants, a few government Ministers and some MPs have hit the newspaper headlines.

Protest

Consultation may not give pressure groups what they want from the government. Sometimes groups want to influence the government *before* policy is formulated, especially if emergencies arise or rumours are spread about what the government is likely to do. In such cases pressure groups may feel the need to move from consultation and persuasion to protest. Groups may act as vehicles of protest in the hope of influencing public opinion in their favour.

One issue which put the spotlight on protest activity developed suddenly in December 1997 when British farmers reacted angrily to the import of beef from other EU countries, especially Ireland. Cheap imports of beef hit British beef farmers hard at a time when they were disadvantaged by the ban, imposed because of BSE, on exports of British beef to Europe. British farmers attempted to follow the example of French farmers by congregating at ports such as Stranraer in Wigtownshire and threatening to block the import of beef. The National Farmers Union (NFU) organised the response of the farming community to a situation which threatened their income and, potentially, the survival of some beef farmers. Strenuous efforts were made to make sure that the farmers did not resort to violence in their 'picketing' at the ports. The government announced a package of aid to farmers losing money because of such circumstances.

Opponents of fox-hunting have demonstrated vigorously against it at strategic times such as the many Boxing Day Hunts up and down the country. Sometimes these demonstrations have led to violent clashes between the two sides. The objective of the protesters is to generate publicity for their cause. Public opinion polls have suggested that opposition to fox-hunting has been growing because of such publicity.

Pressure group activity is likely to be pronounced during the lifetime of the Labour Government elected in 1997 because Labour has promised a radical review of both the welfare state and the National Health Service. These are both widely regarded as among Labour's most welcome contributions to British life since 1945 and are dear to the hearts of Labour supporters especially those on the left wing of the Party. Labour is committed to reviewing health care and welfare because these are expensive services provided by the state at a time when political reality suggests that increasing revenue by taxation in order to finance increases in public expenditure is not electorally viable. Health and welfare are also bound to demand more resources because people are living longer which means that old age pensioners,

who require more health care and welfare, are an increasing proportion of modern society. Both major parties agree that individuals have to be persuaded to start providing more for themselves by way of pension plans, increased savings and health insurance. Labour's review is intended to identify those who are most in need of state provision and those who could afford to provide more health care and welfare for themselves by means of forward financial planning.

Labour's intentions may be defended as 'rational' given the changing nature of society, but inevitably there will be winners and losers from any shake-up of these services. The losers and the potential losers will resort to various forms of pressure group activity ranging from protest demonstrations to provoking backbench revolts in their favour. Before the end of 1997, after only seven months in power, Labour was confronted by its first backbench revolt as MPs voted against a decision to reduce benefit payments to new lone parents by £11 per week. Merely the fear of cuts in disability benefits stimulated protests by organisations representing various groups of disabled people.

PRESSURE GROUPS AND 'PLURALISM': A LEVEL PLAYING FIELD?

On the positive side, pressure groups add to the representative and democratic dimensions of politics and government by widening participation in the decision making process of the state. The political participation of pressure groups has given rise to a relatively new theory of politics which is *pluralism*. The acknowledgement that government and pressure groups interact legitimately gave rise in the 1960s and 1970s to the theory of 'corporatism.'

A 'Pluralist' political system is one in which power is widely distributed throughout society and not confined to the rich, the government, MPs, or powerful groups such as large companies, the 'Establishment' and trade unions. If all sections of society are able to form groups which give them some effective influence when important decisions affecting them are being made, then a strong element of pluralism is present. Society will be that much more democratic if political participation is widespread—if no significant sections of society are excluded from political decision making.

Consultation between groups and government became so commonplace in the era of 'postwar

91

consensus' that the state was pronounced to have become *corporatist* in character. This phrase means that the government granted interest groups, especially those operating in the economy such as employers' federations and trade unions, the right to be consulted intensively when policy was being formulated. If the government could gain the consent of the representatives of the two sides of industry, then policy decisions would be acceptable to society as a whole. In turn, groups would have some influence on the content of government policy. When Edward Heath was Conservative Prime Minister in 1974, there were frequent meetings at 10 Downing Street attended by Government Ministers and leaders of the TUC and the CBI. Mrs Thatcher was scornful of Edward Heath's corporatist attitudes which she saw as weakness, and she did not waste much time trying to persuade either side of industry to accept her radical neo-liberal policies. The TUC and the CBI were both strongly opposed to aspects, often different aspects, of 'Thatcherism'.

The positive side of pressure group activity may be summed up as follows: pressure groups enlarge democracy by representing the views of individuals and social organisations beyond the contribution of voting, parliamentary representation and political parties.

The negative side of pressure group politics is the claim that there is not a level playing field; that in the world of pressure groups God favours the big battalions; that some pressure groups are much more equal than others. Labour's review of welfare will probably stimulate pressure group activity on behalf of some of the most underprivileged sections of British society. If the groups are successful in persuading Labour to protect the underprivileged by watering down any proposals to reduce benefits, then such a development will support the view that Britain is pluralist, that the playing field is level.

MONEY AND INFLUENCE IN BRITISH POLITICS

Groups, rather than individuals, finance British political parties. They provide parties with money to fight election campaigns and to fund other party activities such as publicising party policies in between elections. Some MPs accept remuneration for acting as spokespersons for particular interests or causes. Such financial links between groups and both parties and legislators have long been accepted as legitimate as long as certain safeguards are met. For example MPs have to declare their interests and there are limits on campaign spending by parliamentary candidates.

In recent years, financial links between MPs, parties, groups and individuals have become suspect and open to criticism because of alleged abuses. Groups representing economic and other interests have been accused of attempting to buy 'influence' by being overly generous in their gifts to parties in the hope of policy being changed to meet their wishes. This issue came to a head after Labour's 1997 victory when it became known that the head of Formula 1 motor racing, Bernie Ecclestone, had given Labour £1 million before the Election. Motor racing depends for its survival on massive sponsorship which has been provided mainly by tobacco advertising. Formula 1 racing cars are festooned with the names of cigarette manufacturers such as Rothmans and Marlborough. The new Labour Government announced its intention to ban all sponsorship of sport by tobacco interests because of the health risks inherent in smoking. However, motor sport was to be exempt from this ban temporarily. The reason given for this controversial decision was that a lot of British jobs were at stake which would go to Europe or elsewhere if Britain alone banned the sponsorship by tobacco firms. Labour handed back the £1 million donation but the case for reform of party finances had received a major boost. Ironically, Labour is known to be in favour of such reform.

Party Finances

The fundamental facts about the funding of British political parties and elections campaigns can be stated simply.

1 Both major parties rely heavily on one particular source of finance: Labour gets most of its money from the unions and the Conservatives get their money from 'big business'.

2 There are virtually no restrictions on contributions to parties either in terms of how much may be donated or of who can donate. Parties may accept donations from abroad.

3 Parties are not required to publish accounts detailing where they get their money or how they have spent it. In practice the parties do publish accounts, but are often accused of not being sufficiently detailed and open when they do so.

4 Although there are strict spending limits on parliamentary candidates at constituency level, there are no limits nationally on how much the parties may spend on election campaigns.

5 Campaigning through the broadcasting media is controlled but there are no limits on other forms of advertising such as the press and hoardings. Time on radio and television is strictly limited and is free, though parties have to pay for producing their election broadcasts.

6 The Conservatives receive more income than Labour and both receive much more income than the Liberal Democrats. In 1991–92 Conservative income was £22 million, Labour's income was £12.2 million and the Liberal Democrats received £0.9 million.

7 In 1991–92 approximately 61.5% of Labour's income came from the trade unions in the form of 'affiliation fees' which are related to the number of members in each union, and contributions to Labour's General Election Fund. Another 5% of the £12.2 million total came from the affiliation fees paid by Constituency Labour Parties.

   Conservative income was dominated by donations from firms and individuals who contributed 87% of total Conservative income. Constituency contributions amounted to 6%.

8 Because the Conservatives receive more money they spend more. It is estimated that the Conservatives spent £20 million, Labour £15 million and the Liberal Democrats £3.5 million in the 1997 Election campaign.

The crucial question is: what does this money 'buy'? Does money win elections? Do contributions to parties 'buy' or influence policy decisions when one of the parties controls the government departments which make policy?

At the electoral level, Labour has won elections in spite of being financially weaker than the Conservatives. On the other hand, the Conservatives have had the stronger electoral performance overall in the period since 1945. How much money is available to the parties may be less significant than how well the money is spent. In 1987 and 1992 the Labour Party campaigns were considered to be superior to the Conservative campaigns but Labour did not win. In 1987 there was very little movement in the opinion polls during the campaign which seems to have had little impact on the result.

It is difficult to assess the relationship between policy decisions and financial contributions. The unions and private companies finance the respective parties because the parties stand for their interests. This was certainly true in the heyday of the two-party system. Even now the common interests of the parties and their financial backers becomes clear in an issue such as the minimum wage legislation which was one of Labour's main campaign promises in 1997. Such legislation is designed to improve the incomes of the poorest wage earners and to prevent 'sweat shop' labour which exploits the young and the unskilled. Labour's egalitarian impulse and its long-standing union links explain the party's long-term commitment to a statutory minimum wage. Conservative opposition to such legislation is also understandable in the light of the Party's fundamental philosophy, which is favourable to business, and advocates reliance on the market as a key economic decision maker. Conservative spokespersons argue that a minimum wage means higher costs for some manufacturers and services and could make Britain less competitive in the international market-place. Both parties support their 'natural allies' in their stances on the minimum wage issue. Both claim that their policy is 'good for the country'.

At the collective level the financial links between the two major parties and their backers are a legitimate part of the political process. There is more concern at an individual level. Do donations by individual firms and by individuals bring a reward? Mere suspicion that this might be so explains why Labour handed back the £1 million donation from Bernie Ecclestone so quickly once the story broke.

There have been some changes in the links between parties and pressure groups since 1979. It became obvious during the Thatcherite era that the CBI did not always agree with the Conservative government's economic and industrial policies. A government with radical intentions is less likely to be influenced by any views put to it, even those of groups which are usually supporters of the party of government. Mrs Thatcher was an opponent of the corporatist attitudes of the Conservative Leader she replaced, Edward Heath. It was a sign of the times in Britain that the business community became a little less favourable to the

1990s sleaze?

The financial probity of MPs hit the headlines in the 1990s. The long-standing right of MPs to speak in Parliament on behalf of groups and organisations which they supported fell under a cloud when 'sleaze' became an issue. Some MPs and a few junior Ministers were accused of taking money in return for asking questions on behalf of pressure groups. Some admitted their guilt; others did not.

to represent them in Parliament as long as the MPs record such payments in the Register of Members' Interests. In recent years MPs have found additional employment as consultants working for professional lobbyists. Such behaviour is legitimate as long as it is acknowledged. The twin forces of party loyalty and party discipline were considered to be sufficient to ensure that MPs behaved properly and did not grant undue influence to pressure groups and individuals who paid them.

The 1990s has witnessed a large increase in charges of improper behaviour against MPs accused of taking money and favours without proper acknowledgement. The most publicised case centred on 'cash for questions' allegations against a number of Conservative MPs including two junior ministers who resigned their posts. It was alleged that Tim Smith and Neil Hamilton asked questions in the Commons and performed other services on behalf of Mohammed Al Fayed without declaring their interest or the payments they received for the services rendered. Smith admitted the charges and stood down as Conservative candidate before the 1997 Election. Hamilton denied the charges and refused to stand down. He was defeated by Martin Bell who stood against him as an anti-corruption candidate. Hamilton has been found 'guilty' by both the Parliamentary Commissioner for Standards and by the Commons Select Committee on Standards and Privileges. Ironically, the Commons cannot punish Neil Hamilton because he is no longer an MP.

The 'Cash for Questions' raises two issues:

1 Who should 'police' MPs to ensure that they do not exert undue influence on behalf of groups or individuals who pay them for their services?

2 Should MPs be allowed to work for political consultancy firms and to receive money for political services even if these services and the monies are publicly acknowledged?

There remain strict limits in Britain on what MPs can do for their own constituents, for pressure groups and for individuals. Yet MPs are being allowed to act as 'political fixers'. One solution would be to pay MPs sufficient salaries to justify banning all such paid work as consultants who know their way around Whitehall where many important government decisions are made.

Conservatives in the 1990s. Certain well-known businessmen made substantial contributions to the (New) Labour Party and (fewer) to the Liberal Democrats before the 1997 Election. To that extent the link between pressure groups and parties has been slightly changed in British politics. It is more difficult to envisage trade unions supporting the Conservative Party politically and financially in spite of the reform of Clause IV in Labour's Constitution. Tony Blair and Gordon Brown devoted considerable time and effort before the 1997 Election to speaking at conferences of business organisations whose loyalty had been committed traditionally to the rival Conservative Party.

'Cash for Questions': MPs as Channels of Undesirable Influence

MPs may speak on behalf of group interests and causes in Parliament as long as they declare their 'interest' before they speak. Groups may pay MPs

CHAPTER 9 The Government of SCOTLAND

THERE CAN BE no doubt that the 'Government of Scotland' has been a major British political issue since February 1974 when the SNP's capture of seven seats forced the new minority Labour Government to commit itself to devolution for Scotland (and Wales) in order to minimise further SNP and Welsh nationalist electoral gains which could conceivably have been at Labour's expense. Labour's attempt to reform and enlarge the government of Scotland failed in 1979 when the combination of a surprisingly small majority for the *yes* side in the devolution referendum and the Conservative victory in the subsequent general election handed control over the issue to a Conservative leadership unsympathetic to devolution. The eventual defeat of the Conservatives in 1997 after 18 years in power was followed immediately by the new Labour Government announcing the date of a second referendum and the details of a new devolution scheme.

Devolution

Labour's policy on devolution was profoundly influenced in the immediate aftermath of February 1974 by the electoral background. Labour had won a majority of seats in both Scotland and Wales but 31 fewer seats than the Conservatives in England. This had happened before in 1950 and in 1964. In all these cases Labour was able to form the government only because its electoral strength in Scotland and Wales had made up for its relative weakness in England. Even though Labour did win three more English seats than the Conservatives in October 1974, they still lacked a majority of English seats. It was the net contribution of 40 Scottish and Welsh seats which gave Labour 43 seats more than the Conservatives and an overall majority of three in the Commons. Labour's occasional dependence on Scottish and Welsh seats to ensure or enlarge the Party's majority in the

British Parliament gave the leadership a powerful argument in favour of devolution.

From 1979 until 1997 'devolution' remained on the political agenda with no hope of fulfilment. Four Conservative election victories in general elections were accompanied by a progressive weakening of the Conservative minority position in Scotland. This dropped down from 22 MPs in 1979 to 11 in 1992. Confrontation intensified between a Conservative government in London, including a Conservative Scottish Office under siege in Edinburgh, and the three other Scottish parties, all of which were committed to reform of Scotland's constitutional position. This stand-off was dubbed 'the Doomsday Scenario', a phrase which suggested that something would have to 'give' if the Conservative position remained entrenched. With only 11 MPs to choose from, the Conservatives experienced difficulty staffing the political positions at the Scottish Office. The Scottish parliamentary committees caused the Conservatives even greater embarrassment because either the government had to accept a minority position or appoint English Conservative MPs to ensure a Conservative majority. However, the Conservatives remained totally opposed to demands for devolution from the other Scottish parties who proceeded to push for reform through a *Constitutional Convention*. Labour and the Liberal Democrats cooperated to ensure that constitutional reform was one of the leading points of difference between the two major parties as the 1997 General Election approached.

Labour's 1997 victory ensured that devolution would be enacted though the issue was not without controversy. Only two weeks after taking over at Westminster, Labour announced that there would be a two question referendum which would allow the Scottish people to decide whether there should be a Scottish Parliament *and* whether it should have 'tax-varying powers'. In July 1997 the Government published its White Paper outlining the details of its proposals for reform of the government of Scotland. The title of the White Paper, *Scotland's Parliament*, emphasised that the key feature of the proposed reform would be 'legislative devolution'. This means that the new Scottish Parliament would make policy decisions, which could be turned into law, in the same way as Westminister does. Such a reform requires parallel devolution in the executive and administrative arenas because an elected legislature requires its own executive branch to carry out its policies.

Britain is a unitary state with domestic parliamentary sovereignty vested entirely in the Westminster Parliament. There is no legislative authority superior to the Westminster Parliament within the United Kingdom. Scotland has been part of this unitary state since 1707. Yet the 'Government of Scotland' has been a source of tension between Scotland and the United Kingdom at various points in the almost three hundred year history of the Union. There has always been an element of administrative devolution which was significantly extended in the 1880s and the 1930s.

The enactment of legislative devolution at the end of the 20th century prompts a number of questions about Scottish politics and Scotland's position in the United Kingdom. Why did devolution become a significant issue in the 1970s? Why did Labour commit itself to a Scottish Parliament in spite of claims by the opponents of devolution that it might lead eventually to independence? What differences will Labour's devolution make to the political character of the United Kingdom and to the government of Scotland? To answer such questions one has to look at the development of the Scottish party system since the 1960s and at the details of Labour's White Paper on legislative and executive devolution. We also have to take a long-term historical perspective because the devolution issue, although it has varied in intensity, has been significant at various points in the political history of Scotland since 1707.

A HISTORICAL PERSPECTIVE

The roots of the intensification of the devolution issue in the last three decades of the 20th century are visible in the Treaty of Union which eliminated Scotland's independence and its Parliament but which also recognised that 'Scotland was differ-

ent'. Scotland ever since has demonstrated both 'British' and 'Scottish' characteristics.

There have been 4 principal elements in the evolution of Scotland's relationship with the United Kingdom:
1 Scotland's Institutions, cultural, social and political, which 'survived' the Union of 1707, ensured that Scotland would be, to some extent, 'different' and something more than a region of Britain.
2 Scottish political attitudes and behaviour, including perceptions of national identity, voting behaviour and the party system, which have determined the degree of satisfaction or dissatisfaction with the 'Union'.
3 Administrative devolution—ie. the arrangements for the administration of Scotland's separate dimensions.
4 Legislative devolution—ie. the arrangements whereby 'Scottish policy' in legislative form has been formulated, debated and decided.

For over 250 years Scots accepted the Union characterised by parliamentary sovereignty, the Monarchy and a strong British executive (Cabinet government) without mounting major objections. There was a certain amount of 'tinkering' (minor reforms) with the arrangements for the 'government of Scotland', usually in response to indications of Scottish dissatisfaction with existing arrangements expressed through voting behaviour and the party system. Nonetheless, the 'British' dimension in the government of Scotland prevailed over the 'Scottish' until the 1960s. Then the twin developments of Scotland swinging to Labour from the 1959 Election onwards and the dramatic impact of the Scottish National Party in the 1970s set in motion political forces which could no longer be contained by 'tinkering'. The establishment of a Scottish Parliament and executive represents a decisive strengthening of the Scottish dimension and a profound reform of the British Constitution. The question which remains, and which will dominate discussions about Scottish politics for years to come, is whether the Scottish Parliament and executive will ensure permanently Scotland's position within the United Kingdom or will instead lead to independence and the ending of the 'UK connection'.

The Scottish dimension was prominent from the outset of the British state: "Part of the bargain at the Union in 1707 was that Scotland should retain its social institutions, and indeed it is unlikely that England would have had much success in imposing its own on Scotland". (JG Kellas, *Modern Scotland*, 1980, p.29). The social institutions which were retained at the time of the Union almost 300 years ago are still significantly Scottish today.

The fact that Scotland's distinctiveness amounted to more than mere regionalism required some political recognition which initially took the form of a Scottish presence in the British Cabinet and some administrative devolution, particularly the establishment of the Scottish Office in 1885. Eventually some legislative recognition was granted in the establishment of the *Scottish Grand Committee*. Scottish political behaviour played its part at various points after 1707 by making demands for more political and institutional recognition of Scotland's distinctiveness. Behind such behaviour was a national consciousness which refused to die in spite of the loss of independence and the growth of a strong, centralised British state with its centre in Westminster and Whitehall.

The distinctive Scottish identity was maintained by several cultural and social institutions which survived the transition from independence to Union. Foremost among these are the Church of Scotland, the educational system and the legal system.

The Church of Scotland, Presbyterian in character and the product of a much stronger Reformation than occurred south of the border, is Scotland's Established Church though by no means its only Church. The influence of the Church was particularly strong until the mid-19th century in relation to education, poor relief and moral and social welfare. Today the Church functions politically as a pressure group, especially at the time of meetings of its General Assembly when the views of the Church are extensively reported by the Scottish media. Scotland has become much more heterogeneous in terms of religion. Sixteen per cent of the Scottish population is Roman Catholic (30% in Glasgow).

Education has long been thought of as a key defining feature of Scottish life. The principle of access to education based on merit was accepted in Scotland from the time of the Reformation at the end of the 16th century. Consequently, there was a national system of education open to all in Scotland, largely organised at parish level by the Church of Scotland, long before this developed in England. Accordingly, Scottish education was widely believed to be 'democratic' in character and less socially exclusive than its English counterpart. Nonetheless, the Scottish upper classes opted for English public school education for their children. University attendance was more widespread for most of the 19th and early 20th centuries, though England has caught up in recent decades. Scottish education was, until Thatcherism 'targeted' the English schools, much more centralised and 'national' or nationwide in character. Education remains one of the most significant functions of government in Scotland involving local authorities, the Scottish Office Education Department, and the Scottish Qualifications Authority. Decisions about subject curricula, teachers' salaries, and reform of examinations have long been among the most significant to be taken within the 'Scottish political system', although autonomy has not been absolute when British governments have been adamant about comprehensive education and the publication of school league tables.

The Scottish legal system and Scots Law constitute the third defining characteristic of Scottish distinctiveness inherited from the independent Scotland of the pre-1707 era. The legal system has perhaps been the most significant politically because it has required the passage of separate Scottish legislation through the British Parliament and its implementation by devolved governmental institutions in Scotland itself. Occasionally the distinctive features of Scots Law such as the majority verdict and the 'Not Proven' verdict hit the headlines. There have been efforts to abolish the 'Not Proven' verdict which may demand a greater burden of proof to convict on serious offences than would be the case if it did not exist. The separate Scottish legal system has meant that the education of lawyers and the practice of law have both remained rigorously Scottish. English lawyers are not qualified in or familiar with Scots Law (the reverse is also true) and therefore cannot practice in Scotland without acquiring the necessary training and qualification.

What is significant about education, the law and the Church of Scotland is that decision making in those areas has been largely a matter for Scots living in Scotland and for Scottish institutions based in Scotland. That this has been so generates the belief that this should be so and has maintained a degree of national consciousness which extends beyond the regionalism associated with Geordies in the North-East of England or Yorkshire Tykes or

THE SCOTTISH PARTY SYSTEM: VOTES AND SEATS 1955–1997

PERCENTAGE SHARE OF THE VOTE

	1955	1959	1964	1966	1970	1974[1]	1974[2]	1979	1983	1987	1992	1997
LABOUR	46.7	46.7	48.7	49.9	44.5	36.6	36.2	41.5	35.1	42.4	39.0	45.6
CONSERVATIVE	50.1	47.2	40.6	37.7	38.0	32.9	24.7	31.4	28.4	24.0	25.7	17.5
LIBERAL	1.9	4.1	7.6	6.8	5.5	7.9	8.3	8.7	24.5	19.0	13.1	13.0
SNP	0.5	0.8	2.4	5.0	11.4	21.9	30.4	17.3	11.0	14.0	21.5	22.1

NUMBER OF SEATS WON

	1955	1959	1964	1966	1970	1974[1]	1974[2]	1979	1983	1987	1992	1997
LABOUR	34	38	43	46	44	40	41	44	41	50	49	56
CONSERVATIVE	36	32	24	20	23	21	16	22	21	10	11	0
LIBERAL	1	1	4	5	3	3	3	3	8	9	9	10
SNP	0	0	0	0	1	7	11	2	2	3	3	6

Table 9.1 Note: There were two elections in 1974 in February[1] and October[2]

'Essex Man'. Such national consciousness has also been kept alive by Scottish culture which supports a Scottish element in the broadcasting and news media ('Real Scots read the Record') and by Scottish sport which enjoys separate national status in some sports such as soccer (the World and European Nations Cups), rugby (the 5 Nations Championship), golf (the Dunhill Cup) and so on.

National consciousness has been evident in surveys of whether Scots perceive themselves as Scottish and/or British. One of the first modern surveys undertaken in the 1960s found that many Scots perceived themselves as Scottish rather than British while still voting for essentially British political parties in what may now be described as the last decade of the pre-devolution era.

DEVOLUTION: THE ELECTORAL BACKGROUND

In 1707 Scotland gave up political independence and legal sovereignty to join a much larger state now officially known as the United Kingdom of Great Britain and Northern Ireland. In spite of the centralised nature of the British state, Scotland was to develop politically in two areas in a way which suggested that it constituted a separate, if subordinate, political system within the United Kingdom. Firstly, the Treaty of Union recognised the distinctiveness of Scotland's social and cultural institutions and their right to survive within the new state. This recognition eventually provided the force behind the establishment of the Scottish Office and Scottish committees in the Commons. These Scottish political institutions, however, stopped far short of federalism and did not infringe parliamentary sovereignty. More recently, Scottish political behaviour (political parties and the way in which people voted) acquired distinctive features which pushed the issue of how

Scotland should be governed to the forefront of British politics. Labour's victory in the 1997 General Election was followed by the publication of a White Paper on Scotland's Parliament in July and of the Scotland Bill in December.

There can be little doubt that the voting behaviour of the Scottish electorate over the last 30 years prompted Labour to reform Scotland's constitutional position within the United Kingdom. For this reason, we will look first at the distinctive features of Scottish political behaviour before considering the current government of Scotland and Labour's plans for a Scottish Parliament.

The Four-Party System in Scotland

The Scottish electorate in the 1990s supports a four-party system with the Labour Party, the SNP, the Conservatives and the Liberal Democrats all enjoying significant levels of support, though the Scottish Conservatives have no representation in the Commons following the 1997 General Election. The ebb and flow of the Scottish vote is illustrated in Table 9.1. Since 1974, fluctuations in the relative strengths of the parties within the electorate have had a far-reaching impact upon the attitudes of the parties towards the issue of how Scotland should be governed.

Four significant developments in Scottish electoral politics, which explain the radical changes in the arrangements for the government of Scotland proposed by Labour in 1997, are illustrated in Table 9.1.
- Scotland has developed a four-party system which has implications for the government of Scotland under the proportional electoral system proposed for the Scottish Parliament.
- The Scottish Conservatives have suffered a

long-term decline since the late 1950s which ended in the emergence of Scotland as a 'Tory-free zone' in the 1997 General Election.

- The Liberal Democrats and the SNP have been beneficiaries of the move from two-party to four-party politics in Scotland.
- Labour has maintained a dominant position in spite of the four-party characteristic because the first-past-the-post electoral system employed for the Westminster Parliament works in its favour. In 1997 Labour won 78% of Scotland's 72 seats with 45.6% of the vote.

The four-party characteristic began to emerge in the 1960s when the Liberals and the SNP increased the number of candidates they put up to challenge the two major parties. In 1955 Conservative and Labour candidates together won almost 97% of the vote and all but one of Scotland's 71 constituencies (Jo Grimond won Orkney and Shetland for the Liberals). The Liberals put up only five candidates and the SNP only three candidates so they won less than 3% of the vote nationally in 1955. The Liberals and the SNP put up 47 candidates in 1966 and by October 1974 they were contesting virtually every Scottish seat. The combined Conservative and Labour share of the Scottish vote fell progressively to just under 90% in 1964 when the Liberals won four seats and to less than 70% in October 1974 when the SNP and the Liberals won 14 seats between them.

The 'four-party characteristic' is significant because of the introduction of a measure of proportional representation in the electoral system which will be used to elect the Scottish Parliament. Scotland will have a Parliament much more representative of Scottish public opinion than one elected by the first-past-the-post system.

The Scottish Conservatives have suffered a sustained decline in support since 1955 when they won two more seats than Labour and attracted just over 50% of the popular vote, the only party to do so in Scotland in the 15 elections since 1945. The Conservatives were relegated to the status of the permanent second party in terms of seats in 1959, when Scotland swung to Labour against the British trend, and in terms of votes in 1964. That status was challenged by the SNP in 1974 when the nationalists came second in the popular vote in October and won eight of their 10 gains from the Tories. The Conservatives recovered votes and seats in Scotland in the first of their four consecutive British victories in 1979 but they lost out to

the other parties from 1987 onwards. Their Westminster representation was halved in 1987 and then eliminated in 1997. The limited Conservative recovery in 1979 and a stronger than expected electoral performance in 1992 bolstered Conservative opposition to demands for devolution temporarily but the 1997 result suggested strongly that the Conservatives were out of touch with Scottish opinion. The new Conservative Leader, William Hague, announced shortly after his election that the Conservatives would accept the result of the 1997 referendum on devolution.

Alex Salmond, leader of the SNP

The fortunes of the formerly 'minor' parties have fluctuated since the mid-1960s when the Liberals made inroads into Tory seats between 1964 and 66 and the SNP enjoyed their 'annus mirabilis' in 1974. The SNP have prospered in terms of votes, but the Liberals have enjoyed more success since 1983 in terms of seats won. SNP votes (22.1% in 1997) have been fairly evenly distributed throughout Scotland but the Liberal Democrats have managed to concentrate their strength sufficiently to win more seats than their nationalist rivals. Both have been winning rural and agricultural seats in the North and the South of Scotland leaving Labour dominant in urban seats. (See Table 9.2)

The electoral successes of the Liberal Democrats and the SNP, along with the demise of the Conservatives, have strengthened the pro-devolution forces. However, that camp is itself divided into the British parties, Labour and the Liberal Democrats, who do not wish to proceed any further down 'the slippery slope to independence', and the SNP whose aim is 'independence within Europe'. The pro-devolution forces maintained a successful short-term alliance in the run-up to the September 1997 referendum.

Labour has retained and even strengthened its dominant position within the four-party framework in spite of the transition from two-party to four-party politics. In 1997 Labour won 56 seats, almost 20 more than in 1959, in spite of winning a slightly smaller share of the popular vote than it did then. Of the 11 seats lost by the Conservatives

The Rural & Agricultural Dimension in Liberal & SNP Representation:1997

Liberal Democrat Seats

- Aberdeen West & Kincardine
- Argyll and Bute
- Caithness Sutherland & Easter Ross
- Edinburgh West
- Fife North East
- Gordon
- Orkney & Shetland
- Ross, Skye & Inverness West
- Roxburgh & Berwickshire
- Tweeddale Ettrick & Lauderdale

SNP Seats

- Angus
- Banff and Buchan
- Galloway & Upper Nithsdale
- Moray
- Perth
- Tayside North

Table 9.2

Conservative Seats Lost in 1997

To Labour
- ✗ Aberdeen South
- ✗ Ayr
- ✗ Dumfries
- ✗ Eastwood
- ✗ Edinburgh Pentlands
- ✗ Stirling

To the SNP
- ✗ Galloway and Upper Nithsdale
- ✗ Perth
- ✗ Tayside North

To the Liberal Democrats
- ✗ Aberdeen West & Kincardine
- ✗ Edinburgh West

Table 9.3

in 1997, Labour won 6, the SNP won 3 and the Liberal Democrats won 2. Labour has won the great majority of former Conservative seats in urban areas while the Liberal Democrats and the SNP have 'evicted' the Conservatives from rural and small town constituencies beyond the Central Belt. Labour is represented in the periphery, winning the Western Isles from the SNP in 1987 and gaining Inverness Nairn and Lochaber from the Liberal Democrats in 1997.

Labour's commitment to legislative devolution for Scotland was undertaken in the 1970s with British electoral considerations playing a decisive role. In 1974 the apparent threat to Labour from the SNP (See Table 9.1) forced the Party's mainly English leadership to force-feed devolution to a largely unenthusiastic Labour Party in Scotland. Even though the first attempt to achieve legislative devolution suffered a humiliating failure in 1979, the issue had been established so firmly that it was unlikely to go away. With both the SNP and the Scottish Liberals committed to devolution for its own sake or as a first step towards independence, Scottish Labour became more enthusiastic. The Conservatives' immovable stance against the issue also strengthened the pro-devolution forces.

By 1997 Labour was strong enough to be confident of sufficient public support to proceed with plans for a Scottish Parliament based on a proportional electoral system which is not guaranteed to produce a Labour majority in the new Scottish legislature. A Labour-Liberal Democrat coalition could form the first Scottish Executive, opposed from different sides by the SNP seeking independence and the Conservatives still unenthusiastic about devolution.

THE DEVOLUTION REFERENDA

An interesting feature of the devolution saga is that a Labour government twice gave the device of the referendum a key role in the decision making process.

Referenda have two advantages:

● A referendum is democratic in that it gives 'the people' a direct role in the decision making process which adds legitimacy to the decision taken whether the answer is Yes or No. The Conservatives, who opposed devolution strenuously, quickly moved to accept the result of the devolution referendum in 1997.

● A referendum allows a government not to decide. Basically, this means that difficult decisions may be put to the people and the government does not have to resign if the people reach a decision which the government does not really want. The British government has resorted to referenda in 1975, 1979 and 1997 to decide on issues of constitutional reform.

On the other hand, the critics of referenda in a parliamentary system argue that a government which resorts to a referendum is renouncing its responsibility to legislate. There is a conflict over whether a government should carry out the decision reached by the people.

The disadvantage of using a referendum to decide a prickly issue was demonstrated in 1979 when Labour's first attempt at devolution ended in failure and subsequently in electoral defeat. The Labour Government which felt forced to introduce devolution for Scotland and Wales was weak in the

House of Commons. It started off in October 1974 with an overall majority of 4 which it lost within three years, forcing it to rely on the 'Lib-Lab Pact', —on Liberal support in the division lobbies of the House of Commons. The Labour Party itself was by no means unanimous in support of even the principle of devolution. The Government was forced to hold a referendum and to accept the 'forty per cent rule'. This was proposed by a Labour MP, a Scotsman representing an English constituency, and required that 40% of the registered Scottish electorate, not merely 40% of those turning out to vote, must support the proposals. Worse, a significant minority in the Labour Party took part in a 'Scotland Votes No' campaign.

The result was a narrow victory for the *Yes* camp but the margin was much smaller than anticipated. (See Table 9.4.) The *Yes* vote amounted to only 32.9% of the registered electorate. The Government decided it could not proceed to implement devolution. A motion of no confidence was brought against the Government. The Conservatives and the SNP voted against the Labour Government which lost by 311 to 310 votes. The Government resigned and the Conservatives, led by Mrs Thatcher, won the resulting election by a comfortable margin.

The 1997 devolution referendum provided a vastly different story. Held at the beginning of a Labour government elected by a massive majority, the referendum resulted in comfortable majorities in favour of both the Scottish Parliament and the proposed tax-varying powers. Labour was united—there was no 'Labour Votes No' campaign. The SNP and the Liberal Democrats both supported the proposals even though this was a short-term tactic on the part of the SNP whose objective remains independence. There was no 40% rule in 1997. Almost 45% of the registered electorate voted for the Parliament, but only 38.3% voted for tax-varying powers. The 1997 vote emphasises the near to impossible constraint imposed in 1979 by the 40% rule.

Support for the Parliament ranged from 84.7% in West Dunbartonshire and 83.6% in the City of Glasgow to 57.3% in Orkney and 60.7% in Dumfries and Galloway. Support for the tax-varying powers ranged from 75% in Glasgow to 47.4% in Orkney and 48.8% in Dumfries where the 'Noes' won, narrowly, their only 'victories'. Some local council areas in the 'periphery', the regions farthest away from the densely populated urban and industrial Central Belt were least enthusiastic about the prospect of a devolved Scotland in which they might have different interests from the majority. Thus the Scottish Liberal Democrat Leader, Jim Wallace, MP for Orkney and Shetland and a strong devolutionist, represents an area suspicious of what devolution might bring.

THE GOVERNMENT OF SCOTLAND
Scotland survived as a unified and independent state from the 11th to the beginning of the 18th century. In 1603 the Crowns of Scotland and England were united by an accident of birth. Elizabeth the First had no heirs and the English throne fell into the hands of Scotland's James the Sixth who hurried off to London never to return. For the next 104 years Scotland and England each had a Parliament. However, this ended in 1707 when the Act of Union installed a single Parliament at Westminister. Nevertheless, although legislative sovereignty rested solely with the British Parliament at Westminister, the Act of Union made certain special provisions for the administration of those aspects of Scottish life which differed significantly from their English counterparts.

The Act of Union meant that for almost three centuries Scotland did not possess a legislative assembly to provide any popular Scottish control over Scotland's administrative institutions. This will be changed by the Labour Government's enactment of the Scotland (1998) Act which will add a legislative dimension to the existing administrative arrangements for the government of Scotland. The government of Scotland therefore, has to be analysed in its pre- and post-devolution forms.

RESULTS OF THE DEVOLUTION REFERENDA–1979 AND 1997 COMPARED

		Yes(%)	No(%)	Turnout(%)
1979	Setting up a Scottish Parliament?	51.6	48.4	63.8
1997	Setting up a Scottish Parliament?	74.3	25.7	60.4
1997	Tax-Varying Powers?	63.5	36.5	60.4

Table 9.4

Until 1998 the main feature of the 'government of Scotland' was that it was almost exclusively administrative in character and was subject to the British principles of collective ministerial responsibility and the sovereignty of Parliament.

The Act of Union established one Parliament but it did not transfer all public sector activities to the British executive in Whitehall. Until the Jacobite Rebellion of 1745 there was a Scottish Secretary of State. Following the Rebellion, Scotland came to be administered increasingly from London. In the second half of the 19th century there was considerable feeling that the arrangements made for the government of Scotland were remote and insufficiently Scottish. The post of Secretary for Scotland was re-established in 1885 though it was not promoted to the status of Secretary of State until 1926. Although the Scottish Office was also established in 1885, it was located mainly in Dover House in Whitehall. Until 1939 the Edinburgh wing of the Scottish Office only had 30 or so civil servants. There was a major reform of the arrangements for the government of Scotland in 1939; the Scottish Office was moved to St Andrew's House in Edinburgh and civil servants were transferred north of the border to staff it.

The job of the Scottish Office is to carry out the functions of government which affect Scotland. The Scottish Office has five major departments—Agriculture and Fisheries, Scottish Development Department, Scottish Economic Planning Department, Scottish Education Department and the Scottish Home and Health Department. At the head of the Scottish Office is the Secretary of State for Scotland who has overall ministerial responsibility. He/She is supported and assisted by a small team of Junior Ministers, and Parliamentary Under-Secretaries of State. Similar to other government departments, the Scottish Office is staffed with thousands of civil servants, whose job is to administer to the day-to-day running of the department and its business. The distinctive Scottish executive institutions, though subservient to the British Parliament and the British government, allow us to talk of 'the government of Scotland'.

SCOTLAND IN PARLIAMENT

Scotland has 72 MPs at Westminster for its 5.1 million inhabitants (3,946,113 eligible voters in 1997). Scotland is thus over-represented in the House of Commons relative to population compared to England, Wales and Northern Ireland. The establishment of the Scottish Parliament in 2000 will be accompanied by a reduction in the number of Scottish MPs at Westminster, thus ending the over-representation.

Scotland's special circumstances have required special administrative arrangements, the Scottish Office in particular. Similarly, separate legislation dealing with Scotland's special circumstances such as education is often required. Consequently, parliamentary procedures have been developed to ensure that Scotland's MPs have a major say in the passage of Scottish legislation. These procedures include Question Time, the Scottish Grand Committee, Scottish standing committees and a Select Committee on Scottish Affairs.

Scottish Questions:
The Secretary of State for Scotland, as a member of the British Cabinet, is required, along with other Scottish Office Ministers, to answer parliamentary questions about once every three weeks. Questions on such occasions are not confined to Scottish MPs who are also free to ask questions of other government Ministers.

Scottish Parliamentary Committees:
Scottish Bills, Bills which deal exclusively with Scottish matters, are subject to the same procedures as all other Bills introduced in Parliament. Accordingly, Scottish Bills have to secure the consent of the Commons as a whole before proceeding to the Lords for their consideration. There have been two types of committees dealing with Scottish legislation—the Scottish Grand Committee and the Scottish Standing Committee.

LABOUR'S SCOTTISH OFFICE, 1997

Secretary of State		Donald Dewar MP
Minister of State	Home Affairs & Devolution	Henry McLeish MP
Minister of State	Education & Industry	Brian Wilson MP
Parliamentary Under-Secretary of State	Local Government & Transport	Calum Macdonald MP
Parliamentary Under-Secretary of State	Health, Arts & Children	Sam Galbraith MP
Parliamentary Under-Secretary of State	Agriculture, Fisheries & Environment	Lord Sewel of Gilcomstoun

Table 9.5

The Scottish Grand Committee:

This has been one of the largest committees in the Commons because it includes all Scottish MPs. It was established in 1894 to meet the criticism that Scottish legislation was being discussed and decided by the English majority. Allowing all Scottish MPs to serve on the Grand Committee was intended to convey the impression of an approximation to a Scottish Parliament. However, the Grand Committee was subservient to the will of the House as a whole. It tended to deal only with the committee stage of non-controversial legislation, all Scottish legislation still having to secure the consent of the House at the second and third reading stages. In 1948 the second reading of Scottish Bills and debating the Scottish Estimates were added to the Grand Committee's functions. In 1957 the committee stage of Scottish Bills was assigned to a new Scottish Standing Committee, composed of 16 Scottish MPs, with non-Scottish MPs to be added if necessary to ensure that the government had a majority. The Scottish parliamentary committees ensured that Scottish MPs could have their say on Scottish legislation but their power and autonomy were negligible as they could be overruled by the House as a whole.

The Grand Committee was assigned additional functions in the 1990s when the Scottish Secretary of State, Michael Forsyth, attempted to distract attention away from widespread demands for a Scottish Parliament and meaningful legislative devolution. Meetings of the committee were held in different Scottish towns. Scottish Questions, adjournment debates and Third Reading debates were all added to the Grand Committee's procedures.

The Select Committee on Scottish Affairs:

This was established in 1969 when Labour introduced some reforms of the select committee system in the Commons in order to meet the charge that the executive branch was becoming so powerful that Parliament was in danger of being no more than a rubber stamp. Select Committees have investigative functions and publish reports into executive policy formulation and implementation. The Select Committee on Scottish Affairs did not function from 1972 to 1979 and from 1987 to 1992. The large number of Labour MPs elected from Scotland and the declining number of Conservatives made it difficult for the Tories to staff both the political positions at the Scottish Office and the Select Committee.

The establishment of the Scottish Parliament in 2000 renders the Scottish parliamentary committees surplus to requirements because their functions will be taken over by the new institution and its committees.

Although Scottish issues were provided for at Westminster so that the responsibility or answerability of the executive to Parliament was effectively implemented, the most significant feature of such provision was the absence of a Scottish legislative assembly.

The Post Devolution Government of Scotland

In his foreword to the Labour Government's White Paper on *Scotland's Parliament*, Donald Dewar, the Secretary of State for Scotland, justified his devolution proposals by claiming that the new system of government would "strengthen democratic control" and "make government more accountable". Control and accountability are two key attributes of democracy which should be achieved through elections and the parliamentary process. Elections allow voters to 'control' government by linking the selection of the people's representatives to the policies they stand for and by subjecting the executive branch to re-election. The parliamentary process requires government Ministers to defend their policy and administrative decisions and actions in front of the people's representatives.

The Scottish Parliament is expected to improve both 'control' and 'accountability' in two ways:

● Scottish decisions on Scottish issues will be taken by Scottish governmental institutions based in Scotland. This simply means that such decisions will be made by the elected Scottish Parliament and by the Scottish Executive drawn from that Parliament.

The establishment long ago of the office of Secretary of State for Scotland and of the Scottish Office signified an acceptance of the principle that certain areas of Scottish life were sufficiently distinctive to merit a separate decision making process and separate institutions. The Scottish Parliament extends that principle by vesting much of such decision making in an elected legislative assembly. Government in Scotland should thereby be brought 'closer to the people'.

● It will deploy an electoral system which includes a substantial element of proportional representation rather than the British first-past-the-post plurality electoral system which allows one party elected by a minority of the electorate to govern. A major argument in favour of PR is that it gives more voters an influence over the composition of the government elected and forces the government to listen to more points of view before finalising its decisions.

The constitutional remit—the legislative scope of the Scottish Parliament—is defined in the White Paper in terms of four definitions of 'powers', 'matters' and 'areas'.

Under the heading of *What the Scottish Parliament Can Do* (Chapter 2), particular devolved 'matters' are listed as examples of issues which could be taken up by the Scottish Parliament. No fewer than 47 'devolved matters', "over which the Scottish Parliament will have legislative power", are listed under 9 headings (see Table 9.6).

The White Paper also lists the "reserved matters" which are to be the preserve of the UK government and Parliament—those matters "which can be more effectively and beneficially handled on a United Kingdom basis". Without such "reserved matters" there would be no further need for a United Kingdom.

Reserved to the UK are such matters as the Constitution; foreign policy; defence and national security; macroeconomic, monetary and fiscal affairs other than Scotland's tax-varying powers; employment; social security; and transport safety and regulation.

Furthermore, the White Paper also assigns the Scottish Parliament legislative power over "all matters which are not reserved". This amounts to an open invitation to the Scottish Parliament to take up any issue or problem not falling into the matters reserved to the UK Parliament.

The constitutional relationship between the Scottish Parliament and the British Parliament, in other words Scotland's constitutional position in the light of this substantial constitutional reform, is defined in the following crucial paragraph:

> "... the UK Parliament is and will remain sovereign in all matters; but as part of the government's resolve to modernise the British constitution, Westminster will be choos-

Scottish Parliament

The Scottish Parliament will have control over the following areas

1 Health
2 Education and Training
3 Local Government, Social Work and Housing
4 Economic Development & Transport
5 Law and Home Affairs
6 Sport and the Arts
7 Agriculture, Fishing & Forestry
8 Environment
9 Other Matters

Table 9.6

ing to exercise that sovereignty by devolving legislative responsibilities to a Scottish Parliament without in any way diminishing its own powers."

The Scottish Parliament will be constitutionally inferior to the British Parliament in that the Westminster Parliament will retain the legislative power to overturn any Act of the Scottish Parliament. Sovereignty is not to be divided as in a federal system such as that of the United States. Morever, the sponsors of the Scottish Parliament clearly do not expect that Westminster will have to exercise its veto over Scottish legislation.

The provisions of the White Paper in effect point to a crucial distinction between the 'constitutional' and the 'political'. It has been said of the American Constitution that the Constitution's assignment of the legislative power to declare war to the Congress and the President's possession of the Commander-in-Chief powers are an open invitation to conflict between President and Congress over foreign policy and decisions to go to war. The same might be said of the creation of two layers of legislative authority, the British and the Scottish, within the United Kingdom which remains formally a unitary state with the Queen and her successors as Head of State.

What will happen in practice depends on political developments, in particular on the Scottish and British electorates. If the same party enjoys a

majority at Westminster and in the Scottish Assembly, it is widely assumed that conflicts over policy and the application of law will be kept to a minimum. Conflicts should be resolved through the mechanism of party discipline and common party interest. If, however, there is a British parliamentary majority of one party in London and an opposing majority party in Edinburgh, for instance a Conservative government in London and a Labour Scottish executive, then the stage will be set for outright conflict rather than compromise.

A third scenario lies in the possibility, even the probability, of a coalition government in Scotland.

THE SCOTTISH PARLIAMENT
Members of the Scottish Parliament, who will serve a fixed term of four years, will be known as MSPs in order to avoid confusion with MP (member of the House of Commons) or MEP (member of the European Parliament). The way has been left open for 'dual mandates. This means that an individual may be a member of more than one Parliament.

The role of Speaker will be carried out by a Presiding Officer elected by the Scottish Parliament itself. The fixed term may be cut short if two thirds of the MSPs vote for this or if there is a stalemate when attempting to appoint the First Minister. The procedures and the committee structure of the new assembly are to be left to its membership. The White Paper takes a modern approach to the functions of committees by "envisaging" that they might initiate legislative proposals, scrutinise and amend the executive's policy proposals, and perform "wide-ranging investigative functions". In an assembly without a party majority, which is much more likely in the Scottish Parliament than at Westminster, such committees could develop into real power houses along the lines of the American Congress.

The Electoral System
The Scottish Parliament itself is a major reform of the position of Scotland in the British constitutional system. However, it is rivalled in significance by the electoral system chosen for the selection of its membership.

The White Paper opts for "greater proportionality to build stability into the overall settlement". The Government stops short of the high level of proportionality associated with the single transferable vote system in multi-member constituencies. Rather there will be two avenues into the Scottish Parliament. Out of a total membership of 129, 73 will be elected from single member constituencies identical to the 72 Scottish constituencies in the British Parliament with one exception. Orkney and Shetland, one constituency at Westminster, have each been assigned one MSP. These constituency representatives will be selected by the traditional first-past-the-post counting system

Illustration of the Additional Member Counting System

The counting method for the additional member system is described in the White Paper on the Scottish Parliament.

1   "Each elector will be entitled to cast 2 votes: one for a constituency MSP and one for the party of his/her choice."

2   "Votes for constituency MSPs will be counted on a 'first-past-the-post' basis."

3   The 56 additional members will be elected in eight 7-member constituencies (the existing European constituencies) as follows:

"The number of votes cast for each party within the European constituency will be counted".

"The number of votes cast for each party will then be divided by the number of constituency MSPs gained in Parliamentary constituencies contained wholly within the European constituency plus one". Each European constituency has 9 Parliamentary constituencies.

"The party with the highest total after the (above) calculation is done gains the first additional member".

"The second to seventh additional Members are allocated in the same way but additional Members gained are included in the calculations".

Assume the following result in the first stage of the election with 1,000 voters in the 9 individual Scottish Parliament constituencies which now make up one 7-additional members constituency:

	Votes	Seats won
Labour	490	6
SNP	200	1
Conservative	150	0
Liberal Democrat	120	2
Others	40	

Note: Labour and the Liberal Democrats have profited from the first-past-the-post system because their votes are effectively distributed.

The additional members counting operation:

Additional Members

	1ST COUNT	2ND COUNT	3RD COUNT	4TH COUNT	5TH COUNT	6TH COUNT	7TH COUNT
Labour	$\frac{490}{6+1}=80$	no change: 70	no change: 70	no change: 70	$\frac{70}{7+1}=8.75$	no change: 8.75	no change: 8.75
SNP	$\frac{200}{1+1}=100$	no change: 100	$\frac{100}{2+1}=33.3$	no change: 33.3	no change: 33.3	no change: 33.3	$\frac{33.3}{3+1}=8.33$
Conservative	$\frac{150}{0+1}=150$	$\frac{150}{1+1}=75$	no change: 75	$\frac{75}{2+1}=25$	no change: 25	no change: 25	no change: 25
Liberal Democrat	$\frac{120}{2+1}=40$	no change: 40	no change: 40	no change: 40	no change: 40	$\frac{40}{3+1}=10$	no change: 10
	Conservative elected	**SNP elected**	**Conservative elected**	**Labour elected**	**Liberal Democrat elected**	**SNP elected**	**Conservative elected**

This particular example ends with the 7 additional members distributed as follows: 1 Labour, 2 SNP, 3 Conservative and 1 Liberal Democrat.
The total result for this constituency would be:

	Constituency MSPs	Additional Members	Total
Labour	6	1	7
SNP	1	2	3
Conservative	0	3	3
Liberal Democrat	2	1	3

Professor Richard Rose has calculated how the two parts of the electoral system would work *if* votes were distributed among the parties exactly as they were in the 1997 Election:

	73 first-past-the-post	56 additional members	Total
Labour	56	+6	62
SNP	6	+23	29
Conservative	0	+22	22
Liberal Democrat	11	+5	16

Source: *The Herald*, Friday 25 July, 1997

which awards the seat to the candidate who wins the most votes. In Scotland's competitive four-party system the winning candidate often wins a plurality rather than a majority of the vote.

The remaining 56 MSPs, to be known as additional members, will be elected in 8 multi-member constituencies, seven from each, which will be identical to the Scottish European Parliament constituencies. Voters will vote for 'party lists' rather than individual candidates. The novel feature of this electoral system lies in how votes are counted and seats allocated within the multi-member constitu-

encies. An illustration of how this system works is shown above.

The electoral system chosen for the Scottish Parliament has two likely consequences of considerable significance for the composition of the Parliament and of the Scottish Executive which will emerge from it:

1   A strong element of proportionality in the representation of the parties.

2   Coalition government rather than one-party majority government.

The element of proportionality which this electoral system could produce is illustrated by comparing the percentage share of seats won by each party in the imaginary Scottish Parliament in the example on page 106 with its percentage share of the vote in the 1997 General Election (Table 9.7).

Thus the discrepancies between shares of votes and numbers of seats which are an inevitable part of the first-past-the-post electoral system are ironed out by the system chosen for the Scottish Parliament. The White Paper declares that "Additional Member seats will be allocated correctively, that is account will be taken of the number of constituency seats gained within the European Parliament constituency ...". The 'correction' works against parties which win disproportionately more seats than their votes merit in the first-past-the-post section of the election and in favour of parties which win fewer seats than they deserve.

In the illustration on page 106 the Labour Party falls three seats short of an overall majority (65 seats) and even more short of a comfortable working majority. Coalition government is not inevitable. If the Scottish electorate voted even more strongly for Labour then a majority Labour Scottish Executive would be a strong possibility.

The Scottish Executive
The Scottish Executive will be drawn from elected members of the Scottish Parliament. There will be a First Minister and "a team of Scottish Ministers including Law Officers". The constitutional position of the Executive is defined by the fact that the government of Scotland remains a parliamentary system. Thus the Executive "will be accountable to the Scottish Parliament". The conventions of ministerial responsibility, individual and collective, will apply in Scotland as in Westminster. Their operation might differ significantly if and when the electoral system consistently denies a parliamentary majority to any of the parties. Coalition government, changes of government without recourse to elections, and changes in the combinations of the political parties participating in government are all possible if the four-party framework is maintained by the Scottish electorate.

Implications for the Secretary of State and for Scottish Representation at Westminster
The Secretary of State for Scotland has been the most important politician in Scotland for over a century. He has been described as Scotland's man in the Cabinet and the Cabinet's man in Scotland.

PR & The Scottish Parliament

Party	Share of 1997 Vote	% of MSPs Won
Labour	45.6	48.0
SNP	22.1	22.5
Conservative	17.5	17.0
Liberal Democrat	13.0	12.4

Table 9.7

He was held responsible for ensuring that Scotland got a fair deal when important decisions affecting it were taken in the British Cabinet. He was responsible for the Scottish Office and its administration of Scottish 'matters' including the work of the 5 Scottish Departments. He was responsible for policy proposals which required legislative action at Westminster.

Now many of his responsibilities for legislative policies and Scottish administration will be discharged by the new Scottish executive, effectively a Scottish Cabinet, led by the First Minister. Consequently, the role of the Scottish Secretary will change. The White Paper envisages two roles for the Scottish Secretary. The first is short-term and will be discharged by the present incumbent, Donald Dewar. His main task is to "secure the passage and implementation of the legislation to establish the Scottish Parliament". Thereafter the Scottish Secretary will concentrate on "promoting communication" between Scottish and British political institutions. In other words, the Scottish Secretary will be expected to achieve smooth relations between the two levels of government. The Scottish Secretary will continue to be "representing Scottish interests in reserved areas".

The White Paper also deals with the thorny 'West Lothian' question which cast doubts on the legitimacy of Scottish MPs being involved in decision making at Westminster which concerned only the other three nations within the United Kingdom when parallel but purely Scottish matters are being dealt with by Scottish institutions. Devolution also prompted claims that Scotland's over-representation at Westminster would no longer be valid. The Labour Government proposes to reduce the number of Scottish MPs at Westminster by removing "special statutory provisions" stipulating "a minimum number of Scottish seats".

Financial Arrangements

The most controversial feature of Labour's devolution plan concerned tax-raising or tax-varying powers. In order to give the new Scottish government discretion in its policy making initiatives, Labour decided on two types of funding. The first would be a "continuation of the existing 'Block formula' system of funding most of Scotland's public expenditure programmes which has been applied continuously since the late 1970s". Under this Scottish 'block formula', all Scottish Office expenditure, on such matters as education, the prison service, health and so on was determined by a calculation based mainly on population. The Scottish Office had some discretion on how it allocated its financial resources based on this calculation though many spending programmes such as primary and secondary education did not allow much scope for change.

The crucial feature of the Scottish block was that it paid for spending programmes which both reflected Scottish social and economic realities and British government spending priorities decided by the British Cabinet. The public expenditure decisions to be taken in Scotland under devolution will differ in two ways. Firstly, the political process whereby spending priorities are decided will now involve the new Scottish institutions, the Parliament and the Executive, rather than the Secretary of State and the Scottish Office working within the confines of the British Cabinet and parliamentary systems. The scope for a 'Scottish way', which was always present to some extent will be enlarged. Nevertheless, there will be no increase in the amount of money available for spending priorities decided by the Scottish government in relation to the funds released by the 'block formula system'.

Secondly, the new Scottish government will be allowed to vary income tax rates levied in Scotland by up to three pence in the pound up or down. If it is decided to increase income tax in Scotland, the extra income will be additional to the Scottish Block from the UK Treasury. If it is decided to lower the rate of tax in Scotland, then the loss in revenue will be subtracted from the amount assigned to the Scottish Block. An increase of three pence in the pound would raise £450 million. Here the Scottish government would have much more discretion over spending priorities to be funded by the tax-varying power. However, the discretion will be limited by the fact that the Scottish budget currently exceeds £14 billion and the revenue to be raised from the maximum increase in income tax paid by Scottish resident tax payers would amount to 3% of Scottish public expenditure. In spite of the relatively small amounts of revenue to be raised if the tax-varying powers are utilised, opponents of devolution argued that if Scotland became the highest taxed region within Britain this would have a detrimental effect on employment and on the economy in general.

The White Paper's financial arrangements aroused controversy as they focused attention on Scotland's apparently favoured and privileged position under the 'block formula' arrangement. Treasury figures suggest that public expenditure per capita is higher in Scotland than in any other British 'region' except Northern Ireland. (See Table 9.8.)

Some of this 'discrepancy' is based on differences in geography. Scottish expenditure takes into account the relatively large territorial size of the country in proportion to population. Nonetheless, the 'discrepancy' contains the seeds of a future political squabble along 'national' lines rather than along normal partisan lines. There are 'discrepancies' among the English regions though which suggest that the political issues would be difficult to resolve along simply national lines. The ultimate Catch-22 for any English politicians looking for parity in public expenditure per capita figures is that reducing the Treasury-sourced Scottish Block could drive Scotland along the route to independence.

Government Spending Per Capita in Selected Regions

Northern Ireland	£4979
Scotland	£4461
Wales	£4220
North West England	£3126
South East England	£3000
East Midlands	£2635

Table 9.8   Source: HM Treasury reported in *The Guardian*, 9 September, 1997

CHAPTER 10 Britain and EUROPE

BRITAIN BECAME a member of the European Economic Community, as today's European Union (EU) was then called, on 1 January 1973. The consequences of membership have been and will continue to be far-reaching and controversial—constitutionally, politically and also economically. Constitutionally, Britain no longer enjoys complete legal or parliamentary sovereignty as long as it remains a member because certain EU decisions assume the force of law in the member states automatically. Britain also faces with unease the constitutional prospect of an increasingly federal or centralised Europe. Politically, major decisions affecting our daily lives are taken by EU institutions which many believe are suffering from a severe 'democratic deficit'. This occurs because either they are not elected or, if they are, they have too little power. Economically, Britain's trade with Europe has grown faster than with any other region of the now global economy. Furthermore, the integration of the British economy into what is now virtually a single EU economy may have reached the point of no return.

The 'European issue' in its various guises has provoked bitter internal conflicts in the two major British parties for many years. When Mrs Thatcher was Prime Minister, members of her Cabinet who were strongly in favour of developing the links with Europe (the Europhiles) made her life difficult and contributed significantly to her political downfall in 1990. (See Chapter 7) Conservatives who were suspicious of extending economic and political integration (the Eurosceptics) weakened John Major's government progressively as its Commons majority declined and frustrated the Prime Minister's efforts to rally the Party in the run-up to the 1997 General Election. Critical decisions which will determine both the political character of the European Union and Britain's relationship with it will be taken in the last three years of the 20th century by the Labour Government elected in 1997 and by its European partners.

The Origins of the European Union

Today's European Union traces its origins back to the end of the Second World War. The states of Europe had caused two devastating world wars in less than half a century. By 1945 the world had moved away from the Eurocentric international system which had failed to prevent death and destruction on a massive scale. International politics was now bipolar in structure (there were only two first rank powers). Europe was dominated by the two Super Powers: by the United States 3,000 miles to the west, and to the east by the Soviet Union whose vast territory covered both Europe and Asia. Weaponry had been radically altered by the development of the atomic bomb which had been used by the USA against Japan to bring the Second World War in the Pacific to an end. The costs of developing or buying atomic or nuclear weapons were beyond the means of all but the largest and richest states.

Regardless of these changes, which had reduced Europe's power and status in the world, there were important politicians in Europe who believed that steps should be taken to minimise the risks of world war yet again being sparked off by conflict between the nation states of Europe. They believed that if the nation states were linked more closely industrially and economically, they would be less likely to want to go to war with one another. Economic and political integration (joining together) was to be the means of maintaining peaceful relations among the states of Europe. Interdependence was to replace independence.

Efforts to integrate the nation states of Europe had

European INTEGRATION

The aims of European integration are:

1 Preventing a recurrence of the wars which blighted Europe especially in the first half of the 20th century.

2 Enabling 'Europe' to compete politically on the world stage in the 21st century.

3 Strengthening the economies of member states individually and collectively.

Figure 10.1

to be limited to the western side. Eastern Europe, including the Soviet Union, was separated from the West by the Cold War and its symbolic 'Iron Curtain' which were to survive until the late 1980s. European integration at its birth was both geographically limited and retrospective. In other words it looked backwards to a world which had been largely overtaken by global political developments. Nevertheless, the supporters of political integration also looked forwards to a time when even the larger states of Western Europe such as France, Germany and the United Kingdom would be individually weak economically and politically in relation to larger states such as the USA, the Soviet Union, China and Japan. Integration offered the prospect of 'Europe' being able to hold its own with these global powers. Ironically, developments in the Soviet Union (glasnost and perestroika) and in Eastern Europe (the withdrawal of the Red Army) have led to the distinct probability of former Cold War enemies becoming members of the European Union. Thus 'enlargement' to include some Eastern European states may be one of the central political issues confronting EU members at the beginning of the 21st century.

There may be considerable agreement in European political circles about the aims outlined in Figure 10.1. However, there has been intense argument and political conflict about *how* to achieve them. How much economic and political integration is required? What should be the links between economic and political integration? How much sovereignty or independence should members of the European Union be expected to give up in pursuit of the aims listed? What sort of political institutions should run the European Union? Should all the nation states of Europe give up their independence in order to create some form of European 'super-state'?

Nowhere have these questions aroused greater controversy than in Britain. This chapter analyses the nature of present-day European integration against the background of British unease about the 'European Connection'.

Britain and Europe

When Western European politicians and statesmen were taking the first tentative steps towards economic integration immediately after 1945, Britain remained effectively aloof because of the belief that the United Kingdom was still one of the world's Great Powers and was capable of independent action. Europe was only one of three principal areas of British interest. The others were the Commonwealth of Nations and the 'special relationship' with the United States. Thus the first three European institutions which went beyond the traditional obligations of military and political alliances(such as NATO and the Western European Union which Britain did join)were established without Britain wishing to join. The first such institution was the European Coal and Steel Community (ECSC), founded in 1951. A more decisive move came in 1958 when Euratom and the European Economic Community (EEC) began operations within an agreed framework set out by the Treaty of Rome which may still be regarded as the basic Constitution of the European Union. The creation of the EEC marked the decisive step towards economic and political integration because it aimed to establish a 'common market' which would be characterised by the elimination of all tariff barriers, and some non-tariff barriers, to free trade between its members. Thus the EEC would cover all economic and industrial sectors and would require its own institutions of government to take the decisions which would establish and operate the 'common market'.

The establishment of the EEC was quickly followed by a change of attitude on the part of the British Conservative Government which had come to realise in the immediate aftermath of the disastrous Suez Crisis of 1956–57 that Britain could no longer 'go it alone' in world politics. The Conservative Prime Minister, Harold Macmillan, decided that British national and strategic interests would be better served inside rather than outside the new European organisations. The Labour Party was opposed to joining the EEC on the terms which were thought likely to be negotiated by the Conservatives, partly because of the belief that the EEC was a 'laissez-faire' economic organisation, politically right of centre. Once Labour

110

achieved power in the 1964 and 1966 General Elections it promptly sought to negotiate satisfactory terms of entry. However, British membership of the EEC, which had first been delayed by British suspicions of economic and political integration, was next delayed by French reluctance to accept as a member a country closely allied to the USA. The French President, de Gaulle, doubted the European credentials of 'Anglo-Saxon Britain'. Ironically, de Gaulle's concept of Europe as 'L'Europe de Patries', by which he meant an association of independent nation states cooperating on the basis of total agreement, was not at all far removed from the dominant British view which went beyond party differences.

De Gaulle's departure from the French political scene in 1969 and the election as British Prime Minister of the Europhile Edward Heath in 1970 paved the way for Britain to join the EEC in 1973. Membership was confirmed in 1975 when a Labour government held a referendum on membership. The result was a comfortable *'yes'* vote (67.2%) in favour of Britain remaining in the EEC which was now popularly known as the European Community. Since then the European Community has progressed significantly in both economic and political terms. The first major economic objective, a single internal market, was achieved by 1992. For many Britons that economic objective more or less marked the limit of their aims in terms of integration.

'Maastricht'

The processes of integration gathered pace from the mid-1980s with two major constitutional developments which extended the Treaty of Rome:

1 The Single European Act, which was agreed by the Heads of Government of member states at the Luxembourg Summit in December 1985, and which came into force in July 1987.

2 The Treaty on European Union, which was sanctioned by the Heads of Government at the Maastricht Summit (in the Netherlands) in December 1991, and which has been in force since November 1993.

The Single European Act (SEA) symbolised a major achievement in terms of economic integration. It created a single internal market which went far beyond the elimination of internal tariffs to the removal of many non-tariff obstacles to free competition and trade. The SEA allowed significant

integration on the economic front. However, the Treaty on European Union symbolises a commitment to much more economic and, in particular, political integration than is acceptable to many in Britain. This integration includes *monetary union and a common single currency* (the 'Euro'). This Treaty is often described as the 'Maastricht Treaty' or simply as 'Maastricht' because it was signed at the Maastricht Summit.

'Maastricht' marks the transition from the European Community to the European Union which in 1997 included 15 member states and 370 million citizens. The Maastricht Treaty extended the range of common policy areas by specifying three 'pillars' of integration as the essential foundations of the Union. The first pillar is the familiar European Community pillar which was initiated by the Treaty of Rome. This original pillar is principally economic in character and includes the deepening of economic integration which is implied in the proposals for monetary union. The second pillar is to be in the area of foreign policy—a common foreign and security policy (CFSP). The third pillar will deal with justice and home affairs (JHA), and covers areas such as external border controls, asylum and immigration policies, international crime, and freedom of movement within the European Union. The second and third pillars are more important for their implications than for any policies so far achieved. (Decisions in these two areas are only made if they are agreed unanimously by the nation states and so far this has not happened.) The new 'pillars' deal with areas of governmental concern which were not included in the Treaty of Rome but which have witnessed increasing intergovernmental cooperation between member states. The inclusion in a major Treaty of two new pillars symbolises a widespread determination not to stop the process of integration once the basic economic objectives of the Rome Treaty have been achieved. This has not been welcome in certain British political circles.

'Maastricht' led to harmful divisions within the Conservative Party in Parliament and in the Cabinet throughout the lifetime of the Parliament elected in 1992. The process of parliamentary ratification was difficult. The government came close to losing vital votes and survived only because it successfully negotiated an 'opt-out' from a Social Chapter which threatened to include many social issues such as trade union rights and a minimum wage within the area of European decision making which would be applicable in Britain.

The relationship between 'Europe' and the Conservative governments led by Margaret Thatcher and John Major was frequently marred by conflict over the direction taken by other member states, especially by France and Germany. One of the key questions immediately raised by Labour's victory in the 1997 General Election was whether it would result in any significant differences in Britain's relationship with the European Union. Many people believed that there would be a much more cooperative attitude but that many specific British objections to projected EU policies would remain in place. Immediately after Labour took office the Foreign Secretary, Robin Cook, made it clear that the fact that Britain is an island required the maintenance of border controls which were to be abandoned elsewhere within the EU. Gordon Brown, the new Chancellor of the Exchequer, announced that the VAT rate on energy consumption would be reduced from 8% to 5% (this was a campaign promise) even though the EU objective was a common (harmonised) VAT rate of 15%. The EU Commissioner for Energy pointed out that Labour's proposal was contrary to the 'spirit' of harmonisation but that he did not object on strictly legal grounds. On the other hand, Labour made it clear that Britain would now 'opt in' to the Social Chapter of the Maastricht Treaty.

THE POLITICAL SYSTEM
OF THE EUROPEAN UNION
The Treaty of Rome laid down both the economic aims of its signatories and the decision making procedures and institutions required to achieve them. The previously separate institutions of the three communities (EEC, ECSC and Euratom)

were merged in 1967. Thereafter the three communities were referred to as the EEC or the European Community (EC). The Community was preoccupied for more than 20 years with the task of establishing a common market as the foundation of future economic and political integration. There was little institutional development until the 1980s when significant advances were made with the enforcement of the Single European Act in 1987 and the Treaty on European Union in 1993. These two treaties extended the scope of Community decision making, increased the number of decisions to be taken on the basis of qualified majority voting rather than unanimity, and assigned more influence to the European Parliament in an effort to defuse criticisms that the Community suffered from a 'democratic deficit'.

The Treaty of Rome, negotiated by six states, established the constitutional foundations of a new type of international cooperation. The EEC's institutional set-up appeared to mimic the familiar three-dimensional system of government of the nation state. EEC decision making was entrusted to a Council of Ministers which resembles the executive branch, a Commission which resembles a civil service bureaucracy, a Parliament, and a Court of Justice which is immediately recognisable as the judicial branch of government. These institutions have survived into today's European Union.

However, such similarity to the traditional separation of powers and institutions of the nation state is misleading. The decision making institutions of the European Community are characterised by features of originality which stem from their creation by member states determined to control the processes of integration. Consequently, unlike the American Founding Fathers in 1787, who established a federal system in which the decisive powers lay with the newly established central government (an elected President and Congress), the nation states who founded the three European communities combined the principal executive and legislative powers within one single institution of which they themselves are the members. This is the intergovernmental Council of Ministers. The member governments would be taking the decisions which were to be binding on their own citizens.

In sharp contrast, the Treaty of Rome established an Assembly, soon after to be called a Parliament, which was *not* assigned any legislative powers. The

POLITICAL

Unitary State eg. the United Kingdom. Final law making power (sovereignty) lies with one central institution (Parliament). Devolution will not alter the unitary nature of the British state.

Federalist State eg. the USA or Germany. Legal sovereignty is divided between a national or central legislature (Congress and the Bundestag) and regional legislatures (the states and the Lander).

Intergovernmental decision making within an international organisation. This is based on unanimity and member states possess a veto over decisions.

Supranational decision making within an international organisation. This is based on some form of majority voting and so members face the prospect of being defeated on occasion.

Harmonisation This principle means that national policies should be brought into line. For example all EU members should adopt VAT as the method of indirect taxation and they should apply the same VAT rate on similar goods.

Subsidiarity principle EU decisions should be taken at the most appropriate level. Decisions should be left to member states unless collective decision making would be more effective.

Qualified Majority Voting Decisions to be taken by a margin which is more than a plurality and more than a simple majority (which is 50% +1).

ECONOMIC

Common Market Removal of all internal tariff barriers between member states and the imposition of common external tariffs on imports from third countries.

Single Market Removal of all barriers to free competition and free movement of capital, labour, goods and services between member states.

word Parliament comes from the French word 'parler' which means 'to speak' and the European Parliament was to be mainly what its name suggests—a mere talking shop. If the Treaty of Rome downgraded the role of the Parliament, it raised the Commission above the normal civil service by giving it a highly political profile. The Commission was to propose the policies to be decided by the Council of Ministers and it was also to be the guardian of the Treaty. In other words, the Commission is responsible for ensuring that the member states fulfil their legal obligations. The Commission thus represented a community or supranational (See Glossary of Significant Terms) interest from the beginning. It became the engine of integration and as such stood for supranational interests—interests which transcended the narrower interests of individual states.

In spite of, or perhaps even because of, the central position of the member states in its decision making procedures, the 40 year history of the European Community/Union has been characterised by a persistent tension between the national interests of the individual member states and the overall or supranational interests of the whole community. This tension is clearly visible throughout the European Union: within British political parties (between Europhiles and Eurosceptics), within and between member states, and within the institutions of the European Union themselves. The undoubted progress of economic and political integration as EU institutions take on more and more decision making is reflected in the changing terminology used to describe the growing institution: from Common Market to European Community to European Union. The member states have remained major actors, but the intergovernmental side of the Community which they represent, especially on the Council of Ministers, has been increasingly balanced by the supranationality of the other institutions.

On the Council itself there is a sharp division between those states which actively promote supranationality and those states which are happier with an intergovernmental approach including a large measure of unanimity.

THE INSTUTUTIONS
OF THE EUROPEAN UNION

The Council of Ministers

Both the executive *and* legislative powers and functions of the European Union are located in the Council of Ministers. This is due to the fact that economic and political integration took place as a result of discussions between individual nation states who wanted to control the process of integration. Membership of the Council is vested solely with the individual governments of the member states. Government Ministers attend Council meetings according to the subject matter under discussion. Thus Environment Ministers will attend when environmental issues are to be decided. Agriculture Ministers attend the Agricultural Council and so on. The Council of Ministers is an intergovernmental institution which allows member states to defend their interests more effectively than in the other decision making institutions of the Union.

Important political decisions in the history of the Community have been taken at meetings of the

The progress of
EUROPEAN INTEGRATION
1951–1999

1951 Establishment of the European Coal and Steel Community (ECSC): the first of the European Communities.

1957 Signing of Treaty of Rome by the 'Six': France, Italy, West Germany, Belgium, Netherlands and Luxembourg leading to establishment of:

1958 European Economic Community and Euratom which join ECSC to make three separate institutions.

1961 British Conservative Government led by Harold Macmillan starts negotiations over terms of British entry. Labour opposed to likely 'Tory Terms'. British application rejected by French President de Gaulle.

1967 Labour Government led by Harold Wilson commences negotiations to join but de Gaulle again says 'no'. The three communities are merged, and are now run by common institutions and become the European Economic Community.

1970 Britain begins entry negotiations.

1971 Parliament approves principle and terms of entry negotiated by Conservative Government led by Edward Heath.

1973 First 'enlargement' of the 'Six' as Britain, Ireland and Denmark take up membership.

1974 Labour Government led by Harold Wilson renegotiates terms of membership and holds successful referendum: 67.2% vote in favour of membership (June 1975).

1977 Roy Jenkins appointed first (and so far only) British President of the European Commission.

1978 European Monetary System/Exchange Rate Mechanism commences without British participation.

1979 First direct elections to the European Parliament: all member states except Britain use proportional representation. European Parliament rejects Community budget for the first time.

1981 Greece joins, bringing membership to 10.

1985 Single European Act signed by Heads of Government, came into force on 1 July 1987. Jacques Delors (France) becomes President of European Commission.

1986 Portugal and Spain join.

1989 Delors reappointed. Fall of Berlin Wall.

1990 German Reunification. Britain joins ERM.

1991 Treaty on European Union agreed in principle at Maastricht.

1992 Danish Referendum rejects 'Maastricht'. Britain leaves ERM (Black Wednesday). French referendum narrowly approves 'Maastricht'.

1993 Delors, a strong 'supranationalist', is reappointed yet again as Commission President. Treaty on European Union ('Maastricht') comes into force. European Community now officially designated the European Union.

1995 Austria, Finland and Sweden join bringing membership to 15.

1999 Single currency and monetary system to become operational for those members wishing to and qualified to join.

Table 10.1

Heads of Government of member states, mainly Prime Ministers but including Presidents such as Jacques Chirac (France). These meetings were described as Summit Meetings. The Single European Act formalised the 'European Summit' by requiring that Heads of Government meet twice a year as the European Council. The President of the European Commission also attends such meetings as of right.

The Council of Ministers is not an elected institution in the fullest sense. Member governments are elected in their countries, though even there the electoral connection may be indirect. For example, in Britain the voters select MPs who then determine the composition of the executive on the basis of party strength in the legislature.

In Britain the executive branch (Prime Minister and Cabinet) decides on major policy decisions which are then submitted to the legislature— Parliament—for its consent. This process transforms policy into law. (See Chapter 6 on the legislative process.) The British executive controls the legislative process as long as it retains the support of a parliamentary majority, though the legislative process remains distinct from the executive's policy making activities.

The EU Council of Ministers is both an executive institution and a legislative institution. The Council exercises executive functions when it takes the most important policy decisions with the help of the European Commission. Furthermore, the Council is a legislative institution in that decisions of the Council and not of the European Parliament become the law of the Community and are directly binding on member states and their citizens.

The Council has the potential to be either intergovernmental or supranational in character depending on *how* it reaches its decisions. If unanimity is required before its decisions can become legitimate and binding in the member states, then the Council will function as an intergovernmental institution and integration will be relatively slow.

If the Council of Ministers reaches its decisions on the basis of some form of majority voting, then the Council will be supranational in character. Most states face the probability of being outvoted from time to time. The early history of the Community was punctuated by dramatic rows among member governments, the largest of which would, occasionally, wield a veto over policies agreed by every other member state. Interestingly, the two most celebrated European leaders to make use of the veto were the French President de Gaulle (in office from 1958 to 1969) and the British Prime Minister Margaret Thatcher (1979–1990). Both slowed down the process of integration and both perceived the Community as essentially and necessarily intergovernmental, as an association of independent states determined to hold on to their sovereignty. The Community has, nevertheless, progressed significantly from the almost universal requirement of unanimity to more and more qualified majority voting(QMV).

States are given votes in the Council on the basis of population (see Table 10.2). Thus there are five major countries including Spain. The qualified majority required for the adoption of many of the Council's decisions is 62 votes *and* 10 states in favour. Consequently, two of the largest states could lose as long as they are not joined in opposition by more than one medium sized state with 5 votes or by Luxembourg and one state with 3 votes.

The European Commission

The European Commission is one of the most powerful governmental bureaucracies in the world. It is the European Union's civil service— but it is much more than that. The Treaty of Rome gave the Commission explicitly political powers and duties. The Commission has three distinct responsibilities. Firstly, Community decision making requires that the Commission proposes policy decisions to the Council of Ministers which may accept or reject these proposals. Many of the Commission's proposals are a response to instructions from the Council and the member states. Once the Council decides on a major step forward, such as the creation of a single currency, it is the Commission which works out the detailed policy which has to be submitted to the Council. The Commission also possesses a power of initiative. This means that it may propose major new policies which it believes are in the interests of the Community as a whole. Secondly, the Commission is charged with the responsibility of ensuring that member states abide by the Treaty of Rome and all subsequent Community legislation. Thirdly, the Commission represents the Community in international organisations.

The Commission now has 20 members and a staff of 15,000, most of whom work at the EU headquarters in Brussels. The Commissioners are appointed en masse for five years at a time by member states, subject to the approval of the European Parliament. (It was for four years until 1995.) The Commissioners are appointed as individuals. Nevertheless, there is one Commissioner from every member state while there are two Commissioners each from the five largest members: Britain, France, Germany, Italy and Spain.

Commissioners have to take an oath of allegiance to the European Union and they must not take instructions from their own country. Member states have to agree on the Commission President, who is appointed by the European Council after consultations with the European Parliament. The President is usually a serving Commissioner. When the current President, Jacques Santer of Luxembourg, was appointed in 1995, Britain objected to the nomination because he was believed to be too supranational in his outlook. The Commissioners are the heads of the Community's departments which are called Directorates. The 23 Directorates are like government departments in Britain. They cover the major areas for which the European Union has responsibility. (See Table 10.4.)

The Commissioners have a much higher political profile than senior civil servants in Britain. This is partly because there is no equivalent of ministerial responsibility whereby Ministers are required

QUALIFIED MAJORITY VOTING IN THE COUNCIL OF MINISTERS 1997

Country	Nº· of Votes
Britain	10
France	10
Germany	10
Italy	10
Spain	8
Belgium	5
Greece	5
Netherlands	5
Portugal	5
Austria	4
Sweden	4
Ireland	3
Denmark	3
Finland	3
Luxembourg	2
Total	87

Table 10.2

to take responsibility for the actions of bureaucrats and also because the Commissioners possess considerable political influence. The Commission President is often a controversial figure because he or she is associated with unpopular Community policies. The Commissioners also acquire a high public profile if their responsibilities and actions arouse controversy. Thus Franz Fischler of Austria, Commissioner for Agriculture, became well known in Britain because he was responsible for Community decisions on the BSE crisis.

The two British Commissioners are Leon Brittan, first appointed in 1989 and reappointed in 1995, and Neil Kinnock, first appointed in 1995. Leon Brittan was a Cabinet Minister in the Thatcher Government who resigned in 1986 when he became entangled in the row between the Prime Minister and the Defence Secretary, Michael Heseltine, over the Westland Affair. Neil Kinnock was Labour Leader from 1983 until he resigned after Labour lost the 1992 General Election. Edith Cresson, the Commissioner for Science, Research and Development, was French Prime Minister for a time when François Mitterand was President.

Commissioners can thus be seen to be influential politicians in their own right, not nondescript bureaucrats who never see the political light of day.

The European Parliament

The European Parliament is not a legislature. In the words of an official publication of the EU, "The European Parliament exercises only symbolically the functions of a true parliament such as exists in a parliamentary democracy." The Parliament's functions are essentially *consultative, advisory and supervisory*. Nevertheless, the Parliament's role has been enlarged by recent community legislation. The reason for the Parliament's limited powers is that the states which established the European communities were aware that a Parliament was likely to represent community interests rather than the interests of member states. A powerful legislature, especially one which is directly elected, would limit the capacity of the states to control the process of integration.

MEPs sit in partisan groups, not in national groups. In the 1994 Elections to the European Parliament, Labour won 62 seats, the Conservatives won 18, the Liberal Democrats and the Scottish Nationalists each won 2 seats, while the Ulster Unionists, the Democratic Unionist Party (Ian Paisley) and the SDLP (John Hume) each won one of the three Northern Ireland seats. The Labour MEPs and John Hume sit with the Party of European Socialists. The Conservatives and the Ulster Unionist sit with the Grouping of European People's Party. The SNP MEPs sit with the European Radical Alliance, and the Liberal Democrats sit with the Liberal Democratic and Reformist Party.

The Parliament was the 'poor relation' in EC/EU

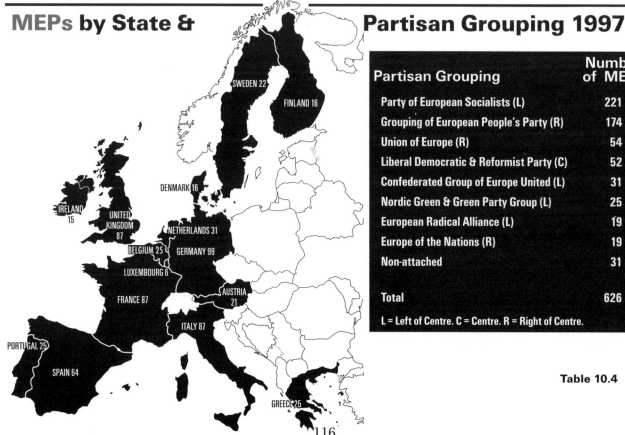

MEPs by State & Partisan Grouping 1997

Partisan Grouping	Number of MEPs
Party of European Socialists (L)	221
Grouping of European People's Party (R)	174
Union of Europe (R)	54
Liberal Democratic & Reformist Party (C)	52
Confederated Group of Europe United (L)	31
Nordic Green & Green Party Group (L)	25
European Radical Alliance (L)	19
Europe of the Nations (R)	19
Non-attached	31
Total	626

L = Left of Centre. C = Centre. R = Right of Centre.

Map labels: SWEDEN 22, FINLAND 16, DENMARK 16, IRELAND 15, UNITED KINGDOM 87, NETHERLANDS 31, BELGIUM 25, GERMANY 99, LUXEMBOURG 6, FRANCE 87, AUSTRIA 21, ITALY 87, PORTUGAL 25, SPAIN 64, GREECE 25

Table 10.4

THE EUROPEAN PARLIAMENT
At the beginning, members of the European Parliament (MEPs) were appointed by the national legislatures. However, the Parliament has been directly elected since 1979. Every member state except the United Kingdom uses a system of proportional representation. This is an example of Britain resisting the pressure for harmonisation. In July 1997, the Labour Cabinet committed itself to introducing a system of proportional representation in time for the elections to the European Parliament in 1999. Direct elections have increased the influence of the Parliament which has 626 members. Membership is distributed among the member states according to population.

The Directorates of the European Commission 1997

Directorate	Responsibilities	Commissioner	Country
I	External Relations	Santer (President)	Luxembourg
	Economic and Political	Brittan (Vice-President)	Britain
		Marin (Vice-President)	Spain
		Van Breok	Netherlands
		Pinheiro	Portugal
II	Economic and Financial Affairs	De Silguy	France
III	Industry	Bangemann	Germany
IV	Competition Policy	Van Miert	Belgium
V	Employment, Industrial Relations and Social Affairs	Flynn	Ireland
VI	Agriculture and Rural Development	Fischler	Austria
VII	Transport	Kinnock	Britain
VIII	Development	Marin**	Spain
IX	Personnel and Administration	Liikanen	Finland
X	Information, Culture and Audiovisual Media	Oreja	Spain
XI	Environment, Nuclear Safety, Civil Protection	Bjerregaard	Denmark
XII	Science, Research and Development	Cresson**	France
XIII	Telecommunications, Information Industry and Innovation	Bangemann**	Germany
XIV	Fisheries	Bonino*	Italy
XV	Internal Market and Financial Services	Monti	Italy
XVI	Regional Policies	Wulf-Mathias*	Germany
XVII	Energy	Papoutsis	Greece
XVIII	Credit and Investments (disbanded)		
XIX	Budgets	Liikanen**	Finland
XX	Financial Controls	Gradin*	Sweden
XXI	Customs and Indirect Taxes	Monti**	Italy
XXII	Education, Training and Youth	Cresson*	France
XXIII	Enterprise, Tourism, Distributive Trades	Papoutsis**	Greece
XXIV	Consumer Policy and Health Protection	Bonino**	Italy

*denotes female Commissioner
**Some Commissioners are responsible for two Directorates

Table 10.4

decision making until institutional reforms were introduced by the Single European Act and by the Maastricht Treaty. The Parliament was only marginally involved in the legislative process, but it was allocated two major powers which it retains today—it could reject the Community budget which is submitted by the Commission and it could sack the Commission as a whole. The recent reforms require that the Parliament confirms the appointment and reappointment of European Commissioners. They also increase parliamentary participation in the legislative process and introduce a new "co-decision making procedure".

The most controversial issue arising out of the European Parliament's place in the EU decision making process concerns an alleged 'democratic deficit'. Today's European Union has become more and more significant as the governmental source of economic, social and other policies which must be implemented by all member governments. The politics of agriculture and fisheries is now a European not a British process. Rules of market competition are European in scope. The institutions of the European Union increasingly compete with the government of each member state as the decisive source of law and policy. Such institutions should, therefore, be 'democratic'. Only the European Parliament is directly elected, and its powers are strictly limited, even after the recent reforms. Nevertheless, election by the people is the route to political power. MEPs tend to be 'Europhile' rather than 'Eurosceptic' regardless of their parties' stands on European issues. This being the case, assigning more legislative powers to a directly elected Parliament would strengthen the supranational or integrationist forces within the European Union.

The Court of Justice
The Court of Justice of the European Union has 15 judges, one from every member state. The judges serve six year terms and are appointed "by common accord of the governments of the member states". Unlike the US Supreme Court, whose selection process is highly partisan (biased) and whose appointees are not required to be at the top of the judicial profession, appointees to the European Court must be qualified to fill the highest judicial posts in their own countries.

Parliamentary Sovereignty

One of the most vital features of membership of the European Union is that it means the end of the treasured British constitutional principle of parliamentary sovereignty or supremacy. This is because EU laws, adopted by the appropriate procedures, are automatically binding throughout the Union. Should the domestic law of any member state conflict with an EU law, the EU should prevail. The legislature of every member state devotes a lot of time to passing 'enabling legislation' which seeks to make domestic law compatible with EU law. Parliamentary supremacy remains in place in so far as there is no law making authority superior to Parliament *within* the United Kingdom itself. However, the superiority of EU law (ie. it has priority) means that the principle of parliamentary sovereignty is no longer absolute. In other words, Parliament cannot pass laws contrary to EU law and hope to get away with it or, ultimately, to remain a member in good standing of the European Union.

The European Court has ruled against Britain on occasion—it has stated that British legislation was incompatible with European legislation. In Factortame Ltd. v. Secretary of State for Transport (1991) the European Court took the highly significant decision that when a British Act of Parliament conflicts with European legislation, the British Statute may *not* be enforced by the courts.

THE EUROPEAN ISSUE IN THE 1997 GENERAL ELECTION CAMPAIGN

The issue of Britain's relationship with the European Community/Union has been one of the most divisive in British politics since Harold Macmillan began the process of seeking membership in 1961. Divisions were especially sharp in the years between the 1992 and 1997 Elections. The European issue was particularly significant within the Conservative Party because it was in government. The Conservative split, worsened by the prospect of further economic and political integration contained in the Maastricht Treaty, weakened the Government in the House of Commons as its overall majority dwindled away to zero by the beginning of 1997. Failure to end or even suspend the conflict between Eurosceptics and Europhiles contributed to claims that the Prime Minister was a ditherer who was forced to make policy 'on the hoof' during the election campaign.

A Single Currency?

The crucial question to emerge almost immediately after the somewhat unexpected Conservative victory in 1992 was what should Britain's attitude be towards the probability of a common or single currency and a common monetary policy within the next decade. The Heads of Government meeting at Maastricht agreed that a single currency and the abolition of national currencies should be the next major objective of those member states economically qualified to join. Such an objective suggested that the supranationalists or integrationists were winning the battle to determine the political future of the Union, and that a federal 'super-state' was a distinct probability. Conservative Eurosceptics wanted the Prime Minister to say *no* immediately. John Major opted for a 'wait and see' policy while admitting that it was indeed very unlikely that Britain would join the projected common currency and monetary system in the first wave, especially in the light of Britain's unhappy experience with membership of the exchange rate mechanism. John Major was deterred from saying 'no' outright by the fact that two of his principal and most popular Cabinet Ministers, Deputy Prime Minister Michael Heseltine and Chancellor of the Exchequer Kenneth Clarke, were strong Europhiles who were likely to resign should the Prime Minister give way to the Eurosceptics.

Labour was hardly more comfortable with the idea of a common monetary system. However, Labour was not in power, and any Eurosceptics in New Labour were not prepared to rock the boat which seemed to be heading towards victory whenever John Major called the election. Both major parties sought to defuse the European issue by promising a referendum on joining the single currency should the government consider such a move to be in Britain's interest.

John Major stood by his non-commital 'wait and see' policy during the election campaign, but he also attempted to make the question of Britain's relationship with the European Union a key election issue. Some commentators, including some Conservative politicians, argued that Mr Major's strategy was severely flawed because it took attention away from his government's main success story, the improvement in the British economy under the stewardship of Kenneth Clarke. It was not clear to everyone that there were significant differences between the two major parties on European Union issues.

A Federal Europe?

The Conservative dilemma on Europe was evident as the campaign unfolded. Two developments symbolised the shortcomings in Major's strategy.

1 A campaign poster depicting a diminutive Labour Leader Tony Blair sitting in the lap of a massive Chancellor Kohl of Germany, a strong supranationalist and one of the longest serving Heads of Government in Europe.

2 A sensational decision by John Major on 17 April, two weeks before polling day, that there would be a free vote for Conservative MPs in the House of Commons on the single currency issue.

The campaign poster explicitly posed several questions which British politicians will be required to answer in the next decade. "Do we want a Federal Europe?" focused on the degree of political integration acceptable to the British electorate. The word 'federal' assumed crucial significance for Conservatives in the 1990s as they were besieged by the probability of devolution at home and further political integration in Europe. Conservative politicians detected unwelcome signs of federalism at both levels. A federal system such as the United States (Canada, Australia and Germany are also federal states) divides legal sovereignty or law making powers between two levels of government—a central or national government (the powers assigned to the American Congress) and the states or provinces (the state legislatures). Conservatives opposed devolution within Britain and accused its supporters of being 'federalists', arguing that devolution would lead to federalism and the eventual break-up of the British (unitary) state.

The Conservatives also argued that Labour and the Liberal Democrats were in favour of a federal Europe in which power would eventually gravitate towards the centre. The Conservatives in turn were accused of being inconsistent, associating federalism with decentralising tendencies in Britain and with centralising tendencies in Europe. 'Federal' became a code for giving in abjectly to supranationalists such as Chancellor Kohl. Mr Blair was careful to reject Conservative claims that a future Labour government would be happy at the propect of a European 'super-state'. On 22 April, during the campaign, he declared that "We want a Europe where national identities are not submerged and where countries cooperate together, not a giant and unmanageable European super-state run from the centre".

"Do we want a single European currency?" reminded the electorate that the party which won in 1997 would have to decide whether to sign up to the next major step in the process of economic integration. This will be monetary union including a single currency. "Or European laws governing British jobs, pay and border controls?" specified social policy making areas in which the EU, after 'Maastricht', was already taking significant decisions which were not applicable in Britain because the Conservative Government had negotiated an opt-out from the Social Chapter. Here a clear difference between the two major parties opened up because Labour was committed to signing up for the Social Chapter (and, in the event, duly did so).

These questions on specific issues were merely the prelude to the poster's principal message to the electorate which is implicit in the question. "Who can best negotiate these issues to Britain's advantage across the table from the immensely experienced leaders of Germany, France and the rest of Europe?". The relative proportions of Blair and Kohl in the poster were designed to emphasise the Tory claim that John Major and the Conservatives would be capable of defending vital British interests much more effectively than the inexperienced (in government) New Labour Leader. The poster suggested that Kohl is strong; Blair is small and weak; the invisible Major is strong. Mr Major asserted that "They (Labour) may claim these days not to wave the red flag, but they are certainly going to Amsterdam (to the next Heads of Government European Council) to wave the white flag." So 'Europe' was intended to be the significant election issue whereby John Major's experience would provide voters with a reason to vote Conservative.

The 1997 Election result suggests strongly that the Conservatives did not succeed in persuading voters that the European questions which the next government would have to answer necessitated a Conservative rather than a Labour victory. Rather the campaign merely served to publicise Conservative divisions on Europe. John Major's decision to permit a free vote on the emotive issue of signing up to a single currency was forced on him by the decisions of many Tory candidates to issue their own campaign leaflets in which they indicated their personal opposition to the single currency. Mr Major's European strategy did not work. Nevertheless, the issues raised by the famous poster will remain part of British political debate for the foreseeable future.